ALL IS WELL

By Julius Lester

Look Out, Whitey! Black Power's Gon' Get Your Mama
To Be a Slave
Revolutionary Notes
Black Folktales
Search for the New Land
The Seventh Son: The Thought and Writings of W. E. B. Du Bois
Long Journey Home: Stories from Black History
Two Love Stories
The Knee-High Man
Who I Am (with David Gahr)
All Is Well

ALL
IS
WELL

by JULIUS LESTER

WILLIAM MORROW AND COMPANY, INC.
NEW YORK   1976

Grateful acknowledgment is made for permission to reprint the following:

"A Letter from Julius Lester," *Broadside*, Issue #84. Reprinted by permission of *Broadside*.

"The Third of September," September 20, 1969; "From the Other Side of the Tracks," September 27, 1969; originally published in *The Guardian*. Reprinted by permission of *The Guardian*.

"To Recapture the Dream," August-September 1969; "Aquarian Notebook," December 1969; "Aquarian Notebook," February 1970; "Aquarian Notebook," March 1970; "Aquarian Notebook," Autum 1970; "On the Suicide of a Revolutionary," Spring 1971; Copyright 1969, 1970, 1971 by *Liberation*. Reprinted by permission of *Liberation* Magazine, New York.

Excerpts from *Revolutionary Notes*, Copyright © 1969 by Julius Lester. Reprinted by permission of Richard W. Baron Publishing Company, Inc.

Excerpts from *Search for the New Land*, Copyright © 1969 by Julius Lester. Reprinted by permission of The Dial Press.

Transcript of Julius Lester's remarks on WBAI-FM on January 20, 1969. Reprinted by permission of "Pacifica Foundation WBAI (FM)."

"The Revolution: Revisited," Winter-Spring 1970, *Katallagete*. Reprinted by permission of *Katallagete*.

"Young, Gifted & Black: The Politics of Caring," from *The Village Voice*, May 28, 1970. Reprinted by permission of *The Village Voice*. Copyright © *The Village Voice*, Inc., 1970.

"Words in the Mourning Time," "Contemplation in a World of Action," "The End of White Supremacy," "Stokely Speaks," © 1971 by The New York Times Company. Reprinted by permission.

Grateful acknowledgment is made for permission to quote from the following:

The Rebel by Albert Camus, translated by Anthony Bower, Copyright © 1956 by Alfred A. Knopf, Inc. Reprinted by permission of the publisher.

The Wretched of the Earth by Frantz Fanon, Copyright © 1963 by *Presence Africaine*. Reprinted by permission of Grove Press, Inc.

Howl and Other Poems by Allen Ginsberg. Copyright © 1956, 1959 by Allen Ginsberg. Reprinted by permission of City Lights Books.

For Whom the Bell Tolls by Ernest Hemingway, Copyright © 1954 by Ernest Hemingway. Reprinted by permission of Charles Scribner's Sons.

"The Philosophy of the Beat Generation" by John Clellon Holmes, from *Esquire*, January 1958, © 1957 by Esquire Inc. Reprinted by permission of *Esquire* Magazine.

Blues People by LeRoi Jones, Copyright © 1963 by LeRoi Jones. Reprinted by permission of William Morrow & Company, Inc.

A Portrait of the Artist as a Young Man by James Joyce, Copyright 1916 by B. W. Huebsch, Copyright renewed 1944 by Nora Joyce, Copyright © 1964 by the Estate of James Joyce. All rights reserved. Reprinted by permission of The Viking Press, Inc.

Disputed Questions by Thomas Merton, Copyright © 1953, 1959, 1960 by The Abbey of Gethsemani. Reprinted by permission of Farrar, Straus & Giroux, Inc.

"Poetry and Contemplation: A Reappraisal" from *Selected Poems of Thomas Merton*, Copyright © 1959 by The Abbey of Gethsemani, Inc., Copyright © 1959 by New Directions Publishing Corporation. Reprinted by permission of New Directions Publishing Corporation.

The Sign of Jonas by Thomas Merton. Reprinted by permission of the publisher, Harcourt Brace Jovanovich, Inc.

Big Sur and the Oranges of Hieronymous Bosch by Henry Miller, Copyright © 1956 by Henry Miller. Reprinted by permission of New Directions Publishing Corporation.

Individualism Reconsidered by David Reisman. Copyright 1954 by The Free Press of Glencoe. Reprinted by permission of Macmillan Publishing Co.

The Day on Fire by James Ramsey Ullman, Copyright © 1958 by James Ramsey Ullman. Reprinted by permission of Doubleday & Company, Inc.

The Outsider by Colin Wilson, Copyright © 1956 by Colin Wilson. Reprinted by permission of Houghton Mifflin Company.

Religion and the Rebel by Colin Wilson, Copyright © 1957 by Colin Wilson. Reproduced by permission of Victor Gollancz, London.

Other portions of this book originally appeared in *Arts in Society*, *Evergreen Review*, *Katallagete*, and *Sing Out*.

Printed in the United States of America.

1 2 3 4 5 80 79 78 77 76

Library of Congress Cataloging in Publication Data

Lester, Julius
  All is well.

  1. Lester, Julius—Biography. I. Title.
PS3562.E853Z515   813'.5'4 [B]   75-40219
ISBN 0-688-03045-9

BOOK DESIGN: H. ROBERTS

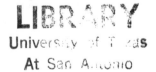

To
Margaret and Carol
who said, "Fly!"

and

Joanne Marie
who came to live in the eyrie

ALL IS WELL

I

1

I was still a child when my mother told me that she had hoped I would be a girl. Though she added quickly that she was pleased that I, and not a girl had been born that Friday afternoon, January 27, 1939 (Sun in Aquarius, Cancer rising, Moon in Aries, and a grand trine in the Earth signs), I didn't believe her. She was almost forty when I was born and whether I was conceived during a night of premenopausal passion, or through the grace of God and a defective prophylactic, I had failed, not only by being born, but doing it as a boy.

Helpless to rectify my error, I did what I could, and in my childhood fantasies became a beautiful girl with long black hair, like my mother's. (I was named Julius Bernard after her, Julia Beatrice, and so identified with her. I was more than her second child; I was her namesake, Julia Beatrice, Jr., heir to the female line, as my brother, nine years my senior and named for my father, was to the male. I felt myself to be her not as she was in the roles of my father's wife, or my mother, but the woman-her, who existed outside social definitions. I used to look at a picture of her holding me as an infant. It was a penny arcade photo, showing a beautiful, young-looking, light-skinned woman, with long, dark wavy hair. She is soft and gentle in that picture, and that was the woman I wanted to be. That was the woman I wanted to know, for only in that photo made in a booth at the railroad station did I ever see a look of love for me on my mother's face.) I called myself Michele, and was very cold and aloof, more brilliant than all the

9

boys in school, and so self-sufficient that I never wanted a boy friend. I tried to keep my fantasy secret, but the day in early childhood when I saw a girl cousin holding a doll, I snatched it from her, refusing to relinquish it until my parents bought me one. (I slept with it until I was nine or ten.)

I was born in St. Louis, Missouri, but when I was two, we moved to Kansas City, Kansas, where my self began to make its dimensions known to me. I pretended to be a boy, and climbed trees, shot marbles, got into fights, and played baseball, all the while envying the girls sitting on porches playing house. Michele was (is?) the real me, and that boy called Julius was the fantasy, a preconceived identity for which I could not be faulted, or held responsible. My sex and name were considered to be me, but my childhood fantasy was an inner language telling me that my definition of who I was was more important than the womb's and the world's.

Though I wasn't a girl, I was still exceptionally bright, and my primary identity was with my intelligence. "That boy is smarter than his teachers," everyone used to say. (It was true. I corrected teachers when they erred, and taught class when I knew more about a subject, generally geography and history.) In a black community in those years, a bright child was special, for these were the days before God manifested Himself in the form of the Supreme Court. The school desegregation decision of 1954 was to be the second Emancipation Proclamation, but during my childhood, there was little hope that the walls of Jericho would ever crumble. The whip did not bite the flesh as often as it had in the days of my father's youth, but it was coiled in the master's hand and did not have to be unleashed to sting and hurt. The omnipresent threat was enough to make the soul cry. But no one lost faith, because it had been that monumental, unshakable faith in God and America which had carried the race through years so bleak that James Weldon Johnson wrote of them as years when "hope unborn had died."

Race progress was measured by the achievements of the race's exceptional individuals. Every time Jackie Robinson stole a base, its effect was more healing to the race's wounds than Jesus' hands on the blind man's eyes, and Adam Clayton Powell's place in our lives was second only to that of the Holy Trinity, and he was crowding them.

The exceptional child was the carrier of dreams for the entire race, and my intelligence was like the star in the East. "That boy's gon' be somebody!" it was repeatedly said of me in my presence. (After I was married, it was fascinating to hear Arlene talk of her childhood, creating images of a golden world of endless summers lived in tree houses made of sunbeams, supported by cool evening winds. I envied her her white childhood and was hurt when she said it was the happiest time of her life. I wanted that to be the years with me, which were supposed to be the rest of her life. It was not to be, and, perhaps, one reason may have been that I was never a child.) There was no time for childhood. (Friday evenings we watched the fights on television. "Gillette Blue Blades and Gillette Razors present [BONG!] the Friday Night Fights! This is Jack Smooth Voice with Harry Cauliflower here at ringside in Madison Square Garden to bring you tonight's fight between another nigger and another white man." Daddy would be sitting in his overstuffed chair and I'd be lying on the floor. "The fighters are moving out to the center of the ring to receive their instructions from the referee." Gladys Goodding sang "The Star-Spangled Banner" ("the home of the brave Negro and the land of the free white man") and the fight was on. [BONG!] It was legitimatized race war. Every blow the white boxer landed, the crowd yelled. Every blow the black struck, Daddy and I yelled. I didn't know what I was supposed to have done to white people, but the crowd cheers for the white fighter told me all I needed to know: They hated me! On an occasional Friday night there would be two white, or two black fighters paired against each other. Such bouts were of little interest to anyone, but Daddy knew how to arouse his and my interest. "Which one we gon' root for tonight?" he'd ask. "The one in the black trunks," I'd reply. He would chuckle contentedly. I'd learned my lesson well.)

There was no time for childhood, and though Mother forced me to put down the omnipresent book and go outside (and give her a respite from me and my questions), I knew that games were not a reality unto themselves. I was going to be "somebody," and I had to prepare for my day in the ring, because they hated me.

Yet, I knew none of them and never spoke to one until I was fourteen. (My first piano teacher, Miss Nye, did not qualify as white, because she accepted black pupils. A real white person would not have done that.) My immediate world was devoid of whites, and so self-contained that even now I do not know where in Kansas City, Kansas, they lived.

They existed, however, and like a young boy preparing for his first camping trip, I was taught how to handle snakes and not be bitten. ("I was in Hot Springs, Arkansas," a minister friend of my father's would begin. "It was right after the war started. I was driving along and made this turn, and Lawd, have mercy! I'd turned the wrong way into a one-way street. [Laughter] And don't you know that before I could make it to the next corner and get the dickens off it—[Minister makes the sound of a siren] [Laughter increases]—I pulled over, you know, and looked through the rear-view mirror, and here came this great big peckerwood cop. Big ol' belly was hangin' down to his shoelaces." ["Must've been the same one stopped me in Cairo, Illinois, one time," someone interjects, to great laughter.] "Yeah, it probably was the same one. Did he look like he just come off the farm down there in Yonky Pen, Arkansas? [Uncontrollable laughter of recognition] I know what I'm talking about, 'cause I had a church not too far from there when I was starting out. Well, anyway, I get out of the car, and he says, 'Nigger, this here is a one-way street.' I looked at 'im, bucked my eyes, and said, 'Yassuh. I'se jus' gwine one way.' [Boisterous laughter, laughter of admiration] He say, 'Boy, I said this is a one-way street.' I gave him one of them big, happy nigger grins. 'Yassuh. Like I said, Cap'n, I'se jus' gwine one way.' Lawd, don't you know that I had that cracker so frustrated and red in the face, he didn't know what to do. He tried to explain it to me again, and I took him back in the same ol' circle. Finally, he said, 'Nigger, get the hell out of here!' [Triumphant laughter] You know, white folks 'bout the dumbest things on God's earth." [Murmurs of assent, as someone else begins his tale of conquest.])

It would not be wholly accurate to say that my father hated whites, but if he lived forever and never saw one, that would be too soon. He had grown up in Mississippi and Arkansas in the first two decades of the century, when lynchings were almost as ordinary as the boll weevil, when the shadow of slavery lay over the southern landscape like a patchwork quilt. He liked to talk of his childhood and I listened, trying to put myself inside his black skin (which his really is), to see and feel what he had known. (Was the then unrecognized writer in me already functioning?)

He was the son of a minister, who died while my father was still a teenager. Daddy's mother died a year later, leaving him to raise the four younger children. He did it, managing to finish school, work his way through college and seminary, and in the fifteen years between marrying my mother and my birth, he had been a teacher, bellhop, barber, carpenter, and undertaker, while pastoring poor country churches. His was an American success story, a triumph against the odds, and he moved with great dignity in a hostile world. Yet, he carried a bitterness which, on the rare occasion when it was expressed, was frightening. One day Mother was reading the paper and lamented aloud the death of some public figure. "I don't see why you care," Daddy said. I tried to make myself invisible, not wanting to be sent out of the room, which always happened when the conversations got interesting.

"Well," Mother said, "he wasn't that old a man." (My mother seldom said a harsh word about anyone, except me, or so it seemed then. Like all black mothers, she had to prepare me to survive, and the gentle expression of love might have made me weak. She could not afford to cuddle the child; her responsibility was the adult who had to enter the ring. There should have been another way, for the child could not understand a mother who never said, "I love you," who never touched him, who never complimented him on his accomplishments, or sympathized with him when he was hurt. So I learned to rely only on myself, not expecting or needing another's approval. My mother never read Greek philosophy, but she knew: Character is fate. There should have been another way to teach it, however.)

"I remember you got upset when Calvin Coolidge's son died."

"That was terrible," Mother said, becoming distressed again.

My curiosity refused to be stilled, and I asked, softly, "What happened?"

"He got a rusty nail in his foot and died of blood poisoning," Mother told me, sorrowfully.

"Your mother cried like it was you or your brother," Daddy said harshly.

"Well, he was only a child," she responded weakly.

"You'll never see me being sorry over the death of somebody white," Daddy declared with brutal finality.

And in the uncomfortable silence, I understood why, sometimes, children shouldn't overhear the conversations of their parents.

My father didn't teach me to hate whites, however, but he sheltered me from them as long as he could. (That was easy, for I wasn't sure what they looked like until I was eight. The problem arose, because my grandmother and one of my mother's brothers were, to all appearances, white. They had Caucasian features and straight hair, and distinguishing between whites and blacks on the basis of skin color was more than my eight-year-old mind could fathom, until the day I asked my third-grade teacher: "What do white people look like?" After the class stopped laughing, she said, "You can always tell a white person by looking at their nose. White people have big noses." I glanced at the blond-haired, blue-eyed, white-skinned "black" girl in the class, and lo, her nose was small. The next time we went downtown shopping, I looked at the noses of people who looked like her, Grandmother, and Uncle Oscar, and damn! White folks had big noses!) That protection was in the form of race-consciousness and race pride. As I grew, I accepted being black as matter-of-factly as I did the sky's blueness. My race was not a disease which needed curing, but a blessing to be defended from all who would seek to regard it otherwise. We read the black press and *Ebony* magazine regularly, and were members of the NAACP. Books by and about blacks were on Daddy's bookshelves, and most curiously, in retrospect, we delighted in Rochester, the black chauffeur on the Jack Benny radio show, and in Amos and Andy. To us, they were not stereotypes, but models for survival. In the character of Kingfish, the creators of Amos and Andy may have thought they were ridiculing blacks as lazy, shiftless, scheming and conniving, but to us, Kingfish was a paragon of virtue, an alternative to the work ethic. Kingfish lived: Amos made a living. It did not matter that my parents lived by and indoctrinated me with the Puritan work ethic. Kingfish had a *joie de vivre* no white person could poison, and we knew that whites ridiculed us because they were incapable of such *élan*. I was proud to belong to the same race as Kingfish.

2

Every summer we went to Pine Bluff, Arkansas, where my grandmother lived. When we crossed into the state, I was always aware of entering something very old. Present was past and past was present. Blacks working in the cotton fields looked like an antebellum tableau, straw hats protecting them from the voracious summer sun whose heat they were supposed to withstand naturally, backs bent as they chopped the weeds away from the young cotton plants. "I've been out in them fields many a day," Daddy would say, waving to the cotton choppers, letting them know that although he was driving a big car, he had not forgotten from whence he had come. "Your back get so sore from bending over that you don't think you'll ever raise up again. And that ol' rough hoe handle in your hands hurts like the dickens until you get calluses." Toward evening we passed trucks loaded with blacks. "Coming from the fields. Ol' white man come down the road in the morning and load'em up. Take'em out to the field, and in the evening, come back and load'em up again. Sunup to sundown. They make about a dollar a day."

Once we went to Daddy's hometown, Brinkley. It was a row of stores fronting on a street across from which were the railroad tracks. There were a few cars parked at angles to the curb, but Daddy didn't stop, though one of his brothers lived there. I knew we had come so I could see what he had escaped from, and, seeing it, I wondered how. Driving through those small Arkansas towns I also wondered how they survived who didn't escape. Everything moved slowly in the towns, if it moved at all. Generally little did, or even could in the thick heat which seemed to have been spread over the land like butter on a piece of toast. People sat, or moved so slowly as to appear like timeless wraiths. Old white men sat around three sides of the inevitable town square, at the center of which was the courthouse, in whose basement was the police station. The summer sun seemed as if it had branded everyone and everything to the spot where it was. But there was nothing serene about the stillness. A sense of dread hangs from a southern sky like Spanish moss from an oak tree.

The dread dissipated at Grandmother's, but the intermingling of past and present remained. Grandmother was old. Her half-black, half-Indian, ex-slave mother had married a German Jewish immigrant peddler. His name was Adolf Altschul, and for many summers when I went out to the road to take the mail from the box, I didn't understand why Emma Smith, my grandmother, had painted ALTSCHUL on her mailbox. One day I was in downtown

Pine Bluff with my parents and saw the name in neon above a jewelry store. "That's the name on Grandmamma's mailbox," I commented blithely. Daddy laughed. "Those are your uncles and cousins." He explained about the white side of the family, how Adolf had been disowned when he married my great-grandmother, but on his death, his family had buried him in the white cemetery. (One day I just might dig him up and bury him where he belongs.)

Grandmother lived with her brother, Rudolph, who was equally old. He rose with the sun, put on a straw hat, cut a plug of chewing tobacco, stuck it in the side of his mouth and sat in his rocker on the front porch, moving only when there was no more shade. He napped, swatted flies, spat tobacco juice and followed the shade around the house, and by evening was back on the porch, feet propped against the same porch support as that morning. At nine o'clock he announced that he was tired and went to bed. He never married and always lived with Grandmother, though they had a sister who lived on the other side of the field, her house plainly visible from the porch. They saw her seldom.

There was no place for a child in that ancient world, and I was left alone each day to bat pieces of coal with a stick and reenact every hit Jackie Robinson had made and all future ones. No one came in the yard, except the iceman every two days delivering a hundred-pound block of ice, and twice a month, a man brought two barrels of water. Grandmother's house didn't have plumbing or electricity.

The big event for me each day was the passing of the freight train. When I heard the churning of its wheels, I ran to the front of the house to watch it pass. I never knew whether to wave at the white engineer, uncertain if he would wave back. If he didn't, was it because he didn't see me, or was it because I was black? Day after day I waited for him to wave to me, and one day he did! Excited as I was, I did not raise my arm, for, at that distance, he might have thought I was a white boy, and if he'd really been able to see me, I didn't think he would've waved.

Though I'd still had no direct contact with whites, one did not have to speak to them to feel their power. In Kansas City our movements were restricted, because we could not eat in restaurants or attend movies in the downtown section. However, we were spared reading our inferior status on countless signs, which were as plentiful as dust in Pine Bluff. NO COLORED ALLOWED. COLORED

ENTRANCE. COLORED FOUNTAIN. COLORED SIT FROM THE REAR. COL-ORED SIDE. To leave the black community was to journey into Negation. Before those trips to town, I became a zombie, refusing to feel even the heat. I emptied my bowels and bladder because Mother would have preferred that I urinate on bolts of cloth in J. C. Penney before allowing me to use the COLORED BATHROOM, which was generally in a dirty corner of a store's basement next to the janitor's mop closet. I willed myself to constipation, an ability I still have. I also learned not to want water, because every black person in creation might go to the COLORED FOUNTAIN (which was never as tall or clean as the WHITE FOUNTAIN), but not only would the Lesters not quench their thirst, they would not even look thirsty. As a result, I seldom drink water now, or look thirsty on the hottest days. And, of course, we never stood at the COLORED WINDOW of a cafe to buy a hamburger, and we looked with undisguised scorn at those blacks who did.

Those journeys to town left me with a dread of whites which will never be wholly dissipated. Though I would learn to move easily, and with confidence, in the white world, and live there exclusively when I became an adult, that little boy remains, unable to understand why NO COLORED ALLOWED. I had a strong sense of myself as an exceptional individual, but it was not that which was being attacked. Racism is impersonal, and its total disregard for individual uniqueness made it more insidious than a personal hatred. Who I was was immaterial to what I was. There was no way for a child to combat that, for it told me that nothing I did would affect how the white world defined me.

But I was fortunate, because my father, as minister of a black church, lived without having to depend on white people for his income. Except for the shopping trips to town, I was able to grow up on the fringes of racism. The black community of Kansas City, Kansas, was a stable one, able to protect, nurture and equip me for my sojourn in the valley of the shadow of death. Consequently, I developed a strong ego and a firm sense of self. The dread was not destroyed, thereby, but I had the necessary prerequisite for the struggle against a society which sought to deny me any existence it did not approve.

So I reveled in myself. I was me! and if I wasn't the smartest person in the world, whoever was, was in danger of being dethroned. I read shelves of books in history and geography, not to mention comics and detective magazines; I collected stamps, studied astronomy and cloud formations, made ink, soap, and various useless solutions with my chemistry set and examined the natural world beneath my microscope. I put on puppet shows, wrote and drew my own horror comics which I sold to my classmates. I studied piano and played first clarinet with the school orchestra. (I wanted to play violin because it was considered a girl's instrument, but to my shame, I weakened when my father and brother called me a sissy.) I sang the role of Dick Deadeye in H.M.S. *Pinafore* in the eighth grade, started a school chess club the same year (of which I was, of course, champion), was president of my seventh- and eighth-grade classes. ("A vote for Lester would be a good gesture.") I was athletic, and was deadly on a basketball court with my two-hand jump shot from the corner. I was the class clown, doing imitations of Milton Berle, Jackie Gleason, Jerry Lewis, Ed Sullivan, and finishing my act with an imitation of Donald Duck imitating Johnny Ray singing "Cry."

None of it, however, stopped the hurting, the knowing that my "I am me!" was equivalent to standing on a beach and demanding that the waves cease their motion. "I am me" did not stop the awful dread that I would be hurt again and again and again. But there was no alternative. I would stand there and shout into the roar of the ocean, knowing that I was doing it for me and not to win the ocean's acknowledgment of the obvious—I am me.

3

We moved south in the summer of 1953. My father had been appointed to the Board of Evangelism of the Methodist Church, whose offices were in Nashville, Tennessee. "The Lord works in mysterious ways," he said, when I complained about moving to the country of NO COLORED ALLOWED. "He might have a purpose for you in the South." I was unconvinced.

We moved into a white neighborhood (I was mowing the lawn one autumn Saturday morning and heard a girl's voice greet me. I looked up and saw a white girl wearing sunglasses and holding a poodle on a leash. Because of the glasses, I assumed she was blind, for she wouldn't have spoken to me otherwise. I'd never heard of poodles being used for seeing-eye dogs, however, but what did I know about white people? I continued mowing the grass. She spoke again. I became a little annoyed with the blind white girl who was going to get me lynched, if I wasn't careful. I continued mowing. Finally, as if she knew what I was thinking, she said something which indicated that she was aware of, and unimpressed with my racial identity. Though terrified of talking to a white girl in full view of the white neighbors, I had to. If she had enough courage (or innocence) to speak to me, I could not do less. We had not talked long, however, before her grandmother called her home. I was more than a little relieved and as I watched her cross the street, I knew she would not be back. A few minutes later, however, she returned, muttering imprecations against her grandmother. During the brief month or two we knew each other, there was never a time she came to see me that her grandmother didn't frantically call her home. There was never a time when she didn't return.

It was important that in my first relationship with a white person, that person risked herself for me. She acted contrary to everything I'd been taught about white people, and because she did, I had to disregard my teaching. Thereafter, I willed myself to trust whites, not wanting to accept or believe that they would not respond in kind. Many didn't, but they were unable to uproot the seed of faith that fourteen-year-old girl helped me plant.

Though I trusted her, the centuries-old fears to which I was heir would not be stilled. We played basketball in my back yard, and though she did not hesitate to push, grab, and hold me to make me miss a shot or lose the ball, I was afraid to guard her closely. What if I tried to steal the ball from her, and accidentally touched those pubescent breasts or alabaster thighs glaring at me from beneath her shorts and she yelled, "Rape!" I'd read too many stories in the black press about black boys and men who'd been lynched for nothing more than looking at white women. Her family sold their house late that autumn, and she moved, undefeated in basketball, waving to me from the back seat of the car until it turned the corner.)

While part of me feared whites, I was also contemptuous of them and their silly segregation. When I rode the buses alone, I sat in the front seat and laughed when whites stood rather than sit beside me. Once the bus driver asked me to move to the rear where, legally, I was supposed to be. I refused, even when other blacks pleaded with me "not to make trouble." But I was young and carried a kernel of resistance to the social order. I didn't know that then, or that there were others my age feeling a similar anger, riding the buses in other cities, precursors of the civil rights movement none of us could imagine then.

I went to the segregated public library often. Whites would move to another shelf of books when I came near, and get up from the reading tables when I sat down. Fools, fools, fools, I laughed, but the laughter could not salve the hurt at being made to feel that I was an unclean thing.

One afternoon while I was watching television, the host of the show announced that they were going to open the back doors of the studio and televise whatever might be happening outside in Art Lane Alley. It was just that—an alley in downtown Nashville where the members of the Nashville Art League exhibited members' paintings. The next afternoon when the camera poked its lenses out the door, it sent into the homes of Nashville the image of a black teen-ager sitting on a stool talking to a white girl. That had not been my intent: I'd only wanted there to be a black person on the television screens of Nashville. However, as soon as I appeared in the Alley that afternoon, a young white girl seized on me with an eagerness that was paralyzing. Having begun drawing and painting that summer, I had my sketchpad with me, and with the sketches in it as a convenient topic of conversation, we talked about art, when we wanted to talk about each other. She was as frightened of me as I of her, and nothing except nervous self-conscious chatter passed between us. We couldn't overcome three hundred years of history and be just a boy and a girl to each other. (Cloudy day. April, 1966. The hill country of Mississippi, off the main road, off the state highway onto a gravel road winding its way up and down, back into the hills with mouse-gray sky of scudding clouds overhead with their adumbrations of rain. No houses to be seen, only the wooded hills. Four Corners, the old man had said, and anybody can tell you. Bob Fletcher, an old friend from college and, that spring, a photographer for the Student Non-Violent Coordinating Committee [SNCC], and I were looking for an old guitar player, one who might remember the songs everyone else had forgotten. Fifteen, twenty miles from the main road until, finally, Four Corners. It was an intersection of gravel roads with a store and filling station on one corner and a store on another. Bob pulled the truck up to the store and we went inside. Three women standing there. The one I saw first was young, with deep sad eyes, and beautiful like the sound of early morning rain falling on spring leaves. I dared not speak to her. Her eyes said too much about Four Corners, the crossroads of nowhere, with its store and glass cases, the interminable days of a bag of potato chips, a piece of bubble gum, a can of string beans and a pound of bacon. I looked to the second woman, who was in her thirties, but already the lines in her forehead testified to the crime of Four Corners. Her mouth was tight, the breasts sagged beneath the print dress, the hair was pulled tight around the head, and she held a baby in her left arm. I turned away to look at the large woman at the back of the store. The progression was complete. The double chin, the rimless glasses, the large bosom, the expression of open hostility. I didn't know if they were related by blood, but they had been mothered by the South, by a constant struggle to stop the hunger, by the leaves falling from the trees. I opened my mouth to speak to the older woman, knowing that no one would come with a lynching rope if I addressed her, but she turned away, deliberately. I didn't know what to do, wanting and not daring to look at the youngest one, for I would not keep my eyes at the floor where they were supposed to be when a black man spoke to a white woman. I would have to look at her, knowing that my eyes would tell her of her beauty and my desire to be a part of it. "May I help you?" I turned and she was moving toward me, smiling, but the eyes retained their sadness, eyes that had either seen too much and turned away, or had seen nothing and knew they never would. I told her who we were looking for and my eyes stroked her face. "Oh, he lives right down the road a piece," she said, pointing. "Go 'til you come to a house with a dog-run. You know what I mean? A porch in the middle of it." I nodded. "You can't miss it. It's on the right-hand side of the road and there's a lot of junk in the yard." I thanked her, smiling, as unafraid as she. I started for the door, but she was beside me, talking. Of what I don't remember, but her voice did not stop in its desperation to find words, any words. I wanted to buy a soda, a few slices of cheese and some crackers and sit with her on the porch. I wanted to take her with me and I knew, I was certain, she would come. But we left her standing in the doorway and when we got into the truck, I asked Bob, "I didn't imagine anything, did I?" If he'd said, "What are you talking about?", I would've known that I had, but he only shook his head, unable to say more than "Uh-uh," quietly, with awe. He had seen it, she and I loving each other and if it had not been Four Corners, I would have taken her to me and washed the sadness from her eyes, dried the tears from her soul, and swum in the life of that body. But she and I were helpless, because one day some white man felt guilty about his lust for a black woman and went and lynched a black man, because . . . He created fantasies about that black man and his fantasies said a black man had a bigger one and could use it better and if you weren't careful he'd be after your wife and sister and daughter and that's all niggers think about anyway because that's all he thought about and they came with ropes and guns and kerosene and knives and they tied the black man with chains across a log, or to a tree, poured the kerosene and set him afire. Sometimes they hung him from the limb of a tree and afterward took his body to his house and threw it on the porch and laughed when the wife, mother, children came to the door to see what that noise on the porch was. Always, though, they used their knives. Because.)

My quasi-sexual adventure in Art Lane Alley was brief. One day the black janitor at the television station called me over and said that the white people at the station didn't like to see me sitting there talking to "that white girl." I told him I didn't care what the white people said. He said he didn't either, but he didn't want to see me get in trouble. The next day I looked at my friend on television and wondered if she would ever know why she would not see me again.

Like a boxer in the early rounds of a fight, I had begun feeling out the white world, testing the limits, irritating white clerks in stores by refusing to address them as "sir" or "ma'am," knowing that blacks have been lynched for something as small as that. But I had to assert myself and refuse to accept the white-imposed proscriptions on my being. My parents were afraid for me, yet admiring. I was afraid, too, but to accept the fear was to legitimatize the white world's claims to my body and soul. I would not do that.

4

Until the spring of 1956, my identity did not change from that of the bright young boy who would grow up to be "somebody." ("Genius at Work" read the wooden plaque on my bedroom door.) To be black and be "somebody" meant that I would become a minister like my father, except that I, of course, would one day become a bishop, a teacher who would become a college president, or a doctor. I had no talent for the latter, no interest in teaching, and a dread that if I entered the ministry, to which I was attracted, I would always be nothing more than "Reverend Lester's son!"

In my fantasies I was a concert pianist, or an artist, but I knew of no black Rubinstein or Picasso I could use as a model, and I did not believe in myself enough to think I could be the first. Then, in the spring of 1956, during my last year of high school, Miss Bass, my English teacher, talked about a poet, Percy Bysshe Shelley, and something within me surged forward to embrace him, like a crowd breaking through police barricades to touch a hero on parade. The writer in me had awakened.

My initial attraction to Shelley was his romantic death by drowning during a storm. There is something fascinating to the young about dying young. How much better to die, your promise unfulfilled, than to live and grow old, your promise unfulfilled. The manner of his dying, however, impelled me to learn of his life, and I read J. A. Symond's biography. Though my hair was not long and curly, nor my eyes saucer-wide and blue, I identified with him wholly as he proposed to Mary Godwin while sitting by the tomb of her mother, Mary Wollstonecraft, when he left his first wife and showed no emotion on learning that she had drowned herself in the river. I identified with his feminine looks, his brilliance, his refusal to live by any definitions but his own. He was a rebel and an iconoclast, and after looking up the words in the dictionary, I decided that I would be, too. I became a vegetarian, as he had been, and remained one until the day five years later when I succumbed to the smell of frying sausage. I became a bohemian, dressing only in jeans and T-shirts and was ecstatic the day someone at school said, "You're becoming an eccentric, just like Shelley."

I had the embryo of a new identity, but equally important, Shelley led me out of an isolated existence whose universe was comprised solely of race and America. My adolescence was wholly contained within "the fifties," when few of our lives extended beyond our own social group, class, or race. Though politics was discussed in my home, it was primarily limited to the fortunes and misfortunes of the race and the evils of Communism, and whatever my father thought, so did I. Through *Life* magazine I was vaguely aware that more existed, but none of it had meaning in my dailiness. I saw only an awesome beauty in the color photographs of atomic mushroom clouds. I was incensed when Truman recalled MacArthur, thought Joe McCarthy was right to rid America of Communists and was the only Eisenhower supporter in my high school. I disagreed with my father, however, about the guilt of the Rosenbergs and was hurt and angered by their execution. I knew little about the case, but perhaps my sympathies had to be with a condemned man named Julius. I was also angered by the violence against my black contemporaries who desegregated Central High School in Little Rock, and I wondered idly if I could have walked through death-threatening crowds as calmly. But when the Montgomery bus boycott and Martin Luther King, Jr., occupied the news, it was of less importance to me than Roy Campanella's batting average.

Later I was to learn that we were the "silent generation," but what was there to be noisy about? I never thought that segregation could or would die, and even the eventual success of the Montgomery bus boycott was not evidence to the contrary (though the Nashville bus company quietly desegregated its buses because of what had transpired in Montgomery). The events of our lives were standing on street corners in the evenings and looking in passing cars to see the legs of those women drivers who'd pulled their skirts and dresses above their knees to more easily operate the floor pedals; sitting on porches on summer evenings and talking about which girls would and which wouldn't; going to parties in dark basements and dancing close while The Platters sang "The Great Pretender" and Johnny Mathis told us how wild was the wind and we thought we heard its whistle in the pressure of a girl's brassiere-hidden breasts against our chests, while hoping she didn't feel our hard young penises against her legs; and after the party, the boys stood on street corners and talked about how closely Grace or Joyce or Caroline had danced and how we knew she wanted to "get up off some trim" and how next time we were going to get "a taste of that," knowing that we were lying and hoping that no girl would call our bluff. Adolescent sexual play in the fifties was brushing your hand surreptitiously across a girl's bosom, feeling her starched cotton brassiere and thinking you'd felt her breasts. Occasionally someone went further, and Jimmy married Beverly and Don didn't marry Norma, and unwilling to become a husband and/or a father for the least "taste of trim," we gave our fledgling passions to pillows in the middle of the night, trying to imagine what a girl's body looked and felt like and would the day ever come when we would know.

There was a small group of us who clustered in each other's houses and listened to records of Charlie Parker, Lester Young, Clifford Brown and Max Roach, the Modern Jazz Quartet, Stan Kenton, Dave Brubeck, Gerry Mulligan, Miles Davis, Chet Baker. Cool jazz was the idiom and we dug the wide, sweet harmonies of the Four Freshmen's "Day By Day," but being black, we liked, even more, Joe Williams shouting the blues every day over Count Basie's solid, rhythmic band. On Sunday evenings we sneaked into Brown's on Jefferson Street to listen to the local jazzmen, and one of us, Waymon Reed, was so good on his trumpet that he began sitting in, and once when Duke Ellington came to town and needed a trumpet player, Waymon got the gig.

Such were our lives, and seldom did we talk or think about anything which occurred outside them. In the fifties, the world was something we read about in the paper, or saw on the six o'clock news, but we did not relate our lives to it, or it to our lives.

Shelley destroyed my isolation. He had been a part of his times, challenging the outmoded and living the new. I could no longer accept who I had been, or what I was about to become—an adult in the same world I'd known as a child. I had been proud of my intelligence, but through Shelley, I realized that I'd used it as an *objet d'art*, to be taken out and exhibited at the request of a teacher, and admiring friends of my parents. Shelley had used his mind to create. Suddenly, the "somebody" I had been told I would be seemed like a dime-store ceramic figurine against the porcelain fineness of Shelley. I was shamed into existence.

5

I entered a wider sphere of reality through the window which had most defined the one in which I had been living—religion. The church was the theater in which black frustrations were released and black hopes renewed with the promise of an eschatological redemption. The world was not the slums spread around the church like a urine stain, but the soul hidden within tortured black flesh. Because God had assumed flesh, come into the sin-sick world and allowed Himself to be crucified, He knew about our troubles, and if we brought them to Him, everything would be all right. "'Come unto ME, and *I* will give you rest,'" Daddy would preach, quoting from the Bible. "He didn't say, go to the *movies* and you'll find rest! He didn't say you'd find rest out at the *ball park* on Sunday afternoon! He didn't say you'd find rest on a *barstool*! NO! 'Take up your yoke and follow ME!'" said the Lord. 'MY burden is LIGHT! My YOKE is EASY!'" It was a theology of survival, but sitting beside my mother in the third pew on Sundays, I wondered how a man could rise from the dead and ascend to heaven. I could not understand how God knew everything, particularly when I could never picture Him except as an old man with the powers of Superman. "Faith can move mountains!" Daddy preached, and imagining the Rocky Mountains which we had driven through the summer of my seventh year, I doubted that anything could move them. I wanted to believe, but did not know in what or whom that belief was to reside. My unspoken uncertainties were irrelevant, however, because that religion of faith was the dominant force in the community, affecting sinner and Christian equally. It embodied a code of conduct, with everyone carrying a psychological monitor of "Thou shalt nots." Most were broken with prosaic regularity, but never without guilt and an all-pervading fear that one had been condemned to a painful perdition. (Being the son of a minister, I compensated by becoming the superstar of profanity among my peers. Each New Year's Day, however, I vowed to expunge my vocabulary, and asked God to help me "speak with a clean tongue." Inevitably, however, there came the day when God seemed to be attending to someone else's prayer just as the bell rang for recess, and before I knew it, my preadolescent voice could be heard the length and breadth of the playground yelling at some classmate, who had missed an easy fly ball, "You goddamned son-of-a-bitch! Your mama coulda caught that in her raggedy drawers!")

Throughout childhood and early adolescence, I had periods of fervent piety, inspired by fear of divine punishment, but when it didn't come, I relaxed into comfortable secularity. (In Kansas City, we played baseball against a group of white boys from the Catholic school once. As the black team's pitcher, I was the one who could not let his confidence be eroded by the white, Catholic boys coming to bat and crossing themselves before the first pitch. I struck out most of them, but it wasn't easy, because I was awed by a religion one could invoke in an inconsequential baseball game. Once, I sneaked up to the Catholic church, which persisted in its segregated existence in our neighborhood, peered inside and was frightened by the lights of what seemed to be hundreds of small candles flickering in the naved darkness. Whatever else Catholicism might be, it was obviously very complicated.)

The vague doubts I'd always had about religion were crystallized by Shelley into one frightening question: Does God exist? Shelley had been a militant atheist, but I could not follow him easily, for in my mind, the act of asking was heresy. Yet, if I was to be an intellectual, as he had been, the question could not be evaded.

The proper place for someone with such a question is college, which I entered the fall of 1956. Fisk University in Nashville gave me a place and resources for four years to answer it and the other questions which logically followed, once I said No. My college life centered on the International Student Center, where foreign films were shown every weekend, lectures, play readings, art exhibits and poetry readings given throughout the school year. The vitality of the ISC came, however, from its habitués, the campus intellectuals, who made the Center their private club.

Though intimidated by the lofty conversations about Sartre, Camus, Baldwin, Kierkegaard, and others whose writings dominated the college intellectual's life in the latter fifties, I brought my questions about God into this arena. The campus intellectuals, a little disdainful of this freshman who dared speak in their midst, dismissed me with the pronouncement that it was impossible to know if God existed, and until it could be proven or disproven,

27

they reserved opinion. I thought that to be an evasion of the question and intellectually dishonest. How could one base his life on the impossibility of knowing? Then, John Brown, a stocky, brilliant history major who usually had only the most brusque remarks for me, said one day, brusquely, "You might find Sartre interesting, Lester." After asking him to spell it, I rushed to the library, and what Shelley had conceived, Sartre midwifed.

Sartre argued that the actual fact of God's existence or non-existence was unimportant when compared to his function in people's lives. A belief in God bestowed *a priori* meaning on life, which he summarized as "Essence precedes existence." Sartre denied this. People exist, and the task of life was to give that existence meaning, i.e., "Existence precedes essence." Because there was no *a priori* meaning, people were "condemned to be free." Most, however, were unwilling to accept the responsibility of innate freedom and, thus, created God to relieve them of the horror of that freedom.

I had never read anything so convincing and was ecstatic at the prospect of assuming responsibility for my life, even if it meant, as Sartre said, accepting the consequences of my acts before I acted. This seemed more honest than acting good because a point would be recorded for me in the Good Deeds column of God's moral ledger, as a Sunday school teacher had once told me.

I became an atheist, not so much to deny God's existence (who can base their life on a teleological denial?), but to wholly affirm my own. When I announced my atheism proudly to the ISC claque, however, they were shocked. I had assumed that they would understand and when they didn't, I understood that I took God so seriously that I would deny His existence. They scarcely regard Him seriously at all, allowing Him neither existence nor nonexistence. Thereafter I knew that intellectuals were merely athletes, using words and ideas instead of balls to play their games. (Mother was taking a casserole from the oven when I told her. "I've been thinking, Mother, and I don't believe in God anymore." She always controlled her emotions carefully, and my words did not cause her facial expression to change, or slow her motion in taking the hot dish from the oven and placing it on top of the stove. She closed the oven door and, reaching in the nearest cabinet to take down the dinner plates, said evenly, "Well, you're no son of mine," and walked past me to set the table.)

Read Huxley's *Ape and Essence.*

Daddy gave me a sermon today which went something like this: "There are times when reason is no good. Now I want you to stop all this mess about not believing in God. Who do you think you are to set yourself up as not believing. You read some fool book and let that tear down all you've been taught. Well, you're going to church whether you want to or not. That's all there is to it. All I get comes from God and therefore all *you* get comes from God. If you aren't going to believe, you won't get what God gives me."

In other words he was saying, "Believe or get out." His approach isn't quite right. He still doesn't think I'm serious. He figures this ultimatum will work. I could live a lie or I could leave. If it comes to that point, I shall do the latter.

Brave and fearless words worthy of an adolescent rebel, but leaving would mean having to go to work, an undertaking for which I was singularly unqualified. But no threat of my father's would have made me recant, and perhaps he remembered the Sunday morning many years before when I, five or six at the time, refused to go to church. Five separate times he spanked me and five separate times I cried and reiterated my refusal, until both our wills broke simultaneously, and just as he was about to relent (so I learned years later), I walked out the door to church, without saying a word. Perhaps he knew that this time I would not be broken and nothing more was said, except that he expected me to continue going to church. Shelley would have refused, but my atheism was not in emulation of Shelley's, nor was I rebelling against my father. I was groping for my life, and it was unimportant whether I attended church, as long as I could follow this incipient stirring of my inner life.

6

By His absence, God now dominated and directed my life more totally than He had when I believed Him present. My unquestioning assumption of His existence had given me a place in the world as a child of God, though I had not known what that meant. Without God, however, I had no place, no moral guidelines, and no knowledge of myself. I was forced to ask, who am I? I did not know then that this was a way of confronting God and challenging Him: "If you know who I am, speak. If You are indeed my Creator and in You and only in You is there meaning, reveal YourSelf. Do it in a burning bush or a pillar of fiery clouds or a red MG, if there're no bushes around and it's a clear day." But no bushes flamed, and the clouds remained unfired. (Since I couldn't drive, I wouldn't have known what to do with the MG.)

Unlike Shelley and Sartre, I could not be an atheist and proceed to live, and I was ashamed of myself. Was I a child, unable to accept a meaningless existence in an uncaring universe? Or did my father know something which I, his intellectual superior, could never know?

I became chaos, no longer defined and unable to define for myself. How did one live without God? I began by trying to create a purpose from the void I now was. It was a Godlike function I assumed, to create something out of nothing. If there was no God, no Judge to pronounce eternal sentence for deeds and misdeeds, why did one act for the good, if one could even know the good? (I had started reading Plato.) What was life itself, and what was its meaning if there was no eternal essence which understood why the sparrow fell and black people suffered?

Most of my days that winter and spring were spent sitting in one of the window seats in the ISC, as dead to myself as a tree embalmed by winter that did not bud in the springing time. I thought only of suicide, because life had no meaning that I could ascertain, and having none, why, then, should one live it? It would be fifteen years before I realized that meaning is meaningless, and as long as one's concern is meaning, life can only be meaningless. But I was attempting to answer with my mind what could only be answered with parts of me I had not yet uncovered.

January 8, 1957
(Journal)
Finished *Life of Nietzsche.*

January 13, 1957
Toscanini died today. Heard an hour of music conducted by him from radio stations in Boston and Cleveland. Read from *The Greek View of Life.*

January 19, 1957
Finished *The Greek View of Life.* Won two games of chess.

January 27, 1957

Today I am 18!! I feel no different. I just wonder if I am a mature 18. I don't know.

I've been wondering whether being an atheist [if] I can still work in the church. I think so. I think that the main thing is a good relation between man and man. God is nothing more than one's conscience.

January 31, 1957

In the last four days I have read *Antic Hay* by Huxley, Mencken's *Minority Report,* Erle Stanley Gardner's *The Case of the Silent Partner* and *My Life and Loves in Greenwich Village* by Max Bodenheim.

Like a lost explorer, I tried every path that looked as if it might lead out of the maze of my mind. I didn't understand much of what I read, being unequipped to understand the complexities of the Greek view of life, or the satiric subtleties of Huxley's novels. (I read all of his novels, and while I could not say that I enjoyed them, I was awed by Huxley's erudition, best exemplified in his essays. He could write well on any subject, it seemed, and he became my literary ideal.)

I read, not to learn what others had thought, for I was not a fledgling scholar, but to understand myself. A book fulfilled its purpose if I underlined one sentence which gave me words by which to know something I'd felt, or an ideal by which I wanted to live. Camus' *The Stranger* and *The Rebel,* Sartre's *Nausea* (which I read the following year), Beckett's *Waiting for Godot* (in which I had the role of Estragon in an ISC play reading my freshman year) were particularly significant. It was strangely reassuring to find others who knew the despair of nothingness.

I tried to read a book a day outside class assignments, for I had decided that college was where you explored yourself, and that didn't occur in most classes. (I was aided in this decision by the "D" I received in math the first semester which ended my dreams of being elected to Phi Beta Kappa, and instead of being disappointed, I found myself free to pursue my education. I went on to compile a most ordinary academic record, based on the theory that if I went to class I would get a "C," if I stayed awake I would get a "B," and if I studied I would get an "A." I went to class.) I read Gide's novels and journals, which were curiously fascinating in their tone (and in the jacket photographs of him, stocking cap on his head, cigarette in his mouth, scarf around his neck, seated on a stepladder beside floor-to-ceiling bookcases, reading, I saw myself as I hoped to be in forty years). Simone de Beauvoir's *The Second Sex* was vital for Michele, who took her as a model, and *The Mandarins* presented me with an historical description of my spiritual problem.

Through Sartre and De Beauvoir, I realized that I had been living in a country of one-eyed people, for racism gives its victims spiritual glaucoma, transforming the multicolored prism of reality into a tiny square of glaring whiteness so bright that one is blinded by it. Sartre and De Beauvoir gave me vision, and though I was black, I began to see that I had been affected by the changes in the psyche of Western people wrought by World War II, Hiroshima and Nagasaki, and the Cold War. While I had been playing cowboy (not cowboy and Indians) in the alleys of Kansas City, the humanistic values of Western civilization had not been able to counter the technological efficiency of Nazism and American democracy. Buchenwald, Auschwitz, Belsen, the fire-bombing of Dresden, and Hiroshima had made the romantic conceit of the goodness of humanity a lie that could never be repeated. Those world-transforming events had occurred outside my consciousness, but I was living the consequences. My atheism, then, was not only an act toward self-definition, but part of a reassessment of humanity's relationship to itself then occurring in the West. I was not the only one who looked upon the world and found no nourishment. It was no longer possible to believe there was a God; it was no longer possible to praise humanity and glorify it as being only a little lower than the angels. Animals did not stoop to people's level.

Some writers, like Beckett, were only able to decribe the void. Others sought to articulate new values, and their works seemed written especially for me.

Underlinings

From Colin Wilson's *The Outsider*:

It is not enough to accept a concept of order and live by it; that is cowardice, and such cowardice cannot result in freedom. Chaos must be faced. Real order must be preceded by a descent into chaos.

32

From Camus' *The Rebel*:

From the moment that man believes neither in God nor in immortal life, he becomes "responsible for everything alive, for everything that, born of suffering, is condemned to suffer from life."

Since the salvation of man is not achieved in God, it must be achieved on earth. Since the world has no direction, man, from the moment he accepts this, must give it one that will eventually lead to a superior type of humanity.

From Colin Wilson's *Religion and the Rebel*:

. . . the visionary disciplines himself to see the world always as if he had only just seen it for the first time.

All experiences can be used as the building bricks of a visionary consciousness if there is a conscious effort at assimilation.

. . . higher consciousness imposes new strains, and the men who have the greatest sensibility often wish they could get rid of it. . . . They are afraid of insanity.

The mark of greatness is always intuition, not logic.
. . . all crises lead to beauty.

It was a long journey, however, from an intellectual understanding of "chaos must be faced" to the emotional apprehension of that particular terror. But the passages I underlined supported my efforts to create values, as well as giving me ideas which would slowly and painfully become mine in the effort to live.

7

Books were my guru, but I needed people to listen to me, to respond and empathize with my struggles. In the English department, where I took my major, I was fortunate to have three teachers whose influence on my life was to be permanent. Bernard Spivack, chairman of the department and a Shakespearean scholar, gave me a permanent love of the beauty and magic of language; Charlotte, his wife, was an artist in the classroom, but I learned equally as much on those Thursday mornings when I sat in her office, where she tolerated me for two and three hours as I grappled with Plato, Spinoza, and always, Sartre. It was she who introduced me to Gide, Camus, Chinese poetry, Graham Greene, and Georges Simenon, who became, and remains, my model for a writer of fiction.

Charlotte Spivack believed in and encouraged my initial efforts to write, but it was the poet, Robert Hayden, who told me bluntly that I was a writer, and that was at the core of my problems. He was a surrogate father, who knew that writing was not only learning the craft of using words, but even more, a psychological condition. A writer was a different kind of person, and it was that person in me he recognized and instructed. To be a writer, one must not only "face chaos," but set up residence within it.

However, I also needed a female contemporary whose hand I could hold during the labor pains of giving birth to myself. But being shy to the point of catatonia, I had accepted that I would never have a girl friend, unless she took the initiative. (One had, at camp the summer before my freshman year. She tired of my lack of aggressiveness and one day kissed me, thrusting her tongue into my mouth and forever changing my life. Ah, Gwen!) Whenever I fantasized about taking a girl on a date, the screen went blank as I arrived on her front porch. What would we do? According to street corner discussions, you took a girl out to "get in them panties." Exactly how this was accomplished was never said, not to mention the more monumental problem of finding some place secret enough to do it, assuming one knew how. If by some act of Divine Intervention (which could not occur since I was an atheist), I "got in her panties," I still had a problem. I wasn't particularly interested in being there. Michele hated boys, for she overheard the vulgar way they talked about girls; I could not regard another girl in a way Michele did not want to be regarded. Moreover, I really didn't want to make love: I wanted to talk. ("Do you think a man on a raft in the middle of the ocean would have a concept of time?" was one of my favorite conversational openers, good for at least a half-hour of silence.) Oddly, though, the girls I knew expected a boy to try to kiss them, and sometimes, more. I didn't understand why they would want to get near that ugly thing boys were so proud of, and Michele swore that no boy would ever stick it in her.

Another part of me, however, ached to feel that flesh which swelled behind the starched white blouses and straight skirts. I masturbated two, three times a day, hating whatever it was that seized and shook my body like a tree in high winds. I particularly hated that thing drooping from the end of my torso like a fat worm, pulsating to an aching hardness as if it lived wholly independently of me. I wanted to cut it off and throw it to a passing dog. I envied Michele, whose organ was invisible to her, hidden, though I was never exactly sure where, unable to embarrass her as mine did me, protruding against my pants with such rigidity that sometimes it felt like a third leg.

Michele prevented me from treating girls as sexual objects, but my own sexual feelings persisted. Not knowing how to accept them as a natural part of myself, and, because of Michele, being unable to wholly admit that I had them, I came to hate girls. My earliest short stories were about young artists so distracted from their work by a world seething with feminine pulchritude that they became murderers of women. The only escape from the dilemma was to find a girl with whom I could talk. Then, if we developed a physical relationship, there would be no shame.

I wanted a female me, a Michele who lived outside me. The fall of my sophomore year, someone said, "That's interesting," when I posed Chuang Tzu's butterfly riddle, and I knew that I had found her. I met Sylvia in the only place my first love should have begun, the library. She was a gentle, soft-spoken, light-skinned girl with narrow, almost Oriental eyes. An art major from New York City, she was a graduate of the elite High School of Music and Art, and we met at the moment when each of us was obsessed with learning who we were and what we were going to do with our lives. "I don't know any of the answers," she wrote me once, "but that won't stop me from trying to find answers that will be true ones. God! This swiftly tilting planet—this green and blue ocean of hope and despair. Of truth? and men. Of truth and life. What am I to do with it? What are we to do with it? Is there only a different answer for each of us—or is there one answer for us all? Is life always a searching and never a finding?"

I had never known one such as her, who cared passionately, who never told me, as other girls had, "You take things too seriously." She was as serious about her life as I was about mine and most amazing, she was as awed by me as I by her. It was the perfect "marriage"; we were two souls in search of our selves and how much less frightening to make that search together. By being together, we affirmed each other and were no longer alone.

She was more than the female me, for her experiences had included concerts at Carnegie Hall, the Metropolitan Museum of Art, folk music, the drawings of Paul Klee, the watercolors of Dufy and the sculptures of Rodin. I envied and idolized her, for she seemed to think, see and feel more deeply than I. "The birds look like black pepper flung against the sky," she said one afternoon as we walked across campus, and how I wished I could open my mouth and speak a poem. She talked more often in images than concepts, and I did not understand her. She showed me her strange drawings of naked, black trees, or of Giacometti-like figures leaping and jumping between asteroids and planets, and I was frightened. She lived someplace I had never been.

Every Saturday afternoon we sat in the ISC and listened to the Metropolitan Opera broadcasts, and one Saturday I borrowed my father's portable radio and we walked to Centennial Park and sat on the steps of the replica of the Parthenon there, to listen to *Tristan and Isolde*. We'd been there about an hour when the park policeman told us to move. I knew that blacks were not allowed in the park, but pretending ignorance, I asked him why. "You just can't," he said, flustered. "Don't make trouble. Just leave." I refused, badgering him until he became angry, and then, in our great love, we laughed and walked away to the strains of Wagner.

She called me "Jay" and told me that my eyes were beautiful and that I had the hands of an artist. I wanted to believe her, because no one had ever said that anything of me was beautiful. I told her that I was going to be a writer, composer, painter, and she did not laugh. She tried to convince me of God's existence, but loved me when I remained skeptical. We pored through art books together and she taught me the humor of Dufy, the passion of Van Gogh, the truth of Rembrandt, and I was overjoyed the day I "discovered" De Chirico and had something to give to her. We clung to each other desperately, fearful of being returned to the desert of our prior loneliness.

And we touched each other, clumsily, and without consummation, but it did not matter. To know myself beneath her hands was to feel myself as a person of beauty, an experience theretofore unimagined. Her breasts were the first I touched and I held them in my hands as if I were a pilgrim to Chartres receiving communion wafers. We found a secret place in the library where we undressed each other and knew ourselves in each other's mouths and tongues, and though I longed to lie wholly within her, we were afraid to risk the child we did not want.

We were going to be married. I would move to New York, get a job and we would make love to Chopin nocturnes, have many children and live happily ever after—painting, writing, composing, dancing, sculpting and drawing. Between us there was scarcely an aspect of the arts we had not studied and we laughed with anticipatory joy at the world's amazement on experiencing our creations.

But the following year, she did not return. She didn't like Fisk, and, also, she wanted to be away from me, feeling that she was being absorbed by me and increasingly unable to exist unto herself. I didn't understand. We wrote constantly for the next two years, still planning to be married until it was evident that she wouldn't marry me until I told her how I was going to earn a living. By this time I was living on North Beach in San Francisco at the tail end of the Beat Generation, subsisting on rice, jasmine tea and an occasional handout of a sandwich from a Catholic priest with a wart on his chin at the church on Washington Square. It was a perfect life, and I couldn't understand why she didn't want to share it. Finally she wrote and told me that I was "immature" and was obviously never going "to grow up." That last letter begged me to return or destroy her letters, and the sketchpads of her drawings. I couldn't. Without them I feared the passage of time would make me believe that I had dreamed her. (The winter of 1963 I accidentally saw her in, of all places, the library on Manhattan's West Twenty-third Street. It had been five years since we'd seen each other and I was surprised at how nervous we were. It was evident that Time had let us remain what we had been, but I was married now and I didn't want to know if she was, too. Afterward I hated myself for running from the library in fear, for not hugging her and telling her that I still had her letters and drawings, the books of mine in which she had scribbled poems and her French book. She had believed in me, had helped me paint the colors on my dreams, and mine were, I had begun to believe, going to come true. But she did not look as if hers were, for the shining intensity I'd known in her eyes had changed to the fright of one being hunted and beginning to gasp for breath. Two years later I saw her again at the same place and this time she ran from me as if she'd seen a specter.

It was the Sunday of July Fourth weekend, 1972. Joanne and I were walking through Washington Square Park in Greenwich Village when I saw Olivia, a classmate from Fisk who was the only person I knew who'd known Sylvia in New York. After exchanging pleasantries and gossip, I asked Olivia what I'd wanted to ask before saying hello to her. "How's Sylvia?"

She looked at me strangely. "You don't know?"

I hoped she was not going to tell me what I already knew from the tone of her voice. "Know what?" I asked, hoping my smile would shield me.

"Sylvia walked into the ocean at Rockaway Beach."

I asked her when.

"Oh, let me see. It was, must have been around 1963 or 1964."

I thought back to the last time I'd seen her. "Must've been after that, because I ran into her the spring of 1965."

Olivia shook her head. "You have to be mistaken. She was dead then."

I asked her if Sylvia had married. She had not.

I came home and that evening, read her letters for the first time in thirteen years. I had forgotten just how much we loved each other. "If I don't love you, where is my home?" I'd forgotten just how completely we were all the other had had at one time, and how desperate our need was for each other. "Just ask the sun and the summer breeze and the moist black earth. They'll tell you. I love you." It was there, in her rapid scrawl, on practically every page, and for the first time, I noticed how often she'd written of one day letting waves cover her. I was too angry at her to cry, for she left me with an emptiness which will never be filled. It was her place and as long as I knew she was somewhere in the world, that place hummed a quiet song. As long as I could walk the streets of New York knowing that one day I would see her, it was all right not to see her. But she had irrevocably deprived me of herself and I wanted to swim into the ocean after her. On that day, I wonder if she knew how much of me she was drowning, also. But I didn't know until she'd done it.)

8

The summer after my sophomore year, Mother decided it was time my brother and I knew each other. Nine years my senior, he'd left home when I was eight to join the Coast Guard (a step I approved, because I would no longer have to share the bedroom), before settling on a career in the Air Force. I'd seen him five times, at most, in the intervening ten years.

I enjoyed being with him on the base beside Lake Michigan, but having none of the shared experiences which meld disparate individuals into a family, we were brothers only because we had the same parents.

Most of the time I sat beside Lake Michigan across the street from his apartment, and it inspired what I considered my first successful poem.

> The lake was calm that day,
> And she made no sound as she brushed
> Upon the rocky shore
> With her easy, gentle sway.
>
> With a tender, tempting voice
> She whispered to the stones,
> But the stones did not have a choice.
> How much better it would be
> If you, my love, were a stone.

(To whom, if anyone, that was addressed, I don't recall.)

After three weeks, I decided to go to Washington, D. C., where my cousin Dorothy lived. Of my relatives, I was, and am, closest to her. The oldest daughter of my mother's youngest sister, she was raised in our family, for reasons still unclear to me. An elementary-school teacher, she taught me to read, gave me my first piano lessons and the first lesson in character that I recall. (I couldn't have been more than six the day I was practicing piano and making mistake after mistake. In disgust I banged my fist on the keys and screamed, "This piano!" Dorothy, who was passing through the room, said, coldly, "It's not the piano.")

That summer became the happiest I'd ever lived, because my whole environment was books. I immersed myself in the cold, wet world of Katherine Mansfield (that's how I recall it feeling), the surreal one of Rimbaud, and the demanding one of the *Bhagavad-Gita*, from which I extracted two important principles: Work without regard for the fruit of your labors; Pain and pleasure are the same. (I understood neither rationally, but something in me recognized the profound truth of them.) I had a passionate love affair with the Library of Congress, wandering through its wide corridors and leaning over the stone balustrades and looking down at the people entering and leaving, convinced that each was working on some important book. I sat in the periodical and newspaper reading room, astounded at the magazines and papers from all over the world, none of which I could read. It didn't matter. To see *Paris-Soir* was concrete proof of a world wider than the one in which I lived. I didn't know how I would become a part of it, but I didn't doubt that I would.

Other afternoons I wandered through the rooms at the National Gallery and wrote Sylvia excited letters about how Gauguin and Van Gogh looked in the original, as if she didn't know. I was mesmerized by the canvases which held Van Gogh's actual brush strokes, canvases that he had stretched, touched and gazed upon with a mind more feverish than I imagined mine to be. I saw medieval paintings and wondered how the people who created them had lived inside themselves. There was an integrity and peace in those paintings which I had never associated with religion. I saw El Grecos, and had to restrain myself from dropping to my knees. I looked at Rembrandts and understood why his name was synonymous with genius, for in his portraits, people were more alive than they had been in life. I sat for hours beside a fountain across from the new Teamsters Union Building and as I watched it arch streams of water into the sunlight, it seemed to symbolize the exultant joy I sensed waiting to burst from me.

As if I'd been locked in a dungeon for nineteen years and fed on bread and water, I felt myself released into a banquet hall. I envied white people, convinced that they came naturally to the art, literature and ideas I was discovering almost alone. In Washington, life mattered. In Nashville, nothing did, but how could it in a place where you couldn't read *The New York Times* as you drank your morning coffee.

I understood why Sylvia had decided not to return to Fisk. Its vision of the world was middle-class and the Holy Grail was a new car. It was not committed to the pursuit of Truth, but the care and feeding of the next generation of "niggerati." Only in Sylvia, a few friends, and the white students who came to Fisk on exchange programs from small liberal arts colleges like Pomona and Oberlin, did I meet people who lived for inner realities.

When I returned to Fisk in the fall, I was a man at war, stoning the high-heeled properly coiffed girls with profanity, wearing my jeans like Jeanne d'Arc carrying the Croix of Lorraine into Orléans, and being as different from my classmates as I could, afraid that if they liked me, I would succumb to the virus of black "respectability" and be entombed in some black suburbia and written about in *Ebony*. The only way to affirm something in myself, which I could not yet name, was to live with hatred against that which I could. The evening the Dean of Men would not allow me to attend a concert because I didn't have on a tie, I knew that we were not engaged in a petty struggle over a piece of cloth, but in a battle for control of my life. Fisk equated dressing well with living well; I was not so misguided. Finally, Anna Harvin, the Dean of Students, called my parents to complain about my dress and "antisocial" behavior, but they could do nothing. Having been raised to resist the efforts of whites to control my soul, I was not going to give that right to blacks.

I was a rebel in a cause whose outlines were vague, until I happened on an article in *Esquire* by John Clellon Holmes called, "The Philosophy of the Beat Generation."

> Everyone who has lived through a war, any sort of war, knows that beat means, not so much weariness, as rawness of the nerves, not so much being "filled up to here," as being emptied out. It describes a state of mind from which all unessentials have been stripped, leaving it receptive to everything around it, but impatient with trivial obstructions.

I didn't wholly understand Holmes's words, but when he wrote that the Beat Generation was on a "quest" for spiritual values, I trembled with self-recognition. He quoted Jack Kerouac telling an interviewer, "I want God to show me His face," and though I was loath to relinquish my bitter atheism, I had to admit that, perhaps, my denial of God was a longing to meet Him.

The Beat Generation was a positive response to the nothingness delineated by Beckett. It was not only a reaction against the spiritual depression engendered by Auschwitz and Hiroshima, but, also, the vapid world of conformity and fear which covered America

41

like poison gas in the fifties. Fisk University was Uncle Tom in a gray flannel suit, and one night at a meeting of the Philosophical Society (of which I was organizer and president), Dean Harvin and I argued over individuality and conformity, she, in a lapse of professionalism, yelling at me, "Mr. Lester! You have to conform to society's standards!", and I responding with equal fervor, "All I *have* to do is die!" The Beat Generation told me that there were people who had faced the chaos and emerged, dancing. In the now famous second issue of *Evergreen Review*, "The San Francisco Scene," amid the poetry of Brother Antoninus, Gary Snyder, Phillip Lamantia, Ferlinghetti, and a beautifully lyric story by Kerouac, "October in the Railroad Earth," there was a poem whose greatness was unmistakable: "I saw the best minds of my generation destroyed by madness,/starving hysterical naked," began Allen Ginsberg's "Howl" and Bill Lewis, my best friend, and I would shout those lines in unison as we walked across campus, knowing that would be our epitaph if we allowed Fisk to have its way with us.

I now had a name for myself—"beatnik"—and began dressing even more sloppily, and lay awake nights fantasizing about driving nonstop across country, though I still hadn't learned to drive. But I did not delude myself into believing that I had wholly uncovered my identity. I was black, and could take from the Beats what I might need to fashion a self, but I was incapable of belonging to them. The best minds of my generation had been lobotomized by a dread different from any a white person might have known.

The discovery of the Beat Generation would have been enough to transform my life, but more came the day I was browsing in a bookstore and picked up D. T. Suzuki's *Zen Buddhism*. In it I found a perplexing, incomprehensible non-philosophy which was exhilarating. It had no ten commandments or admonitions to do good and shun evil. I understood nothing of it, but was compelled to know more.

That same day I bought another book, *Haiku*, and in the three-line, seventeen-syllable Japanese poems, I heard my voice. Like Zen, haiku was a different way of perceiving experience, a way of being, in which one lived the poetry of every minute, for the world was infinite possibility.

That fall, my hands picked up books and magazines as if guided to them. All thought of being in control of my life vanished completely, however, the December day the university informed me that I had been selected to be an exchange student to San Diego State College for the next semester. I had applied to go to Oberlin in Ohio. I knew that I was being sent to San Francisco and North Beach, via San Diego State. ("The Lord works in mysterious ways," I could hear a certain voice saying.)

I almost didn't go. That fall I had been elected editor of the campus newspaper and in November, Bill, who was managing editor, and I decided to publish an issue satirizing the university. The newspaper's staff vetoed the idea, and I fired them. I wrote all the articles, except two or three contributed by Bill and, surprisingly, the paper's faculty advisor, Lutrelle Palmer (now a prominent broadcaster and newspaperman in Chicago).

I don't know if the satire was good, but the paper was a resounding success. The students had not been as excited since I'd been there, and though I'd headlined the paper, EDITOR TO BE EXPELLED, I was sure I wouldn't be. I appreciated, however, the many assurances from students that if such was attempted, they would go on strike. I deliberately released the paper on the last day of classes before Christmas vacation, knowing that the students would take it home to show to their parents, many of whom were prominent alumni. It was my hope that they would be so disturbed, pressure would be brought against the president to sit down with a group of students and discuss the quality of education at the school.

There was no doubt that the paper reached the alumni (and several years later, I was told that a copy was read approvingly by Fisk's most important alumnus, W. E. B. Du Bois), because when school reconvened, Stephen Wright, Fisk's president, called a special convocation. Its sole purpose was to reprimand me, and when he declared, "I am certain that not one student, besides the editor, agrees with the views expressed in the paper," I sat, waiting for students to leap to their feet and shout him down. The silence fell in torrents from the nave of the chapel. Even Bill seemed to move away from me in his seat.

Later that day I was informed that the university did not want me to represent it as an exchange student, and someone else would go to San Diego State in my stead. The bureaucracy at State, however, could not rearrange itself for such a simple matter and informed Fisk that if I didn't come, there would be no exchange program. Fisk would not yield. I formally transferred to San Diego State.

On the eve of my twentieth birthday, I boarded the train on the first step of my journey to North Beach, vowing never to return to Fisk and Nashville and the violations on my being they represented. Existence precedes essence.

II

1

In San Diego I encountered the white world directly for the first time. No one had prepared me for being one of seventy-five blacks on a campus of fifteen thousand whites. I was eager, however, to test myself intellectually against whites, confident that I would triumph. I was well prepared for the wrong war.

The battleground was not the southern white hostility I'd always known, but the indifferent and unassailable certainty of whites that my identity was wholly contained in the pigmentation of my skin. I had been trained to parry the blows of overt hatred, but my drillmasters had been black southerners who did not know that there were ways of being called nigger which left you bloodied and you had not seen a weapon or its wielder.

I was not flattered to be the only student my teachers knew by name on the second day of classes, for from their mouths, "Mr. Lester" sounded like "the colored boy," the one whose absence from class would be as apparent as if the sun died. I walked across campus day after day, sending my self winging toward others and no one noticed it fluttering before them. It went from pairs of blue eyes to hazel, green, and brown ones, and was stamped by each, like a box proceeding down an assembly line to the press where the product name was imprinted on its sides—COLORED. No one looked down when it plopped at their feet, gasping for the life which only recognition could give. Soon I looked at that self, and where I had once marveled at its morning-glory fragility, the powder of its butterfly wings, I now saw a fantasy I must have

45

created for my own entertainment, for no one else saw what I had believed was me.

Suddenly, I heard words come from my mouth with a slow laziness, minus endings, noticed that my hair would not lie flat beyond the first class, no matter how many strokes I gave it in the mornings, and though I'd never been in a cotton field, I wondered if there was lint beneath my fingernails. I started using the deodorant my mother had put in my suitcase.

Living outside the black community for the first time, I ceased to exist in any familiar way. I knew myself as a thought of others, and only in the way they conceived me to be. (One morning as I slept through Seventeenth-Century Drama, the teacher woke me. I was more than a little embarrassed, for I had failed the race and probably returned us to slavery.

The teacher, however, smiled at me. "Do you work at night?" he asked gently.

I was working in the college library to earn money for my pilgrimage to North Beach, but I didn't think that was what he had in mind. "Yes, sir," I replied, seeing myself bending over filthy sinks washing dishes in a restaurant until two A.M.

"And you probably come from a large family, too?" he continued kindly. "A lot of brothers and sisters making it difficult to study or get rest?"

This shit's getting a little deep, I said to myself, but I had to lie. He would look like a fool if I didn't. Too, he was trying to help me. "Yes, sir," I answered in my best colored-boy-struggling-through-school voice.

He nodded. "Well, I understand. I think it's admirable that you're trying to get an education and if the only place you can get some rest is in my class, go right ahead."

If I'd been a white student, I was one nigger I would've hated. Being the nigger in question, I thanked him in my white-folks-sho'-is-nice-to-me voice and went back to sleep for the remainder of the term. I got an "A" in the course.

But who had made a fool of whom, I wondered for years after. Had I really "put one over on 'im," by being what he thought I was? If so, why did I loathe myself as he smiled at me? Yet, what was my choice? The teacher was sincere, and he thought he was helping me. Why, then, did he make me feel like crying, and for whom were the tears?)

I was a neophyte in the white world, unable to recognize paternalism, and worse, white girls titillating themselves with subconscious erotic racial fantasies of which I was the stimulus. I had a casual relationship with two girls, and mistakenly thinking they were responding to *me*, I asked one to go to a Bach concert. After an embarrassing pause she said, "My mother would literally go insane if I went out with you." Having been told that by girls at Fisk, I understood, and undaunted, asked the other girl. She smiled her pretty white smile, looked at me with her sky-blue eyes and said, "Oh I can go out with almost anybody. Why should I go out with you?" I stood there, a nigger grin on my face, unable to think of one reason why she should.

I thought a friendly relationship was developing between me and two of the librarians with whom I worked. I enjoyed talking with them about St. John Perse, Hemingway, Joyce and Robinson Jeffers, all of whom I "discovered" that spring. The relationship with one librarian ended the morning he asked me, apropos of nothing, "Do you know James Baldwin?" True to my meek nigger soul I quietly said, no, and felt guilty because I didn't. I ceased speaking to him, however, but didn't know why.

The other librarian was an attractive young woman on whom I had a crush, and the night she offered me a ride home, my fantasies danced arabesques around the farthest stars. Bent over by the weight of unrelieved erections, I was, at long last, going to be seduced by the experienced older woman (Frame One on the screen of adolescent male sexual fantasies). I walked beside her through the parking lot in a daze, but not so much so that I didn't see the man standing in front of me when we got to her car. Before my anticipatory erection could shrivel, she said, sweetly, "Julius, I want you to meet one of our Hungarian friends." With those words, the love affair of her life ended. In 1959, no Hungarian could be a friend of mine. For two years America had rolled out the red carpet and uncorked champagne bottles to welcome Hungarian "freedom fighters" fleeing from "Iron Curtain domination," and I was painfully conscious that people who spoke no English had more opportunity in America than I did. I forced myself to shake the Hungarian's hand, knowing that it was not his fault that he was free in my country, but I wondered how many months would pass before he became truly American and hammered his nail into black people. To my librarian friend, I never addressed another word and I knew why.

Yet, I did not understand myself, for while I resented being regarded solely as a colored thing, I was angered when someone, like the female librarian, assumed there was *no* difference between us. I wondered if I was becoming one of those "sensitive Negroes," who saw an affront in any word, gesture or facial expression of a white. I didn't have the words to tell myself that I was reacting against relationships based on white definitions and the unquestioned assumption that their definitions were, also, mine. This was a denial of life at its source. I knew, with that felt knowledge which I trusted, that I wanted to have my assumptions about myself respected, at the very least, and, at the most, accepted as the only legitimate basis for a relationship.

But when someone is smiling at you, how do you say, "Stop calling me nigger"? How do you stop hurting when you can't see the blows striking you? How do you stop bleeding when you don't know what is opening the wounds?

One evening, however, I found myself on familiar ground, and I howled my outrage. It was the night of the Spring Sing of the Greek letter organizations. I sat in the darkened amphitheater while fraternities and sororities followed each other onto the stage and, among the usual standards from musicals, sang spirituals. Even then I didn't approve of whites singing black music; it was like citizens of the Third Reich singing "Kol Nidre." But I maintained a fidgety silence until a fraternity in blackface makeup walked on stage and sang "Joshua Fit the Battle of Jericho." At long last, an identifiable and unquestionable insult! "What th' fuck is this shit?" I said loudly. "Muthafuckas! Fuck this shit!" The audience stirred audibly, but I wouldn't stop. Blacks sitting near me tried to shut me up. "Stop acting a nigger," I was told in anxious whispers, but if there'd ever been a time to act like one, this was it! The fraternity finished to tumultuous applause, which I took as a personal rebuke, and I walked out angrily, now cursing the blacks who were relieved to see me go. I wrote a letter to the school newspaper that night which said, in part, "Possibly in fifty years a presentation such as that can be made and no one be offended because the memories and emotions it evokes will be buried. Unfortunately, however, the funeral is a future event, and SAE [the fraternity] seems to desire the funeral to be in the unforeseeable future. . . . The Greek organizations that sang the spirituals seem to recognize the great music that came from the soul of oppressed people, but isn't it slightly ironic that the people themselves are not recognized?" The letter was published, but no one, not even the fraternity, took it seriously enough to respond.

My salvation at San Diego State would have been to recreate my black world with the other black students, but in 1959, blacks avoided each other when they were in the white orb, not wanting to be accused of segregating themselves. We were "integrated," sitting next to and being seen with a white person at every opportunity. We tried not to notice that the white students did not sit beside us, or ever smile in our direction, and kept our anguish private, scarcely acknowledging it to ourselves, never offering or seeking the solace we could have given each other.

2

My personal environment was equally enervating. The exchange program at the school was sponsored by the Methodist student organization. They maintained a three-room apartment adjoining their chapel and center at the edge of the campus, and it was here that I lived with four others: a neurotic white minister, the director of the center, who drank milk from the communal bottle "to satisfy my oral needs" (I told him breasts were far superior); a Panamanian black, who seemed to fear the loss of his meager knowledge of English if he ever stopped talking; a Palestinian Arab who began and ended each day with an anti-Semitic litany flung in the general direction of Israel, and as the weeks passed, curses toward me as I goaded him by becoming more pro-Israeli than David Ben-Gurion; and a Thai artist whom I liked because he was never there.

It was a Third World menagerie, a living example of the liberalism of the Methodist Church, Proof A in its *Summa Theologica*. I'd never had to live with other people, however, and not only lacked the desire, but considered their presences as unwarranted violence. (Even though Fisk University required that students from Nashville live one year in a campus dormitory, I refused, willing to relinquish my degree rather than be subjected to sharing the dailiness of others.) I needed a significant portion of each day to be alone with myself and living with four others almost made that impossible. I robbed sleep, staying up each night when the apartment was quiet, listening to Bach on the phonograph and letting the solitude restore me as sleep could not.

49

Having no friends, my only home was inside myself, and if there is no other country except that of your self, you are in mortal danger. Some instinct told me to write, to put my self on paper where I could see it and touch it, to place it where it could not harm me, as it would if it remained wholly inside, to begin to create a self through words, one which would never again need others to tell it who it was. Thus I began my apprenticeship as a writer.

The first step was learning to read critically, and instead of reading my class assignments at night, I analyzed the different uses of consciousness in Faulkner's *The Sound and the Fury*, Joyce's *Ulysses*, and Virginia Woolf's *The Waves*, compared the varied ways Langston Hughes, James Baldwin and Richard Wright treated black subject matter, and tried to define what the qualities of good writing were. During the first two months in San Diego, I read all of Hemingway (responding only to *The Old Man and the Sea*), Mann's *The Magic Mountain* (an overwhelming experience), Joyce's *Ulysses* (the Mass in B minor of Western literature), novels by Pär Lagerkvist (whose treatment of religious subject matter intrigued me), as well as the poetry of Rilke, Pound (neither affected me), Sappho and Edna St. Vincent Millay (who continue to sing in my romantic soul).

I began writing haiku. Its unadorned simplicity, lyricism, and inherent discipline against projecting one's emotions onto poetry and reality appealed to a reticence in me. I did not understand precisely who I was that I could love haiku and Bach, whose mode was pure classicism, and equally love Sappho and Millay, for whom emotion was life. Both modes, however, existed with equal intensity in me, and I denied neither, hoping to learn when and how to speak through each.

I completed a short story about a lynching, a subject that practically every black writer then had to confront, because it was the metaphor of the black experience. My story was from the point of view of the lynchers, a feeble attempt to explore what Hannah Arendt would later call "the banality of evil."

April 2, 1959
(Journal)
This is my first effort at Negro subject matter and I think I escaped the trap of sociological propaganda which is the downfall of most Negro writers. I think I'll use my people as source material more if I can use it in a catholic sense. After all, Joyce

wrote about the Irish and who is more catholic! White writers have been more successful at writing about Negroes. A certain amount of detachment is necessary, but this is true of any work of art. The balance of detachment and involvement must be there for it to be really great.

I was not impressed by black writers, for I was not angry like Richard Wright and James Baldwin, and didn't want to be a people's poet like Langston Hughes, though I liked his work. I wanted to explore how black people lived inside themselves, without having to be the attorney for the defense against a prosecuting white society. White writers were freed of this burden, and in the work of Faulkner, and, later, Shirley Ann Grau and Ellen Douglas, I saw aspects of my racial self which black writers, who had no choice but to be advocates, had not been able to show me. I responded deeply to Dilsey and the Easter service in *The Sound and the Fury*, for here I touched my own childhood experience as a black minister's son listening to a great preacher, my father, and being totally oblivious of the beauty and majesty of what I was hearing. Faulkner showed me that, and for the first time I understood why my father had admonished me not to despair when we moved south. Shirley Ann Grau gave me the South as a place of ageless lyricism, and Ellen Douglas' work was permeated by a tone of compassion I hoped eventually to find within myself. The black writers of previous generations were defined by anger and outrage. Though I had experienced it, it did not sit at the core of my being burning like phosphorous. Wright, Baldwin and others had expressed the rage with unmatched eloquence and freed me, at age twenty, to sit in the silence of night and dream of writing a black *Ulysses*, of plunging so deeply into the black collective unconscious that, in so doing, I would draw a map of the human soul.

To write, however, was more than learning to order reality through language. It was, also, as Bob Hayden had taught me, an attitude of living for the act of writing, not for one's self.

Underlining

From James Ramsey Ullman's *The Day on Fire*:

I say that one must be a seer by a long, immense and reasoned derangement of all the senses. He seeks in himself every kind of love, suffering, or madness; he exhausts all the poisons in himself in order to keep only their quintessences. Unspeakable

51

torment, in which he has need of all faith, all superhuman power in which he becomes, of all men, the great Sufferer, the great Criminal, the great Damned—the supreme Scholar! For he comes to the unknown. . . .

In that novel based on the life of Rimbaud, I found the most extreme description of what it was to be an artist. It was a philosophy of amorality, with no values except those dictated by the urge to create. Van Gogh, Beethoven, Gauguin and every artist of whose life I knew anything had conformed to this philosophy. I didn't know if I could.

3

My reluctance to hand my soul over wholly to the urge to create was rooted in that part of me which was searching for God. I hated to admit that this was what my atheism was, but a true atheist, it seemed to me, would have achieved a unity of self in the ultimate denial. I had not. To know God was to know myself.

God was obviously so well-hidden, however, that if I was to know Him, He would have to stop me as I crossed the campus one day and introduce Himself. Occasionally, I talked with Virginia Schmitz, an older woman I'd met at the Methodist student center. A devout Christian, Ginny impressed me, because she was never fazed by any blasphemy I uttered, sensing perhaps that I was pleading with her to convince me of her faith. She couldn't, but in her, I experienced a different quality of being than with any person I'd known, besides Janeice, Bill's fiancée. Both gleamed with a love so startling I could not accept it as genuine. No one was truly good; some were merely better at pretending they were.

One Saturday I went to La Jolla, the beautiful and wealthy community on the Pacific in the San Diego suburbs, and walked until I found a lonely place on a rock extending into the ocean. I sat for hours, watching the waves crash into the rock, not flinching when large waves sprayed me. I sat, thinking that I wanted to be like the sea. It needed no one to look upon it and call it ocean. Before anyone had seen it and called it by a name, it had rolled against the rock on which I sat, and if ever again there were no people in the world, the ocean would continue to be the ocean. It was telling me something vital to my search, but deliberately using a language I could not understand.

Soon afterward, however, I found some of the words I needed. One afternoon in Modern British Literature class, I happened to be awake, and the teacher mentioned, in passing, a book by my idol, Aldous Huxley. I don't remember what he said about *The Perennial Philosophy*, but instead of going to work after class, I rushed downtown, hurrying in and out of bookstores until I found it in a second-hand shop.

It was my introduction to the literature of Christian and Oriental mysticism, and through it, I realized something which should have been obvious: Religion is not what transpires in churches, but the direct apprehension of God.

Underlinings

From Huxley's *The Perennial Philosophy*:

My Me is God, nor do I recognize any other Me except my God Himself.

—St. Catherine of Genoa

In those respects in which the soul is unlike God, it is also unlike itself.

—St. Bernard

Goodness needeth not to enter into the soul, for it is there already, only it is unperceived.

—*Theologica Germanica*

You are as holy as you wish to be.

—John Ruysbroeck

I was not convinced, but the fact that the intellectual I respected more than any other affirmed the existence of God was the precise sanction I needed. If Huxley, the paragon of reason, believed, then it was all right. On the afternoon of June eighth, I boarded the train for San Francisco, but with none of the anticipated excitement. I knew no one in San Francisco, except friends of my parents in Oakland, with whom I would stay for a few days. I had no job awaiting me and had been able to save only a couple hundred dollars from the library job.

I was afraid and ashamed of my fear, and in my journal, copied a quote from Joyce's *Portrait of the Artist as a Young Man*:

53

You made me confess the fears that I have. But I will tell you also what I do not fear. I do not fear to be alone or to be spurned for another or to leave whatever I have to leave. And I am not afraid to make a mistake, even a great mistake, a lifelong mistake and perhaps as long as eternity, too.

My fears would not be stilled by a quotation from a great book, for the process of an individual's growth is a continual venture into uncertainty, and the fact that Stephen Dedalus had succeeded was no guarantee that I would. Stephen was existentially free, knowing that only the act of freedom was important. I knew only that I wanted to be back in my room in Nashville. But the only way to live without fear is to do that which is frightening.

To give myself courage, I thought of the white exchange students I'd known at Fisk who hitchhiked around the country as readily as I crossed the street. How I wished I could go into the world with such confidence. But they were white, and self-confidence was something white people had like blue eyes, I thought. They were inoculated with it as infants. I was black and had only had diphtheria and smallpox vaccinations, and fear was the amniotic fluid in the wombs of black mothers, who conceived and bore children despite that implacable, hating white force which stood as an all-pervasive negation of black life. I had learned to fight the fear, but it was a battle whose outcome would never be more than a stalemate. I had to carry the fear in me, like a baby to which I could not give birth. It would kill me if I did.

4

June 10, 1959
Oakland, Calif.
12:30 A.M.
(Journal)

I'm here and I have so much to say, but I don't know if I can say it all.

I left San Diego yesterday at 4 and Judy and Ida met me at the station [in Los Angeles. They were close friends from Fisk]. Oh, I love Judy; I don't think I've ever met a more human person. She isn't profound or intellectual, but if a person can make you feel love, intellect isn't necessary. . . .

. . . twice since yesterday I've felt acutely alone. The first time was after we left Pomona and were driving along the freeway. I wanted to cry. I don't know why. Maybe because I didn't ever want to leave the people I love so much. It's strange that Judy and I are tied together by a sense of humor, because she isn't intellectual. But there's something more there, because I feel that she loves me. All that she's done for me I can never repay, but she's done it, seemingly not caring if I repaid her.

The second time I felt something which I will give the name of loneliness was on the train today. I wondered what was I, Julius Lester, an emotionally ill 20 year old, doing out here facing the world. You strike out for "the territory ahead," but the utter futility of it all . . . I was glad to leave San Diego and as I left it seemed that as the city passed by my window, it passed out of existence. It's strange, but whenever I return in body or thought to a place I always think that these people have been living from day to day, struggling, maybe or maybe not existing, but they seem so irrelevant.

Coming up the coast I was clobbered by the fact that Man is so egocentric and for no reason. Let me try and describe the coast. To my right, ugly domineering mountains staggered upwards and then stumbled down to the very skirts of the ocean. There was no beach. A little sand here and there, but most of the time it seemed that the sea had vomited the mountains from its bowels. Imagine the scene at high tide! The sea raising herself to a huge bursting point, then with a loud roar and yell, crashing and charging the indomitable mountains—they scarred, rough, not budging but seeming to embody all eternity. What had man with his reason been able to do? He'd carved a paltry railroad on the mountain and a pitiful two-lane highway. I could see abandoned shacks.

I saw one happy sight. A man and a woman sitting at a table that must have been picked off the dump. He had on an undershirt and pants and she, a ragged dress, both obviously from the same junkpile. Their appearance was quite a contrast to the proper embodiments of the organized society in my coach. But they looked at the train as they ate breakfast. Behind them was their tent and to the side, the fire which served as their stove. Their truck was nearby and all their belongings inside. They weren't the type who would make the society page, but they were free. People who have that courage have to have a soul that struggles to understand what the mountains are saying. The ocean was pacific and where where where did it stop? See why I felt alone and scared? I wanted to go home. Back to the world where I had no responsibility. But no . . . I can't. I must press on, even though it hurts, hurts to the point that I don't know who I am or what I want. It hurts so that I can do nothing but endure the pain and then I sleep and wake and feel again my fate moving within and know that the pain is inseparable. If only I can find an adequate means of letting my soul speak. I want to talk in music, paintings, sculpture, poetry, the dance, those whom I can call friend. But I fear insanity will be my eventual end. Sometimes I know nothing but chaos confusion anxiety fear. I'm alone!

Only after I had been made to know my minuscule finiteness in every fiber and corpuscle of my being did God lift the veil of self to reveal Himself. I knew myself as a grain of sand in the presence of infinity, and I cried out: I am alone!

The God I had rejected in my adolescent atheism was a concept which had to be destroyed, for it had no relationship to God's reality. I understood now why it was easier to disprove God's existence than prove it, because anything which could be approached with the mind and called God, was not. Anything which I could understand as being God was not. Then, what was God? God was!

I mistook, however, the inception for the climax, and assumed that because I now believed, God would always be present. He was, but I did not know that one must tend the God within as if it were a bonsai tree. I would be dismembered in the vortex of terror repeatedly, until I accepted the poverty of my heart as something to be loved, until there was no escape from knowing that my need of God was not a condition of weakness.

On that June day in 1959, however, I knew that I had seen an aspect of God, and heard what the ocean had been saying: I am that I am. There was no joy in my first mystical experience, nor did I tell anyone of my new knowledge. Part of me was ashamed of it and I could see Shelley looking at me disdainfully. But I could not deny what I now knew, or convince anyone else of its truth. It was a secret I would share with very few during the next eleven years, yet I knew it to be my real self. My mistake was to continue living as if I did not know.

5

Talk about tired! I've been hunting for a place all day and one possibility. The most disgusting thing is that most people seem to read the sign that flashes over my head. It flashes so bright that soon it'll be inside of me and this'll make me bitter, which I don't want. Went in one place and got the proverbial, "Somebody just took it. Just hadn't had time to take the sign down." The lie is too obvious. If I'd been thinking, I would've gone to the window and politely removed the sign. The amazement on his face when I entered said quite loudly, "What th' hell is this nigger doing in here?"

Well, I'm sitting in one of the North Beach places now. When I first hit this part of town I wanted to laugh. The people are so ludicrous! The first thing that occurred to me was, "What is their motivation?" And all the Negroes! But it's no wonder! Here, at least, you're accepted, but it's more because you're a Negro and not so much as an individual. I want to be accepted as plain ol' me, and rejected on the same basis. But it's a little better to be accepted because you are a Negro rather than rejected for the same reason.

I would like to get an apartment over here, but price will probably eliminate me. But North Beach, I think, is like Montmartre with its narrow streets and hidden alleys. Also it's near the bay and you know my passion for water. Naturally, I bought some books today—Baudelaire's *Intimate Journals, Beat Zen, Square Zen and Zen* by Alan Watts and *The Dwarf* by Lagerkvist.

The characters that stroll in and out. Long hair, beards—do you take them seriously? They seem to me to be bums masquerading under the banner of the avant garde. . . . It is a masquerade because obviously they're wearing this mask for some reason. This is all like watching something on the stage. But these also will die like the poor, ignorant Negroes on Fillmore, but at least the latter are without pretense. These here may be without pretense, also, I really can't say.

The Negro and the "beatnik" attitude toward him is interesting, because it creates a new Negro. America's born Outsider can now belong. He who accepted before his position of unacceptability in society is now made to know consciously that he is oppressed. But we accept you. We, the beatniks are "white Negroes." We are emulating your reaction toward society. So now the Negro is a paragon of sorts and what develops is a new Uncle Tom. Not the obsequious old man down South, but a "balling fool" who can ball and be praised for it.

It's strange, but I had to leave the South before I realized that I was Negro. In the South you accept segregation as a granite fact, but here it's more subtle, more cruel. And what you previously realized through reading the paper becomes a fact as you feel the signs above you blinking and soon your heart beat and the blinking of the sign are synchronized. When that occurs, the sign is within and then you have to fight to accept and see yourself as an individual and not a kinky-headed, brown-skinned innately inferior person without a culture. You become an individual whose racial background ends with a bill of sale for some slaves who took the name of their master or anybody or anything else at Emancipation. Will I have to look in the mirror every morning and say, "I am Julius Lester!"

I rented a room on Grant Street, the main thoroughfare of North Beach, near the corner of Columbus Avenue, and very soon knew that I belonged there. No one found my presence odd (and if I appeared to others as a "poor, ignorant" Negro, as I in my adolescent intellectual snobbery described the blacks I'd seen, I didn't know it). I was the youngest person living on North Beach, not even old enough to go in the bars where much of the community's life was, but I did not resent my youth. Being among people who insisted on living their lives as they defined them was enough. I did not have to chant my name like a mantra each morning to reiterate my existence.

Nowhere was this new way of life more exemplified than at the Bread and Wine Mission, a storefront at the top of Grant Street beneath Coit Tower. Founded by an Episcopal priest-poet-writer, Pierre de Lattre, the Mission was a place where one could go to talk, drink coffee, read from Pierre's enormous library which lined the walls, or just sit and be quiet. On Saturday evenings there were poetry readings, and I heard Robert Duncan and was more shocked by the coterie of young men around him than impressed with his poems. Bob Kaufman, the Martinquean poet, read several times, and I was jealous of his enormous popularity. Other evenings, there were theatrical improvisations, in which I participated with some success. In the afternoons, the Mission was generally empty, and I practiced Bach on the piano. At least, that was my excuse. I simply wanted to be in the same place as Pierre.

He was one of the first of what would come to be called "street ministers," and the most singular exemplification of who I wanted to be as a person. In his hooded sweatshirt and jeans, he emanated gentleness and caring. I wanted to sit at his feet and learn from him, participate in the *agape* love feasts he held each Sunday, but I could never think of anything to say to him. So I played Bach on the piano.

Pierre and the people who came to the Mission seemed to care about the world and what was happening to the people in it. I'd only known people who cared what happened to them and I couldn't believe the people at the Mission were really any different. One evening I was exhilarated, having just read in the paper that a white man in South Carolina had been sentenced to the electric chair for the rape of a black woman. It was an unprecedented event, deserving commemoration as an annual holiday. Almost as soon as I entered the Mission, someone asked me if I'd seen the article.

"Yeah," I replied grinning, choosing to ignore the implicit racism in his assumption that I would naturally know about it.

"That's equality, I guess," the young man said. "Equal murder."

His words were a slap to my joy, and though I lacked the self-confidence to argue with him, to myself I countered quickly that it was about time a white man paid with his life for the thousands of raped black women. I wasn't going to feel sorry for one white man, particularly when no tears had been shed for the thousands of black men murdered for alleged rapes of white women. And, anyway, more white men had raped black women than black men had white women. ("And on the Rape Scoreboard tonight, Rape Fans, the White Team is still ahead One Hundred Million to Ninety-nine. Now, over to you, Bill, for the Mugging scores where it looks like the Blacks are leading." "Right you are, Roger. . . .")

My unspoken tirade was interrupted: "If we're going to have equality, let's have equal right, not equal wrong."

He was right, though I couldn't admit it aloud. For a moment I wished I were white so I could take an absolute position against capital punishment, so I could fight for good, no matter how much vengeance clawed at my soul for release. But when no genie appeared to grant the wish, I wondered if I could get the job of pulling the switch on the "cracker."

Another evening I walked in during a discussion of what to do on August sixth. I maintained my usual silence and eventually surmised that that was the day the atomic bomb was dropped on Hiroshima. I was embarrassed that I hadn't known and ashamed that I would not have thought to observe the anniversary. Being black did not give me carte blanche to be indifferent to the pain of others. Because I suffered, I was not exempt from caring about another's suffering, not even a white rapist's.

A silent demonstration was held in Union Square on Hiroshima Day, but I didn't go. That was not my way. But I didn't know what was.

6

For the first time since the previous summer, my outer reality was beneficent, but how could it not be in San Francisco? Though I intended to get a job and stay forever, I walked out onto Grant Street each morning, looked at the sky, and the mere thought of work was a sin for which I quickly asked forgiveness. I walked the streets of Chinatown, smelling the aromas of strange foods, listened to the singsong of Cantonese, learned to eat with chopsticks in cheap basement restaurants; I climbed the city's hills, some of which were so steep that steps had been substituted for sidewalks, and on reaching the top, winded, my breath was taken wholly from me by the view of the bay; I sat in small parks and watched the sea gulls, young mothers playing with their children and was sorry that Michele would never be a mother; I sat in Aquatic Park at night, listening to the foghorns, the tolling buoys and watching the searchlights on Alcatraz, which I thought would be a perfect American Mount Athos; I walked and walked, not knowing where I was going and one day came upon the Golden Gate Bridge so close to me that I saw that it didn't stand in the water but leaped from it with an ecstatic shout; and on another sanctified day a walk brought me to Rodin's *The Thinker* sitting alone on a lawn before a many-columned building, the Palace of the Legion of Honor, and I longed for Sylvia. I went to coffeehouses and heard folk music, vowing that one day I would cradle a guitar like a lover and sing sad songs in minor keys; I fell in love with every woman dressed in black, or who had long dark hair, perceiving each as a Madonna carrying beauty like an offering I would never be worthy to receive; and there was the Sunday morning I walked up Broadway at five A.M., after an evening in Berkeley listening to folk music, and as I turned up Columbus and happened to look behind me, there, coming through the fog, was Allen Ginsberg!

With North Beach as home and San Francisco surrounding it, my inner world existed for the first time without sentries patrolling its walls, and inside, I continued to explore the two paths of my life—religion and art.

My new religious life centered on the statue of St. Francis by Beniamino Bufano, which stood in front of a Catholic church on Vallejo Street, around the corner from my room. It was fifteen to twenty feet high, thickly proportioned but with flowing lines. St. Francis' arms were raised, and it was as if he were not only welcoming the birds, but the universe itself. Most remarkable was the broad silly smile on his face. Never is a religious figure depicted in a state of joy, but Bufano's St. Francis was a real person, approachable and lovable. (The statue now stands in front of the Teamsters Hall on Fisherman's Wharf.) I was almost converted to Catholicism by that statue. If the Church could produce a man like that, what might it not do for me? But I was afraid to attend Mass or talk to a priest, not knowing what to say, except, "Teach me to be Saint Francis." Somehow, that didn't seem to be right. (It was.)

My journal records thirty-five books read during the two months I was in San Francisco: Francoise Sagan, whose simple style was greatly appealing, William Carlos Williams (a bore), Rexroth's incredibly fine *One Hundred Poems from the Japanese*, Mailer, Gide, a biography of James Dean, who'd recently been killed, Rilke, Baudelaire, Rimbaud, Maugham, Stendhal, and most important, Henry Miller. In *Time of the Assassins*, his study of Rimbaud, and *A Devil in Paradise*, I met a robust human being whose intensity and joy in Being were qualities I felt to be my own, if I could ever find them. I considered Miller the first American Zen Master.

Underlinings

From Henry Miller's *A Devil in Paradise*:

I am not interested in the potential man. I am interested in
what a man actualizes—or realizes—of his potential being. And
what is the potential man, after all? Is he not the sum of all that
is human? *Divine*, in other words? You think I am searching for
God. I am not. God is. The world is. Man is. We are. The full
reality, that's God—and man, and the world, and all that is, including the unnameable. . . .

Every so often I revolt, even against what I believe in with
all my heart. I have to attack everything, myself included. Why?
To simplify things. We know too much—and too little. It's the
intellect which gets us into trouble. Not our intelligence.

A man can only prove that he is free by electing to be so. And
he can only do so when he realizes that he himself made himself
unfree. And that to me means that he must wrest from God the
powers he has given God. The more of God he recognizes in
himself the freer he becomes. And the freer he becomes the
fewer decisions he has to make, the less choice is presented to
him. Freedom is a misnomer. Certitude is more like it. Unerr-
ingness. Because truthfully there is always only one way to act
in any situation, not two, not three. Freedom implies choice, and
choice exists only to the extent that we are aware of our inepti-
tude. The adept takes no thought, one might say. He is one with
thought, one with the path.

More than anyone else I was to read, until I found the writings of
Thomas Merton, Henry Miller affirmed me. He wrote about Freedom, Truth and God as if they existed with the same palpable
presence as the sex he celebrated. He did not write like an intellectual, with calm detachment and reason, but with passion and
this was an important example for me in an age when emotion was
feared. "Cool" was the dominant virtue of my contemporaries in
black America. Jazz turned "cool" with Miles Davis' muted trumpet
sketching the Spanish landscape; on street corners young blacks
leaned against parked cars so loosely that they almost merged into
the simonized finishes. "To be cool," wrote LeRoi Jones in *Blues
People*, "was . . . to be calm, even unimpressed, by what horror
the world might daily propose. . . . In a world that is basically irrational, the most legitimate relationship to it is nonparticipation."
The problem with the world was not that it was "irrational," I

thought, but that it was rational, living with the lobes of its brains rather than the aorta of the heart. I hated the dispassion of my contemporaries and cried with Millay, "Oh, world! I cannot hold close enough!" In a world of people who consciously refused to feel, I was determined to feel every emotion to its source.

I completed my first novel that summer, *The Sea, The Rock and The Hurricane*; and in a letter the autobiographical hero wrote to his closest friend, I presented myself as I was near the end of my season with the Beat Generation.

> I have found God. . . . I think it all started when I read Spinoza's *Ethics*. The ideas immediately found fertile soil. All he says I'd felt previously, but didn't know exactly what it was I was feeling. I've described the Maine coast to you many times. This is where God spoke to me. I was sitting on a rock that was about six feet above the sea. The waves were crashing on the rock and running up to me before they slid and tumbled back down. As I sat there it struck me as forcefully as the waves slamming themselves against the rock: This is God talking to me. I was partaking of eternity. "Before Abraham was, I am." The indomitable rock said this. It stood there, unconquerable. The ocean said it also. Everything around me breathed the essence of eternity. I knew then why I loved Bach and Michelangelo and Basho. They were telling me what the ocean and the rock were saying. I started improvising on my recorder and all I knew was the music. I didn't exist. I became a part of infinity. Athene, Apollo and Aphrodite were in me and I in them.
>
> This happened last month and since then I've been composing music for the recorder. Gregorian chants and Jewish music have always appealed to me very deeply and I'm sure that my compositions show elements of both, but whatever they show, they're very religious. I've done several paintings of Jesus because now I feel close to him. Not in the usual religious way, but in the sense that he was a poet, a man who felt what I did. I'm writing nothing but haiku now. I've found my poetic voice. You know how crazy I am about Shelley and how I've tried to imitate him. But his rhetorical passion is not mine. Haiku seems to have been waiting for me to discover it.
>
> Now I feel love everywhere. Before I talked about it and thought I knew what it was, but I realize now that I had just begun to taste it. Love is the one universal. It is God. My entire becoming now is *consciously* directed toward manifesting this Love I feel. Art is a love letter to God telling Him He sends me

like nothing else. I must spend my life loving Him. It's completely irrelevant if He loves me. I must love in every way I know how. I can't spend my life loving just one individual, but every person in whom I feel a soul. I must love. . . .

7

It was time to leave. I had ventured into the world and ingested as much as I could. I needed time to let the California months filter through me. This could be done only in Nashville, for there I would learn if my fictional mouthpiece was real, or merely a product of another place, a flower unable to grow when placed in different soil. It was easy to be a new person when I walked down the streets and nobody knew my face. I had to know who I would be where everyone knew not only my face, but me.

The August morning I left San Francisco, I went to City Lights bookshop to sell some of my books. I was broke, and it was a three-day train ride home. Lawrence Ferlinghetti had seen me in the store often enough to recognize me, though he didn't know my name, and he was a little surprised when I said I was going home. I couldn't explain why, and only said, "I have to. It's O.K." He nodded, and it was good to be understood.

I bought several pounds of grapes to eat on the train, but they were soon gone, particularly after a flash flood in the desert delayed the train for twenty-four hours in Needles, California. But a black woman sitting beside me shared her bag of fried chicken. (These were still the days when blacks who traveled carried their own food, a habit from the years when we were not allowed to eat in railroad dining cars, or had to sit behind a screen to do so.) When she got off the train, she slipped me a dollar and wished me luck.

I had to change trains in St. Louis, the city of my birth, and, with my dollar, left the station looking for a cheap luncheonette. I found one a short block away and ordered a bowl of chili, which was only fifty cents.

The waitress hesitated a moment, then asked, "Take out?"

I smiled. "No, thank you. I'll eat it here."

"We don't serve colored," she responded, flatly.

I sat there, my flesh burning as if it had been laid on the griddle

64

behind her. If I had thought, before entering, I would have looked through the window to see if there were any blacks inside, as my father had taught me to do. My San Francisco sojourn had lulled me into forgetting my lessons.

I left hurriedly, blinking my eyes rapidly to hold back the tears, angry for having exposed myself needlessly to being hurt by the white world, angry at the city of my birth where the Hungarian friend of the librarian could eat a bowl of chili and I couldn't. As hungry as I was, though, I wouldn't order the chili to go. To walk down the street eating chili with a wooden spoon from a paper cup would have been eloquent testimony that I agreed to being a nigger. Far better to double over with the pain of hunger, to die even, than that.

8

I came home and was not surprised to learn that I had changed. When I was readmitted to Fisk on the condition that I not "create trouble," I had difficulty recalling why the registrar would think I would. Fisk had no reality for me anymore. School began, and I didn't buy books for my classes. In several of them, I turned my chair away from the instructors and toward the window to look at the magnolia trees. I could no longer play the game. When one has an encounter with Being, life is suddenly too precious to squander on the unimportant.

Released from the painful introspection of the previous three years, I became a sea gull, flashing white as I soared and dipped over the curling ocean. I became the sky, sparkling in glitters of blue over the world. I became All and each step I took was the most graceful pirouette ever done by a mere mortal. Where before I had been empty, now I was so full that I seized every instrument of expression I could find, and I taught myself guitar, spending hours in the music room of the library poring through its excellent collection of books on spirituals and learning that being black did not mean I knew black music; I studied voice, sang in the Fisk choir and arranged spirituals, one of which the choir performed; I resumed studying piano and learned Chopin nocturnes, Bach two-part inventions, Bartok's "Mikrokosmos," and the Bach Piano Concerto in D minor, the first movement of which Janeice and

I performed in a two-piano arrangement at a school convocation the following spring. I completed a minor in art, studying under Aaron Douglass, who had been the most prominent artist of the Harlem Renaissance, and, of course, I wrote—poems, short stories and a novella, "Don't Dilute the Bourbon."

There was no time for class assignments, not when I was confirming my identity as an artist, a miner in the soul of humanity. In the music of Bach, my fingers discovered the order of the universe, balancing and unraveling the lines and harmonies of three-part fugues. In spirituals, I sang myself as a racial being, one unsullied by the malevolent white force, and the old ones lived in me as I voiced the lives I'd touched in the dust of Arkansas back roads, in the sound of train whistles on summer nights, in my father's preaching and storytelling and I understood God's mysterious way of working, for by moving south I had sunk my roots in the historical and psychic bedrock of my people. I was rolling away the stone from the tomb of my slave ancestors, singing the magical notes and allowing them to rise and tell of the troubles they'd seen, of how they'd been 'buked and scorned, and how they had overcome.

At long last, I was living with the intensity and passion of Shelley, Henry Miller and Rimbaud, and feared that God would chastise me if I allowed one minute to pass unnoticed. I hated the death of sleep and succumbed to it for no more than four hours a night. I hated the classes which I was forced to acknowledge with my bodily presence, but refused to give one iota of myself.

November 13, 1959
(Journal)

The day is so magnificent. Autumn's death is even more beautiful than I ever thought. The serene cirrus clouds talk to me of Zen and the Tao as they languish on the blue infinity which is so blue that it tingles dances sparkles. The wind has been caressing my body all day. My body clothed in tight jeans and thin shirt heaves ecstatic spasms in reply. I'm sitting in Shakespeare class, my feet propped up in the window feeling the wind skim playfully inside my pants leg. I had a midterm in Neoclassicism today which has left me completely indifferent. I haven't read all year—just practiced my guitar—the epitome of quiescence. And last night read some of Van Gogh's letters and Zen koans and writing haiku.

And feel Aphrodite ravish me and Athene telling me that poetry music art Love are the only important things. All else is irrelevant and I listening to her say yes yes yes and I ache inside with undiluted joy as I look at a mackerel sky with wisps of cirrus and piles of cumulus and I must talk tell someone that yes yes yes Shakespeare is second-rate and so is Dryden and Pope and no no no don't please don't forget to look up and no no no don't please don't forget to feel and love. Burn all the libraries and let's start again like Patience Sparks who is asleep while Dr. Moses drones profoundly on ancient Rome who doesn't care. I don't want to be a scholar who has read forty books on the use of the metaphor in Act II of *Midsummer Night's Dream*. No, let me be despised by men. Reject me and in so doing you'll let me alone and I'll be happy lying in a park all day with the drunken rejects scribbling haiku on a stolen roll of toilet paper which the wind will blow blew blown my poems into gutters trash cans garbage trucks fires into some sensitive pre-existent soul that will exist and wipe himself with the paper and I'll smile and say, "Hi, Rimbaud," and now it's getting cloudier but the blue is singing and guess what, Vincent Millay?

I love you. . . .

The only lack in my life was a woman with whom I could share my new self, and to my surprise, she was to be Bill's fiancée, Janeice. (The previous autumn, she and I were alone in the Music Building one Sunday morning. I don't remember why we were there, but our being together was casual, for I didn't like Janeice. Not only was she not intellectual, she was a Christian. We wandered into a classroom, and when she sat down at the piano and started playing, I expected her to falter and quit after a few measures. Instead, the Brahms Intermezzo in B minor unfolded beneath her fingers as if it were being created at that very moment. The brooding moodiness of the composition reverberated within my own troubled existence and when she finished, I loved her.)

A year later I had grown enough to recognize in her what I had responded to in Pierre de Lattre and found so unbelievable in Ginny. Janeice had an infinite capacity for love, and I wanted to learn from her, to be like her. We found ourselves together more and more, sitting beside each other in a Philosophy of Religion class (for which I did buy books) and discovering Tillich's concept of "ultimate concern." It was she, a psychology major, whose study of piano convinced me to return to the instrument. The more we were together, I realized that she was an artist, but her medium was living. She, too, knew that life had to be lived intensely, for we lived on Death's lap.

January 17, 1960
(Letter to Janeice)

Were you out this evening while it was misting? Maybe you don't like mist. I don't know, but I do. Mist is so quiet, even quieter than a slow rain. Mist is beautiful because it's so tiny and it doesn't wet you all at once like rain, but it just keeps falling, those tiny, grain-like moisture drops and soon you're damp and later, soaking wet. I walked home in it. For me you're like the mist. . . . It's taken me until last fall to get gloriously wet in you. Love is determined largely by the fact of two people meeting at the moment in each of their lives when each is in the best position to appreciate the other. I met Sylvia at the moment when she needed someone to talk with and I needed this, also. Now there is you, when I need someone my own age whom I can respect. Someone who, like me, is possessed by something that refuses to let you go and you'd die if it did let you go. This sounds so mundane, but for me it's the greatest thing that has happened to me since California. Whenever I see you I know that here is one person who has done and learned something today. And just seeing you means a lot to me, because you serve as an example to me.

Through her, I began learning to be more than mind.

9

On February 2, 1960, a small item in the back pages of the daily paper reported that four black students from A & T College in Greensboro, North Carolina, had been arrested the previous day for not leaving a dime-store lunch counter after being refused service. I read it with less interest than I did the evening's television listings.

Since the previous fall a small group of students from the black colleges in Nashville had been trying to negotiate the desegregation of lunch counters with the managers of department and variety stores. With the news from Greensboro, the students decided to do the same. ("You gon' sit in?" someone asked me as the day of the first one neared. "What th' fuck I want to sit next to a white man and eat a hamburger for?" I shot back. I'd already forgotten the incident in St. Louis a few brief months before, but I was convinced that the desegregation of a lunch counter had nothing to do with the transformation of souls. Anything less than that was not change, but the illusion of it.)

The last Saturday of February, seventy-eight students were arrested in Nashville in the first mass arrests in what was to be a decade of such. I had a date with Candie that evening. She was an exchange student from Pomona College (Calif.), an attractive, blond art major and a close friend, whose involvement in the sit-ins was offensive to me. "You're an artist," I would argue. "Your job is to paint, not sit in." "Changing society is more important than all the masterpieces in the world." "Slavery was worth it, because out of it came the spirituals," I would retort. She would look at me as if she didn't know whether to cut my throat in anger, or her own in despair at my obtuseness. That Saturday evening as I walked toward her dorm, I heard that she'd been among those arrested. I turned around and went to Bob Hayden's house, where I spent the evening sight-reading compositions for four hands by Ravel with Irma, Bob's wife. Near midnight we heard that the students were being released on bail, and Irma and I went down to the jail. We'd scarcely walked into the lobby when Diane Nash, who later became a prominent civil rights leader, walked over to me and said, with menacing coldness, "We'll all be in next week, won't we, Julius?" The hostility in her voice hurt, but not enough that I couldn't respond, "I doubt it very seriously." As the students walked out of the jail and into the lobby to be greeted with loud cheers and hugs from those released earlier, I knew I was witnessing the baptismal rites of a new religion. I was the only sinner present, however, and stood to one side against a wall, Tonio Kröger at the ball. They belonged, but I didn't. I wanted to and was not comfortable with my nonparticipation as the sit-ins continued through the spring. I should be involved, I told myself, and once, I joined a pray-in outside the Mayor's office, but afterward, could not understand why I had gone, or what I had accomplished by being there, particularly knowing that the Mayor was out of town. I could not give myself to a movement for social change, however, for I had other work to do. James Joyce had not stopped writing *Finnegans Wake*, though the Nazis were goose-stepping over human lives. His alloted task was *Finnegans Wake*.

69

. . . my piano lesson was good. Mrs. Kennedy [my teacher] enjoyed my Bartok and I was so happy. The Mozart is coming, but there's so much in it. I'm so excited and want to work so hard on it and the Scarlatti. Studying baroque and Mozart is good for me because to play them one needs control and understanding and as Mrs. Kennedy said, "This comes from within." It's doing a lot for me as a person and I can apply it to painting and writing. I want to give a recital because none of the pieces Janeice and I are working on are difficult technically. Therefore the audience could not be thrilled with our virtuosity. The pieces are all simple and therefore deceptive and elusive, requiring understanding. A romantic piece can be successful purely because of its bombast and musical rhetoric. Not so Bach, Scarlatti, and Mozart.

There's so much to do! I'm so afraid that I'll flunk Senior Comprehensives. I can't see them as being important. I'm living on a level where exams, school are non-existent. At times I can feel my greatness moving within me. Is this conceit? If so, it is, but I can. I tell myself that I'm a genius and believe it and work to exemplify it. I can feel it physically—the excitement of realizing the gifts I possess are many and that I must use all of them somehow. And I want to use all of them to their fullest. I want to continue studying piano and give recitals; I want to paint, draw; I want to talk with people. I want to love love love.

I look at my hands and think "They're beautiful and soft—feminine in a way and Bach flows through them, words, too, colors and designs." I listen to my voice and like it. It's soft and resonant and the soul of my people issues from it. I think of my eyes and the many books they've seen and the many clouds, the faces of girls. My eyes have seen many things—mountains at dawn and the tide at night; telephone poles running by a car train bus window in New Jersey and Arizona, Kansas and Tennessee and my eyes have seen nothing. I've heard many things—the rhythms of train wheels, trees at all hours of a day; the bay at night with foghorns; I've heard the sun and I've heard the moon since I was eleven years old; I've heard God on a train in California and on a jukebox in a bar; I've heard Bach, Beethoven and Dizzy Gillespie; I've heard God talking to me everytime I see Janeice and I've heard God everytime Sylvia bit my ears and neck in excitement and cried and I've heard nothing. I've felt many things disguised, but they're all the same—Love. But each time I've seen, heard or felt, must be the first time. Everything is new. I must be a virgin. Never should anything be commonplace. Each depression must be unendurable and each ecstatic spasm must be an orgasm. I must never sleep. Passion should and must be the vehicle for living.

Yes, I celebrate me, Julius B. Lester, because I feel in me a combination of elements that have marked me for an ability of expression unlike anyone else's I don't know what it will be, but I must never stop until I find it and once it is found, lose it and start searching again.

I feel more and more that there is not time for trivialities. There's too much to do, to know to waste time, but how does one determine what is a waste of time? Any experience is valid if you are receptive to it. I must make myself a powerful receiver. I have been given by some strange accident, many gifts and a sensitivity to go along with the gifts. For this reason, I feel my genius, my greatness. I am one of the chosen ones. I've been given many things, enough for a crowd of people, but they're mine and I must and will use them.

Ah, it's so wonderful! Everything! I'm listening to Ravel now —the duets Mrs. Hayden and I have played. I'm very happy, extremely so. I'm no longer afraid to be happy. Therefore I am happy often.

I think the peace of the Buddha is with me. I smile like him now. Is it permissible to cry? I'm so happy.

The spring passed like snow at the sudden rising of the thermometer, and I worried about my life after graduation. On successive days I decided to join the Coast Guard, go to medical school, the New England Conservatory of Music, and to graduate school in Comparative Literature. I didn't want to do anything, though, except what I had been doing—reading, writing, painting, singing, composing and being supported by my parents. Almost every day, however, a classmate asked, "What you doing in the fall, Julius?" "I don't know," I'd reply, a little embarrassed, particularly after the classmate listed the job offers he'd had and the graduate schools to which he'd been accepted.

Ironically, it was through the very political movement I scorned that a way presented itself. In March, Candie attended a meeting of students who'd been demonstrating throughout the South. They met at Highlander Folk School in Monteagle, Tennessee, and when

Candie returned, she talked of little else except Guy Carawan, a folk singer she'd met who worked there. (They were married a year later.) On his frequent visits to Nashville to see her, we became friends, and through him I learned that Highlander was planning a summer camp and needed counselors. Though the school was oriented to social issues, I applied, for it would mean being with Guy for two months, from whom I was learning guitar strums, chords, and songs.

I lived the last weeks of college painting a watercolor of a staircase leading downward to an Exit sign, the symbolism of which was not obvious to me at the time, sight reading from *The Well-Tempered Clavier*, practicing for the folk music concert I gave in May at the ISC, reading, writing, and wondering where I'd be the next year. Would I look back at that young man and hate myself for leaving his dreams unfulfilled? In the dreams of adolescence one creates an idealized self, a crystal goblet that shatters against the unyielding wall of reality into fragments so small that, looking at them, one cannot see that they were once a vessel of dreams. Would the dreams so passionately expressed in my journal remain words on a notebook's lined pages, a monument to adolescent exuberance and excess?

Afraid, I willed myself to resist the doubts and fears, and a few nights before Commencement I wrote Janeice and summarized my journey on the eve of my life.

Night brings shadows of past nights in past places of past Me's —of gutter trash on dark D. C. streets at two A.M. following a drunk; of trains moving surreptitiously behind the mask of black and me watching out a window; of a man with a hook for a left hand taking a "fix" in a one A.M. Pittsburgh, Pa., bus station; of bongos and Shakespeare and the Pacific Ocean in San Diego; of Alcatraz looking like the Tao; of unquiet sleep as a mind refuses to turn itself off; of books (there have been many)—Simeone de Beauvoir in Gary, Indiana, Steinbeck in Michigan, Zen in San Francisco, the *Bhagavad-Gita* on a bus, haiku on a train, Fournier in D. C., Sartre in Tennessee; of music —a noisy, coffeehouse, jazz in somebody's pad without someone I loved, classics—Bach on an old radio vainly transmitting an out-of-town station, a concert on the Potomac, and there was Vaughan Williams, too, let us not forget Ralph and his Tallis. Yes, night when a man meets himself for odd conversations, or sighs of regret, stabs of longing. There have been nights when sleep denied its presence to me and my mind denied all answers; nights when I contemplated the infinite while looking at the full moon; nights when I walked because I liked night and walking and the police liked neither. Every day has a night although electric lights want to prove different.

What is an experience? What is a soul? Why am I the way I am? What is music? Why is it so unreal? What is a cloud, a blade of grass, a worm? What is love? Why is there a God? Why do I sit here writing? Why do I want to marry you? Why is Beauty beautiful? Why is an E minor chord so disturbing and soothing?

I live and I'll die, unable to find one answer. A minute is so important and so many pass me, unused. I compare my aspirations and my abilities and realize: I am one person among billions living one life, about 65 years out of a million which have preceded mine and will come after. Yet I do not despair. My 65 can help shape the million to come.

III

1

When I awoke the morning after Commencement, my bold confidence in being a wearer of destiny's mantle evaporated in the new day's sun. The future fell on me, and I disintegrated. My dreams, bleached of their iridescence by the glare of reality, paraded mockingly through my mind like plucked peacocks. There was no objective proof of my exalted destiny. If I was so brilliant, why had I failed a course in Romantic Poetry and graduated only because Bernard Spivack prevailed upon the instructor to pass me? I had, also, failed the American Literature section of the Senior Comprehensive exam, and Bob Hayden gave me a passing grade on it, anyway. (When I looked at the exam, saw that I knew none of the answers, I wrote my name on the cover of the blue book, turned it in and walked out.) If I was such an intellectual, why had I not graduated *summa, magna,* or *cum laude,* instead of "Thank you, Lawdy!", like the majority? My academic record was so undistinguished that I had not admitted, even to Janeice, that I hadn't applied to graduate schools because I feared that none would accept me. As for my self-proclaimed identity as a writer, I had not even won the creative writing award given a graduating senior. There was an infinitesimally thin line between self-confidence and self-delusion, and I wondered how long ago I had crossed it.

Despair increased when my father told me that he'd made an appointment for me to meet the head of the Methodist Publishing House: "I heard on the grapevine that they are looking for a black editorial assistant." I wanted to cry out against his pulling a sheet over my life, but as he explained what a good job it was, that I would be the first black there in an editorial position, and how I could write at nights and on weekends, I allowed myself to be convinced. He was older and knew about the uncertain and unknown future waiting outside the door like a rapist. I had to grow up, be practical; it would not be a disgrace if my dreams were not fulfilled. That was life.

Until one learns, however, to say no to everything which doesn't affirm his/her sense of self, one agrees to self-destruction, and when I left the publisher's that afternoon, assured of the job, my body stiffened and began to grow cold. Had I suffered and struggled in San Diego to become the first black editorial assistant at a church publishing company? Had I known San Francisco, Pierre, and St. Francis to sit at a desk and read manuscripts of ministers' sermons? I called the publisher the next morning and refused the job.

I had reclaimed my integrity, but, having heard nothing from Highlander, I was still without a job. I refused to think about it, and let my eyes search the titles on my bookshelves, hoping they would be guided to the one I needed.

It seems now that Thomas Merton has always been there, standing over my life like the statue of St. Joseph which sits on the hill at the entrance to the Abbey of Gethsemani. But I had not known him before that day when I opened *Disputed Questions,* a Christmas gift from my mother. (I'd told her that I wanted to be a monk, a notion I must have conceived in San Francisco. She'd responded with characteristic bluntness: "Monks don't do anything." I was too young to know what a virtue that was, and was surprised when she gave me the Merton book. A friend is one who, after telling you what he/she thinks you should do, helps you do what you want to do. Such were my parents.)

The first essay was a brilliant analysis of Pasternak's *Dr. Zhivago,* and I was amazed that a Cistercian monk, cloistered for twenty years, knew so much about the outside world. This was no sanctimonious priest mouthing pieties, but a man more involved than those who lived in the world. There was a purity in Merton's vision and literary style which a young twenty-one-year-old would find appealing, because the young listen only to those of pure ideals. Merton's idealism was not, however, expressed in simple dictums.

He confronted me with the necessity to be courageous, but without offering formulas by which that duty could be lived.

Underlining

From Thomas Merton's *Disputed Questions*:

... our job is to love others without stopping to inquire whether or not they are worthy. That is not our business and, in fact, it is nobody's business. What we are asked to do is to love; and this love itself will render both ourselves and our neighbors worthy if anything can.

This was the quality I envied in Ginny, Pierre, and Janeice, and for a few days I wanted to enter the cloister, for only there could I wholly devote my life to that kind of love. I knew, however, that the greater part of my impulse to be a monk was a fear of failure in the world. One only joined a monastic order when there was no other way to live his life and be fulfilled. My abbey would have to be of my own building.

Underlining

From Merton's "Poetry and Contemplation":

... true contemplation is inseparable from life and from the dynamics of life—which includes work, creation, production, fruitfulness and, above all, *love*. Contemplation is not to be thought of as a separate department of life, cut off from all man's other interests and superseding them. It is the very fullness of a fully integrated life. It is the crown of life and of all life's activities.

The contemplative is not the man who sits under a tree with his legs crossed, or one who edifies himself with the answer to ultimate and spiritual problems. He is one who seeks to know the meaning of life not only with his head, but with his whole being, by living it in depth and in purity and thus uniting himself to the very Source of Life. . . .

What we need are contemplatives outside the cloister and outside the rigidly fixed pattern of religious life—contemplatives in the world of art, letters, education and even politics. This means a solid integration of one's work, thought, religion, and family life and recreations in one vital harmonious unity with Christ at its center.

Though I did not know what he meant by "contemplation," what I read sounded like the teasing call of a bird that seemed near but was hidden from me by the thick foliage of the trees. I nodded my head in agreement with his words, but could not say what it was I was assenting to.

My confidence in the kind of life I had chosen was restored, however, but not enough that I ceased fretting about a career. For a few days, I considered the ministry. There I could combine my interest in religion, be free of the routine of most jobs, and still have time to write. I was not unmindful, either, of how pleased my father would be. But I made no decision. "The most beautiful life possible," wrote Simone Weil, "has always seemed to me to be where everything is determined, either by pressure of circumstances or by impulses . . . and where there is never any room for choice." Three days before the Highlander Summer Project was to begin, Guy called. I had been hired.

2

The Highlander Summer Project would be unusual today, but in 1960, when it was still illegal in the South for blacks and whites to even have meetings together, fifty-five black, white, Indian, and Chicano teenagers lived, worked, and traveled together for two months. Because of the environment which was and is Highlander, we were not aware of how extraordinary it was for us to be together on that beautiful plateau in the Cumberland Mountains outside Monteagle, Tennessee, where Highlander was then located. Highlander created an atmosphere in which we were regarded not as ethnic categories or sociological abstractions, but as people with different cultural experiences. We shared those in the way we played, what we talked about and how we talked, but without racial self-consciousness. In a moment of inspiration, I wrote Janeice: "Race is an abstraction!" Twelve years later I would understand that in my soul.

At Highlander I was myself for the first time ever. (Until your identity is like the ocean's, who you are is determined by where you are and who you are with.) I was accepted and liked for who I was, because I had found my compeers—teenagers. Like me, they fluttered through the world on butterfly wings, afraid of being caught, mounted and displayed in the cases society had reserved for them. They returned the same image of myself to me that I saw.

I didn't realize it then, but I felt at one with them because emotionally, I, too, was fourteen, not a counselor but another camper standing in the doorway of puberty. This was confirmed when I found myself in love with two fourteen-year-old southern white girls, Charis and Lolita (her real name), the inception of what was to be, it seems, a lifelong erotomania for teenage girls. But I had never seen the miracle of a young girl's body in the season of its birth, when the woman in the child is made visible. I didn't want to have sex with them: the thought was repugnant. I wanted to be them, to walk around with a body warm like dawn and softer than fog. I blushed when they teased me, and hoped I wouldn't die of joy when I held their hands for fleet seconds during square dances. Charis and Lolita were my unrecognized introduction to my sexuality, a force so overwhelming that I would avoid confronting it for another six years.

More immediate, in its consequences, was the introduction to radical politics I received that summer in the late-night conversations with other counselors and the Highlander staff. They were like the people of the Bread and Wine Mission, caring about others, the conditions in which they lived, and wanting to do something about it. They read newspapers and magazines I'd never heard of, talked about labor strikes, peace, Cuba, and, of course, civil rights. (Every evening after supper, Guy lead singing for a half hour or more, and taught us songs coming from the nascent civil rights movement, always ending with "We Shall Overcome," which had been Highlander's theme song for twenty years and was introduced into the civil rights movement by Guy. We sang it slowly, majestically, and I was never able to retain a separateness from its quiet strength and expression of determination and hope. Singing it, I would remember much that I had wanted to forget— the COLORED signs sticking out of my childhood like gravestones, the times white drivers had tried to run me down when I was hitchhiking home from school, the nights I'd been stopped by policemen for no reason, except that I was black and walking down the street. I'd shrugged off those incidents, I thought, but "We Shall Overcome" released the demons from my past, and my voice soared with the others as I tried to exorcise them. I knew, as I sang, that people had to sit in, picket, demonstrate against, and change a society which bound our wrists with baling wire, and made us live with swords down our throats. I would look at some of the kids of the Summer Project, who'd had their homes dynamited because of their parents' civil rights activities, who'd been arrested for riding in the front of buses, and I felt that the life I'd projected for myself was equivalent to fiddling while others fought the conflagration. But, weren't fiddlers needed, too?)

The Summer Project ended in August, but I remained at Highlander through the Labor Day weekend for a folk music workshop Guy conducted. I'd come to the school primarily to learn from him, and I had. Often, he had me lead the singing in the evenings, but I looked forward most to the nights when, after the campers were in bed, Guy took out his guitar and banjo and sang songs from the southern mountains, spirituals, blues, English ballads, and love songs. When he frailed "Cripple Creek" on the banjo, I wanted to go live in "some dark holler," and in the English ballads, I saw Michele in a long dress and shawl, walking at the edge of a misted moor. Folk music is the psychic history of a people, and though I didn't think that black me could, or should even try to convey the songs of any people except my own, I wanted that history and its truths for my private moments, when I sang only for myself.

During the Labor Day weekend workshop, I met topical song-writers from the North and a joyous young woman named Ethel Raim, with whom I would study guitar when I came to New York. (She became a close friend and was responsible for the first essay I would publish.) Pete Seeger was there, too, his neck looking almost as long as the one on his banjo. And there was me, learning a guitar run from this person, a chord change from another, and songs from everybody.

But the workshop ended, and though I dreamed of going to New York or Cambridge to seek fame and fortune as a folk singer, I returned to Nashville. This time my fears were too great to be nullified by quotes from Joyce, or quelled by an act of will. I was a fledgling in the wider world. During the Summer Project and the music workshop, I'd met young whites who talked of New York, autumn in New England, socialism, anthropology, and Supreme Court decisions with such ease that I despaired at the deficiencies in my knowledge and experience. I could not understand why people with lives so rich seemed to enjoy talking to me. It was flattering, yet disturbing, because they talked without any awareness that I had not spent summers on Martha's Vineyard, or discussed Cummings while crossing Harvard Square. I wondered who they saw when they looked at me. Couldn't they see that I was not one of them, and never would be? Couldn't they hear in my voice the distant trains tracking the night? Couldn't they see in my eyes the coal-oil lamps flickering like lightning bugs in cricket-sung-darkness? Why didn't I exist as vividly for them as they did for me? Why did they assume that because I talked about Art, I was like them?

Yet, I knew that I was going to have to move into that wider world and stay. I needed to talk about theories of aesthetics, the differences between Chinese and Japanese poetry, and the Zen tea ceremony, and there were no such conversationalists in my black world. I hated myself for no longer having a place among my people, and I knew that no roost was waiting in the white world. But I had watched the hawks that summer and knew myself as them, always alone, descending to earth in a furied streak only for sustenance, and returning to the sky to glide on the currents of an unseen wind.

3

September. I thought of my classmates going to their prestigious jobs, enrolling in graduate schools, while I sat in my room looking at my life as if it were a poisonous snake waiting to strike me if I flinched. My parents did not seem concerned, but they must have been embarrassed when others asked, "What's Julius doing now?" and Daddy had to call upon all of his ministerial eloquence to find a way of saying, nothing, and make it sound like the best job in the world. Not knowing what to do, I went to Washington, where I knew I could easily get a Civil Service job.

Since my only skill was typing, I took the Civil Service typing exam, and repaired to the Library of Congress, while waiting for the results and a job assignment. One day while wandering the corridors, I saw a notice that interviews were being conducted for the job of Library Poetry Assistant. The title itself was enough to make an English major swell with self-importance, and I went for an interview.

The job was to be host to the poets invited to the Library for public readings, and I didn't know that I lacked the necessary prerequisites of the summers in Paris, autumn on the Cape, and meals in at least one other language besides English. Nor was I able to conceive that some of America's distinguished poets might not wish to have a nigger as their host-guide. (That poets can also be racists remains incomprehensible to me.) So I, who did not know the difference between *a la carte* and *table d'hote* (and still ain't too sure), was interviewed to be Poetry Assistant of the Library of Congress.

After the interview, I walked slowly away from the Library and across Capitol Hill, knowing that my parents, the Spivacks and Bob Hayden would be so proud of me, assuming I got the job, which I was sure I would. Suddenly, my fantasy was interrupted by an audible voice: "You don't want to work." I stopped. "You don't want to work," the voice repeated, and before I could wonder where it had come from, or if I was, at long last, going crazy, I recognized the truth of what it said. I did not want to work, now or ever, no matter how grandiose the job title. I did not want to do anything which required giving five days of my life each week to the ignominy of earning money.

By ten o'clock that evening I was on a bus for Columbus, Ohio, where Bill lived. Three days later, I was back in Nashville.

4

It was good to be in my "monk's cell," where one of my paintings hung on the wall, a copy of a medieval manuscript of a Gregorian chant on another, the black FM radio on a night table beside the bed, the typewriter on a card table in the middle of the room, my books and records shelved along one wall. I was reunited with myself.

October 20, 1960
10 P.M.
(Letter to Janeice)
Things have been as they should be I think. . . . My life is uncomplicated now. I'm deliberately avoiding intimate social

contacts. I can't write and live, too. But wait until spring! I'm learning that I need blocks of time to write prose, whereas poetry for me doesn't require this. Of course, I'm beset with much self-doubt. This is nothing new, though. Mr. Hayden informed me several years ago that a creative person always has this problem. So I'm learning to live with it.

I'm learning the real meaning of patience, too . . . real in the sense of a deeper aspect of. I guess it was exemplified in a 15 pp. story I finished last week. I didn't like it. I rewrote it three times before it hung together poetically. Even now, I'm deleting sentences and adding a few. I'm learning that patience is not only working with one sentence until each word is the one right word, but patience is knowing that your potential cannot be realized in a few days. The great work I feel within me (I hope that's what I feel) requires years of producing lesser works. Patience is not only a relaxed waiting, but a vital perseverance.

I completed several short stories and a novella that fall, and read intensely: Durrell's *Alexandria Quartet* (marvelous!), Jessamyn West, Austin Wright's *Islandia*, Alan Lomax's *The Rainbow Sign*, a biography of Goethe, James Purdy, Henry Miller, Katherine Anne Porter (whom I loved), D. H. Lawrence (whom I didn't), Flaubert, Isak Dinesen (still a favorite), Kerouac, Robert Graves, and Mary Renault.

I was writing away from the typewriter now, learning to keep a part of myself separate, to observe and make notes. Sometimes I felt like an agent, pretending to share another's reality but being involved only in operating the microfilm camera hidden in my mind. My life could not be lived for itself. Like a pregnant woman who lives mindful of the life she carries within, so I lived, nurturing and protecting the artist in my soul's womb.

October 23, 1960
11 P.M.
(Letter to Janeice)

Saturday night I went to the ISC film as usual. It was *The Brink of Life* directed by Ingmar Bergman. It's the story of 3 women in pregnancy. When I left I felt as if I had had a child. (One scene is of natural childbirth.) I left holding my abdomen and it still aches. Of course, you know how much I'd like to have a child, but alas! My intellect or will won't help me. Therefore I experience it through a film.

In my writing I've become increasingly interested in women

. . . I find men so insensitive and indelicate. I could never write Bill about the film. He isn't feminine. Men are intellect and reason, but a woman is so much more. Even at Highlander I experienced so much with girls 14 and 15. I could talk with them like I talk to you. It was so new for me and so beautiful. I envy women. Their bodies are beautiful. And some have the corresponding feeling. . . . I guess I feel close to women because they know through childbearing what it is to paint, compose or even scribble. I've had some strange experiences. I can feel the sexual experience of a woman. Physically I can feel it by simply concentrating. In the film I felt Cecelia's miscarriage when she said, "It's leaving me," or the other woman when she was being taken to the delivery room—"This is life itself."

I hope someday that I will be able to live the nine months with a wife, but I'm afraid my hopes won't be realized. There're three ways to serve God—through Man (this is you, I think), through the Devil and the direct apprehension of the Godhead. I'm afraid my way is through the Demonic. . . . It's because of the demonaic in artistic creation which consumes the artist as if he were a match lighting a fire that I hesitate to even consider marriage, a family. It seems that Art has the power to destroy the artist, in that he is so consumed that all else is irrelevant to Art. In a way, one stops being what is called human. Who has been able to live with those creative ones that are called great? All of those that we have detailed biographical data of have made the lives of those around them miserable— Gide, Van Gogh, Gauguin, Wagner, Beethoven. A few people stuck by them. Such love is equal to that of Jesus. They did lay down their lives for the sake of a Beethoven. I wouldn't ask anyone to do that for me. . . .

I cared for nothing else that fall but writing. The people I talked with, the young women I dated, had no existence of their own except as specimens to be examined. I wanted to know the texture of every emotion, how much it weighed in this person's life, and how much less or more it weighed in another's. I opened myself to people as I'd never done before, curious to see what I would feel with different ones. I wanted to be a mirror and hold the perfect reflection of whoever stood before me, not for them, but for the writer in me.

Yet, I was uneasy with the parasite hiding behind my warm smile. Equally as much as I wanted to be a good writer, I wanted to be a good person, like Pierre and Janeice. But how could I be both? Each required the totality of one's being. In a moment of terror I shared my fears with Janeice.

> . . . I've destroyed myself for the artist. I experience on two levels—as Julius and as a creative person. The creative person is always observing Julius and Julius knows it. I can't integrate the two and it makes Julius seem like a hypocrite, a liar. Like Zola said at his father's deathbed: "What a fine scene for a novel this would make." This is me. . . . All this leads me to wonder whether or not I, as an individual, have a genuine emotion—a feeling in and of itself, an experience which is complete in itself. For me a poem or a story is more important than a person, if it has to come to a choice. . . . It is so painful and hard to live with, Janeice. It makes me loathe myself and suicide seems desirable. Self-acceptance when you know the evil within you is a difficult thing. . . .

Afraid of what I was becoming, I stopped writing. I didn't want to be an object to myself, or know others as corpses upon which I performed autopsies. I didn't know how to live as a writer without maiming myself, and once again, I longed for the safety of the identity a career would confer upon me. More seriously than ever, I thought of the ministry, sent for seminary catalogs and decided to apply to the University of Chicago and enter its program in Religion and Literature. I even decided to write my dissertation on "Primitive Christianity in the Beat Generation." Having decided all that, I waited to see if the decision would be confirmed in some way. Early in January, Septima Clark, the Director of Education at Highlander, called and asked me to assume Guy's duties as music director until June. (He was in South Carolina working at Highlander projects in the area and collecting music.) Without hesitation, I accepted and never thought of the ministry again.

5

Winter at Highlander was quiet.

> Looking out, I could
> Only see the fogginess
> of the fog.

❋

In the fog I
Try to walk
Quietly.

❋

The horses graze as
If it were not
Raining.

❋

The only sound in
The fog—moisture
Dripping from the trees.

I wrote little more than those few haiku, for I was involved with
the people who came to the workshops. They were rural blacks,
and like the cypresses of the Big Sur coast which grow in wind-
sculpted beauty, those people breathed an eternal essence, too. My
world of books and ideas was artificial beside theirs, for they lived
in Death's shadow and did not quail. They worked as maids,
laborers, ministers, farmers, fishermen, and at great personal risk,
organized literacy and voter registration schools in small southern
towns. What had I done?

After a workshop in February, I went to the South Carolina
Sea Islands to be with Guy for a week. It was night when I
arrived on Edisto Island, and morning brought the sight of aged
oak trees, mournful Spanish moss hanging from their limbs; long,
uncurving country roads loud with silence, and frame shacks,
some of which, I learned, had stood since the days of slavery. I
went to church that morning and throughout the long service in
the cold building, I stared in awe at the faces of the old people,
faces which, if they had been crowned by kerchiefs, would have
been those of my slave ancestors. Each one looked wise with the
knowledge of winds and clouds and earth, and after church an
old woman walked up to me and, with no greeting or introduction,
said, "Son, you look like you could turn water to wine." I laughed
at the joke I didn't understand, but she repeated her remark
solemnly and walked away, leaving me shivering with fright. But
the atmosphere on Edisto and the other islands was such as to
make the remark sound like normal conversation, because this

was another country and another time, more Africa than America, more then than now, and if crows had descended from the trees to converse with me, I would have answered.

I wished I could be wholly a part of the world there. The people belonged to something, as did my father, but I had stepped away from the generations of history lined into their faces. I was no longer an integral part of the culture, and when I listened to the singing in the churches and homes on John's Island, I could not help but try to analyze the harmonies and the complex rhythms of the hand clapping and foot stomping.

But I loved them whose lives I could not fully share, and wanted whatever I did to acknowledge them in some way. They were my people and always would be. The sorrow of our lives was as eternal as the waves washing onto beaches our foreparents had stumbled across, after the terror-fraught voyage from Africa.

6

February 27, 1961
10:30 P.M.
(Letter to Janeice)

A year ago today you were in Detroit and I was at the Haydens'. It was a snowbound Saturday. I'd had a date with Candie, but she stood me up. She was in jail.

Since February a year ago I've been more and more involved with social action, a way of life that had before been completely dismissed by me. After a year of being in a social action climate, being involved with people who are as intensely involved in it as I am with music and being on the staff of Highlander, which is dedicated to social problems, I can no longer give it a cursory dismissal. I have consciously and unconsciously absorbed non-violence, integration and all the rest. And I can no longer consider these problems unimportant. I can no longer be unconcerned. I can no longer consider the contemplative way of life as the most important.

And because something new has forced its presence into me, I face new problems in an attempt to digest it. But I still cannot become overtly involved . . . but in a real way, I've never been uninvolved. My involvement with people has become deeper, so much so in fact that I find it difficult to leave the South, although I want to.

Sartre and Camus both speak, that the artist must be engaged, i.e., to be involved and deliberately committed. To rephrase it, in the words of Ralph Ellison, the artist has a moral responsibility. And I guess it is the recognition of this that creates a problem. It creates a problem in that you don't shove Bach in a man's ear while he can only hear his stomach growling. And I'm finding it difficult to write in a climate of social revolution, because my mind refuses to let me be unaware of what is going on. This is good, in that I'll be able to write in the future, but it sorta makes writing difficult now. One gets tired of absorbing, of being a spectator. Thank God, I can sing.

But none of this I'm saying is coming out to say all that I'm feeling. You see, once I think I've found myself, I immediately find yearnings within me that have just awakened. And right at this moment, I wish I were talking to someone. That, obviously, is something new in me. But more and more, people have entered my life and I wonder now how I could have been so content with my intellectual tower of years past. I don't have your way with people, but yet, I've met more people since June than in all the years previous.

One hears that a life should have a sense of direction. I puzzle over this, not quite understanding it and not having it. Where is my life leading to? I have hitched my wagon to no star that I know of. I have no golden dream which I want to make manifest.

If genius is the concentration of all of one's faculties on one act, then I have no claim to genius. The only act I can pour all of my powers into is the one I happen to be doing.

I dunno, Janeice. I'm not happy, nor am I depressed. I'm drifting and it's hard getting accustomed to the feeling that drifting will be my way of life. But I can see no other that will allow me so many intense experiences.

As spring came, I knew that I had to leave the South if I was going to maintain the vision of myself as an artist. Who you are depends on where you are, I recalled, and, in the South of 1961, I was perilously close to becoming a worker for the Student Non-Violent Coordinating Committee (SNCC), the group of young college blacks who'd left school to spearhead the civil rights movement. I had finally recognized the importance of what they were doing, but my doubts about "the movement's" ability to effect significant change remained. (I listened to many discussions that spring about non-violence as a tactic versus non-violence as a way of life. I was saddened when the majority consensus in every discussion rejected non-violence as a way of life. In my emotions I knew that it was the respiratory system of the spirit, but I did not have the words to say it.) Yet, despite my reservations, I could not remain in the South and be outside "the movement." To join, however, would have been to deny some truth about myself.

I was haunted by the memory of Sylvia that spring and knew that when it was time to leave, I would go to New York to be close to her, to walk through the Metropolitan Museum of Art and see the Rodins she'd described so often, and, perhaps, regain her inside myself, and, consequently, myself.

I could only call that self, writer, and I didn't like it. Writer was not a fixed point, but an invitation to uncertainty and self-destruction. But it was the only word in which I knew who I was, and without it, I would be swept out to sea.

IV

1

It was early June, 1961, when I arrived in New York with my guitar and typewriter. I had only fifty dollars, but during those first days there was too much to see to worry about the future. I set out each morning from the apartment of Mac Sturges, a friend from Highlander, and walked the streets, discovering Madison Avenue with its shops and galleries of Tibetan sculpture, African masks, Indian blankets, tapestries, antique furniture and paintings by Picasso, Braque, and Pollock. I peered into Fifth Avenue mansions at high-ceilinged rooms, where chandeliers twinkled like the Milky Way in an August night sky, and made my fantasy trip with Sylvia through the Metropolitan Museum, where I saw Rodin's "The Kiss" and knew our love had been remembered even before it had begun. On Sunday afternoons, I went to fabled Washington Square Park in Greenwich Village and listened to guitar, banjo and mandolin players and folk singers, but was too shy to bring my own guitar. I rode buses, not knowing where they went and thus discovered Carnegie Hall, on whose stage Toscanini had conducted the music I had listened to every Sunday during my adolescence. I made a ritual pilgrimage to Harlem, the black holy city. ("If I could only get you in Harlem," Daddy had said behind the backs of white people who'd insulted him.) For a day I walked its streets, my mouth gaping in amazement at this infinity of blacks. The census claimed there were twenty million of us in America, but there had to be that many in Harlem!

More overwhelming than Harlem's blackness, however, was its poverty. Like some great orator, Harlem spoke eloquently of life for which each breath was struggled, of hard times coming incessantly like Arctic blizzards. I did not think it was possible to dream in Harlem, and I hurried back to Mac's apartment on East Eighty-third Street.

For a portion of each day I walked along the Hudson River in Riverside Park and in Central Park. I needed to rest in these burrows, for New York's hard visage, constantly moving crowds, and ceaseless noises were abrasive, as was the loneliness which trailed me like a shadow. I had no friends in New York, except for Janeice, and after seeing her once, I realized that I loved her more through letters. So I lay in parks and called the grass my friend, gazed at the river and knew it as my sister, and wondered if I would ever find my place.

2

My money was near depletion by the end of the month, but I got a job at Camp Woodland, a progressive camp in the Catskill Mountains outside Phoenicia, New York. I was reunited with my adolescent compeers, and with so many bright and nubile young girls around, love blessed me and this time, profoundly. Karin was a fourteen-year-old dancer with long hair, a voice quiet as an autumn Catskill morning, and a maturity exceeding her years and mine. There was no artifice between us, no attempt to hide the emotions we evoked in the other. When I came in to breakfast each morning, she was there to place a dew-shining tiger lily behind my ear, and when I looked into her eyes, I knew that her gesture was not the innocent one of a girl with a crush on a counselor, but that of a woman who knows. If I have one regret about my life, it is that I allowed myself to be intimidated by her chronological age (and the statutory rape laws).

While I wanted to lie in the dew-heavy grasses of dawn summer mornings with Karin, I did so, at least figuratively, with Anna, a work camp counselor. A large-eyed girl with dark hair which she wore in a bun, she was also a dancer. A junior at Vassar, she was unlike any girl I would ever love again—cold, arrogant, affected, snobbish—and though she ridiculed and mocked my cultural ig-

norance ("You've never *heard* of Martha Graham?") I loved her
with a masochistic passion. She represented that wider world
whose ways I wanted to learn, and I accepted being treated like
a footman so that I could learn to move as easily as she through
the New York cultural world of concerts, dance recitals, plays
and restaurants. That autumn she introduced me to the Leningrad
Kirov Ballet, the Martha Graham Dance Company, Indian music,
as well as sex as we rid ourselves of the burden of virginity,
clumsily but ardently, one afternoon that September.

Though we professed love, we never perceived the other as a
person. She gloried in my blackness, wearing me like a mink stole,
and indulging in fantasies of her mother's apopleptic attack if she
knew that her daughter was going with a black man. She enjoyed
showing me off that autumn to her classmates at Vassar and doted
on the stares we elicited in public.

We were emotional cripples using each other as crutches. We
shared what little of ourselves that we could and took what we
needed for our individual sallies at the windmill. Late that autumn,
nothing remained. (I saw her several times the following spring,
and occasionally we spent nights together. The last time I saw her
was on the street one day after we were both married, she to a
now well-known black writer. We laughed as we puzzled over
this new, strange experience called marriage. Then suddenly she
laughed that wonderful, free laugh of hers and said, "I was an
awful bitch, wasn't I?" I smiled wryly, the hurts still there, pulsating with lives of their own. I nodded, unable to tell her just
how much of a "bitch" she had been, but because she could
acknowledge it, everything was all right, and I loved her again
and she knew, loving me, too, and perhaps wondered, as I did, if
this were not the moment at which we should have begun.)

3

When I returned to New York after the camp season I started
looking for an apartment and hated myself for not having the
courage to rip out the lying tongues telling me, several times a
day, "It's just been rented." (How warmly people smile when
they say it.) I accepted the inevitable and carried my dreams to

the Harlem "Y," where, if I were told there were no vacancies, it would be the truth.

Moving to Harlem was a bitter defeat, a retreat from the world in which I wanted to find a perch, because Harlem was the home of the vanquished, and I feared that I had taken the first step to becoming one of them. I knew that existence is precarious, and that I could easily awake one day to find that I had become a wino or a junkie, leaning on a lamppost cursing "Whitey" for having taken my life. On the warm evenings of early autumn, I stood with others on the corner of One Hundred Twenty-fifth Street and Seventh Avenue, at what was then called African Square, and listened to the speakers mounted on stepladders declaiming against "the white man" and proclaiming the new black world a-coming. Everything I would hear in the last half of the sixties, under the rubric of Black Power, was expounded on those nights by anonymous men painting black dreams on the canvas of evening before dreamers, skeptics, and hostile policemen, whose white faces floated through the darkness like sour milk in black coffee. I listened and agreed that we should buy black, love each other and be proud of ourselves as black people, but the next day when I walked among the winos, junkies, crapshooters, and thousands of unemployed men, the dream seemed to be a sand castle standing too close to the tide line. Others could love Harlem for what it could become; I couldn't. I was bewildered by its enormity and frightened by its impersonality. Though I had been segregated in the South, I could not say, as James Baldwin did, that "nobody knows my name." Why did he care if anyone knew his name? I sensed that it had something to do with Harlem, with existing and doubting that you really did, and if I remained in Harlem too long, I feared that I would dissolve into that unseen, unknown and undifferentiated black mass, like land taken by a flood.

To leave Harlem, however, I needed money, and each morning I went downtown to answer wants ads which read, "B. A. in Eng no exp nec." I was eminently qualified, but was not surprised when the jobs were "just filled by a young man you probably passed on the stairs."

In the evenings I took my guitar to Greenwich Village's Mac-Dougal and Bleecker Streets, where coffeehouses flourished. It was the beginning of the folk music revival, and if one were willing to pass the basket after performing, work could be had for walking through the door. My pride wouldn't allow me to do that, but, oddly, it was absent when I agreed to sit in the window of a coffeehouse and sing from nine P.M. to three A.M. for five dollars a night, six nights a week. I could have earned more passing the basket, particularly when I quit after not being paid for three nights.

Eventually, I was hired as a stockboy and mimeograph machine operator at the business school of City University. I was elated to be "gainfully employed," though two weeks had not passed before I wondered what I had gained. For eight hours each day I stood at a mimeograph machine and ran off exams, memos, notices, and announcements. I quickly became an expert machine operator, and there came the fateful day when I finished the day's quota of stencils by noon, told the boss I was through and would see him the next day. He looked at me as if I'd suddenly unzipped my pants and taken out my penis. "You can't do that!"

"Why not? I don't have anything to do."

"But you can't go home. You're paid for eight hours a day."

"Uh-uh." I shook my head. "I'm paid for my work."

"Well"—he paused—"go up to the storeroom and count the boxes of paper clips. We may have to reorder soon."

I looked at him as if he'd just taken out *his* penis. "You got to be kidding!"

He wasn't, and neither was I. I went home. I was not surprised when I was fired a few days later.

During that brief period of employment, however, I escaped from Harlem to a furnished room on West End Avenue near Eightieth Street. Though the room's only window looked onto an air shaft, I didn't care. At least it wasn't a Harlem air shaft.

4

Because it was near the Christmas season, I quickly found a job as a temporary clerk in the record department of the Double-day bookshop at Fifty-seventh and Fifth. I went to work each morning, stood behind the counter and looked at the people who walked in with small poodles, whose shampoos and manicures cost more than the thirty-six dollars I took home each Friday. But

I learned to smile at the imperious ladies of the upper East Side, who wanted to know, "What's new that I would like?" I learned not to say, "How should I know?" and showed them the latest albums by Lester Lanin, Peter Duchin, Ferrante and Teicher, and Broadway show cast albums, and when they asked, "Is this new Duchin really good?" I assured them that "This one is far superior to the last album," though I'd heard neither. At noon, unable to afford lunch, I sat in the winter cold beneath the fountain in front of the Plaza Hotel, surreptitiously eating the sandwich I'd brought and hoping that any blacks walking by wouldn't be too ashamed of me. At six, I left work. The early winter darkness transformed the crowded streets into ominous forms rushing toward subway stations like maze-trapped rats looking for an exit which didn't exist. Hunching my shoulders against the cold, I walked across Fifty-seventh Street, past Carnegie Hall whose concerts I couldn't afford, past the Art Students League where Sylvia might have been in class at that very moment, to the subway at Eighth Avenue, all the while being bumped and jostled by the other rats, hating them, for there was nowhere in New York one could go and be alone, and hating myself, for I was lonely. I looked at the faces on the street and in the subways, but could I stop one and say, "Hi! I need you!" Or, "Hi! You need me!" Or maybe, "Hi! We need each other!" There was one young woman at work, a music student, whom I asked to go to a Bach concert with me, and before saying no, she paused an instant too long, and I remembered: I had bad breath, but there was no mouthwash which could eradicate the odor of niggerness.

I went to my room each evening, lay on the bed, and let the loneliness thread its way into my bloodstream and soon there was no other reality except loneliness. I knew, however, that it was important to go to work each day, wrap records, make change and pretend that I saw, heard and believed in the people around me. Always threatening to leap from behind the mask, however, was me, and if that me spoke, it would be an agonized crying, a sobbing without shame or embarrassment, wrenching itself from my body while I was reaching for a Mable Mercer album, going through a subway turnstile, or in front of the newsstand where I bought *The Times* each morning. So, I acted myself, sensing that if one day I did not, I would be dragged into the farthest fathoms of loneliness from where no diver who ever retrieve me.

December 25, 1961
(Journal)

Tuesday night I knew that one day I will commit suicide. The realization came over me quietly and I found myself not debating over self-murder, but wondering when I will do it. I know how. I know why. When, I don't know. But one day I'll do it quietly, calmly and without previous forethought. It'll be as natural as yawning.

The knowledge gave me a certain satisfaction, for it was a recognition of a psychological defect in myself, a weakness of the spirit, a fragility of being which could not withstand too much adversity—"Here Lies Julius Lester, Too Fragile To Live." Or was I merely a spiritual coward, who cried when he scraped his soul on the pavement?

I went as often as I could to the Cloisters in upper Manhattan. I walked the corridors of the reconstructed Spanish monastery, imagining myself in scapular, face hidden in the cowl, arms clasped across my chest, going to Compline. I sat in the gardens, looked at the statuary of the Virgin Mary and the saints and knew a modicum of peace, but the Cloisters was a museum, and most who came were tourists, not supplicants, and the tiny peace always slipped from the needle's eye of my soul.

I bought an FM radio, a Christmas present to myself I could not afford, but I vaguely remembered that I had always used classical music as a means of ordering my being, of touching something outside my pathetic self.

Music replaced loneliness as reality, and slowly, as the dark days of winter waned, I backed away from the edge and could begin to see where I had been. There was nothing mysterious or profound about what I had experienced. My idea of myself was being tested in the world. I had created the outlines of a self in the isolation and security of a college campus, fashioning that self from a myriad of sources: Rimbaud, Colin Wilson, Merton, Henry Miller, Tillich, Sartre, Zen, Taoism, haiku, Kerouac, the Golden Gate Bridge, spirituals, prison songs, hawks, and sea gulls. This agglomeration could not be real until it learned to live in the uncaring arena where everyone is dispensable. I had come to New York and, for the first time, was unprotected by the benevolent concern of teachers, parents and friends. I entered the world as naked as I had been that January afternoon twenty-three years before, but this time, there were no doctors waiting to sponge me, and no nurse to wrap me up in warm blankets. The world was not a sterile delivery room but a germ-infested tenement, and if you survived with your dreams still glowing pink, you did so alone. The world demanded that its rules be obeyed, and you went to work on time, paid your rent, bought food, or suffered the consequences. No one was exempt from the rules. Whatever else you did with your life was your concern and your struggle, and the world was indifferent, as long as you paid the rent on time.

I recognized anew the enormity of what I was attempting—to carve my life out of nothing but myself. "It would be so much easier to mold my life around a career," I wrote Janeice. "Instead, I was chosen to have living as a career. Thus each step is always the first step."

I could look back, pleased that I had not given up in my first battle, though I had mounted the gallows. "God will not have his work made manifest by cowards," I read in an essay of Emerson's, but I was not sure that courage was required as much as the ability to withstand pain, something I was not sure I could do too much longer.

I received a letter from Pat Downs, a friend who'd been an exchange student to Fisk from Colby College (Me.), inviting me to ride to Nashville with her and Nancy Rowe, another former exchange student. I knew that I wanted to go. Just as I had had to return to Nashville from California to measure myself, I had to once again place myself against the past to better know my present.

I quit the job at Doubleday. The time had come, anyway, for not only had I been retained after Christmas, but promoted to manager of the record department at the store in Grand Central Station. Promotions and raises were some of the more obvious traps the world set.

We left New York the next afternoon and spent the night in Georgetown, at the home of Pat's aunt. Pat and Nancy went to a party that evening, but I remained behind. I happened to pick up Nancy's copy of David Riesman's *Individualism Reconsidered*, not a book I would normally read, since I was not interested in sociology. The title was provocative, however, and I leafed through it, stopping at an essay called, "A Philosophy for Minority Living." I read the first paragraph.

The "nerve of failure" is the courage to face aloneness and the possibility of defeat in one's personal life or one's work without being morally destroyed. It is, in a large sense, simply the nerve to be oneself when that self is not approved of by the dominant ethic of a society.

The course of my life was reconfirmed, for Riesman's statement was a variation of the quote from *Portrait of the Artist as a Young Man* that I had copied into my journal three years before. Riesman's was less romanitc, however, and without heroic overtones. Stephen Dedalus was not afraid; I was, and Riesman acknowledged that which I was ashamed of, and on it, he predicated a philosophy—to fail and not be destroyed. I did not have to succeed to prove the value of my life; the struggle was all. As I sat in the quiet light of that Georgetown living room, I didn't need to return to Nashville anymore. I would continue the trip, but at the city limits I would wonder why I had come. Let the next winter be bleak. I would persevere.

5

Spring was the resurrection. I now had a piece of the sky from a new room two floors higher from where I could watch pigeons court on the sloping roof of a church, sea gulls, and, at night, the moon. I wasn't working, hoping that the money I'd saved from Doubleday's would last until June, when I would get another camp job. "I'm happy and full," I wrote Janeice in the middle of April. "The struggle brought me to another level of Being and the plateau is filled with deep grass—slim-limbed stalks luxuriating in light and air, feasting on the sun and being what they are—tall grasses."

I lay in Riverside Park each day, reading, writing haiku, and at nights, worked on a novel called *Michele*. But as spring opened itself, my certainty that I had come "to another level of Being" diminished. I'd retreated so far inward during the winter that the outer world was still inhabited by eidolons. Anna came and stayed the night and we made love and I was aware of myself as a man acting the role of a man making love. Afterwards, when I was once again alone, it was with effort that I recalled that she had been there, or that we had made love. I carried on a desultory affair with a fourteen-year-old girl, intrigued by it and her, but feeling nothing inside myself. Like a ragpicker, I gathered experiences that spring, going to parties, playing guitar in Washington Square on Sunday afternoons, but the only impresses were left during the times of solitude—walking by the Hudson River in the early morning, listening to music, reading and writing. "I feel sometimes as if I am irretrievably lost," I wrote Janeice in early June. "Lost from what, I don't know, but just lost. Even though I crave people in my loneliness, my inner world is more vivid and meaningful to me. Somehow the world doesn't exist anymore. I know it is there and it affects me, but yet, it isn't there. I'm really scared for me. I don't know why, but I'm just scared. I don't quite know what to make of what I am."

But, without realizing it, I did, for in another letter to Janeice, I wrote: "I don't exist. I have no life of my own." It was true, for I lived only when I was writing. I hated the fact, but writing was my only bridge to the world, and without it, I was an atoll.

I could not survive another winter with no other reality except that of a dead self. Or, at least, I did not want to. I made vague plans to visit the *Catholic Worker* in the fall and see if I might want to live and work there. I would, also, make a retreat at a monastery. Perhaps the pain of the past winter was God's way of showing me where I belonged.

I got a job at a summer camp in the Catskills, and the first evening, June 22, I was sitting in a corner of the recreation room, playing the guitar when a young woman with short blond hair and bright blue eyes walked over and asked if I knew any blues. I didn't, but improvised one easily, knowing that this white girl wouldn't know the difference. She didn't. Six months later, to the day, we were married.

V

1

What could I have known of love that summer of 1962? I thought it was another function of the autonomic nervous system, something you did at a certain age, like walking. It was that way in the movies, and where else in American society could I have learned of love? I looked at her and liked the aggressiveness of her walk, the sun-glistening-goldness of the blond hair on her arms and legs, her azure eyes, and heard a Dimitri Tiomkin score swelling from the strings of an invisible orchestra. (She wore sandals, with long laces twining the calves of her legs, reminding me of the ethereal women of North Beach. I looked at her (ah! those sandals!) and didn't see a person, but an idea. Would I have fallen in love with her if she'd been wearing shoes? Sadly, I cannot say.)

Arlene was twenty-two, a dropout from Reed College, and had been living in Cambridge for the past year. We had read the same books, thought the same thoughts, and shared a passion for ideas and conversation. How serious and intense we were, adolescent idealists wanting to create a world of human perfection, or one, at least, that loved dreamers like us. What could we have known that summer of gathering another into yourself? If we had known, it would have been obvious that friendship was our language. How were we to know that a marriage was more than a movie made from the script of our fantasies? We did not see each other, but images of security and identity, as well as someone whose strengths complemented our weaknesses. (The second night of camp, we walked into town to drink beer, and coming back in the darkness, she asked me what I was going to do after the summer. I told her that I thought I wanted to be a monk and planned to visit a monastery. "You don't believe in God!" she exclaimed. "Yes, I do." There was no moon, and we stopped in the darkness, scarcely able to see each other, and she challenged me to prove God's existence. I couldn't and felt no need to try, and while I was disturbed that she insisted on proving to me that there couldn't be a God, I was excited by the quality of her brilliant mind, by her willingness to disagree with me and probe for the fallacies in my thinking, of which there were many, according to her Marxist-Leninist detector. After we were married, she told me she decided that night to save me from the monastery. Our end grew from our beginning.)

We mistook our intellects for our selves, a common adolescent error. Beyond that, however, we had nothing to give to each other, having no real selves. We were magnets of needs, requiring, most of all, someone to tell us what we could not tell ourselves: There is nothing wrong with you. (Laurie was a sixteen-year-old junior counselor. She was quiet, and my attraction to quiet women had always been profound, for I could rest with them and share the silence which I loved more than words. Laurie and I would lie beside each other in the summer grasses, speaking little. It was enough to be there and cover ourselves with the sky. She never believed that I loved her, experiencing nothing in herself worthy of love. What would have happened if she had believed me? I do not know, for while I could *be* with Laurie, I needed Arlene.)

Adolescent love is the attempt to define one's self through another, and that is why "I need you" is the ultimate declaration of that love. Adolescent love is a shelter from the terror of trying to be a person, and while such a haven is necessary, it is not adequate for a marriage. But neither is love.

When another counselor and I were fired at the end of July for protesting against the camp administration by wrecking the sound system and draining the artificial lake, I was distraught at leaving Arlene. I was convinced that I would never see her again and I dreaded being alone to face the trees of winter.

August 27, 1962
5:30 A.M
(Journal)

A Monday morning and I enter the seventh month of my twenty-third year and I find myself wondering once more will I make it? . . . It has been rough. I [can't] take any more pain and suffering. I've had more than my share and I just don't want any more. I don't want to feel myself treading unsteadily on the edge of insanity. All I want is to continue to be happy.

Of course, I've been reproaching myself for feeling this way, telling myself that pain is necessary, but all I say sounds empty. To suffer doesn't make sense. To be alone as I've been alone is equally senseless. I'm just tired of it. The struggle has sapped me and I really wonder if I can emerge whole from another struggle.

10 P.M.

Am reading Malcolm Lowry's *Hear Us, O Lord, From Heaven Thy Dwelling Place* and in the story, "Strange Comfort Afforded by the Profession," there is a moving passage built around a line from a letter Edgar Allan Poe wrote to his stepfather—"For God's sake pity me." And I quote a revealing sentence from the story —"It was questionable whether poets especially, in uttermost private, any longer allowed themselves to say things like 'For God's sake pity me.'"

I know. . . . Why should I be ashamed to cry out in my loneliness? Why will I be too ashamed to say it to Arlene? I guess because she might think less of me. But how I need her!

This afternoon I tried to think of someone I could go to just to lay my head in their lap, just to sit near them and not say a word, just to sit and know that here was someone who loved me, someone who cared.

I'll never make it through another winter of complete loneliness like last winter. Another desperate fight to maintain my sanity would end in failure I'm sure.

"For God's sake, won't someone pity me?"

And so, Arlene came to live with me.

2

I called her *la hija del sol* and myself, *el hijo de la luna* and did not understand what I was saying, except that she liked the day, and I the night. But the differences between us were as profound as the separation of the celestial lights. She was extroverted, open, affectionate, enjoyed the company of people in a way that was almost offensive to me. She was radiant, like a fifteen-year-old girl,

101

life emanating from her as if she were its source. Like the moon, I was subdued, quiet, emotionally reserved, and almost cold in my ability to be detached from others. ("What do you *feel?*" she demanded to know during the arguments which characterized our eight years together. I felt nothing except an impatience with her anger which forced me out of my inner world.) She was brash, aggressive, quick to anger and tears: I had long periods of self-pity and depression, and was so shy that I could only talk to her in letters. Her qualities were male, and I referred to her as the husband in our relationship, and I, at long last, could be a woman, cleaning the apartment, shopping, doing the dishes, taking the laundry. She called me Julie, and I delighted in my feminine name. We complemented each other, she enticing me from my inward reserve, while I tempered her emotionalism. She was the day, the child of the sun, and I, the night, the child of the moon, and not incidentally, she was white, and I, black.

I'd known since I was nine years old that I would marry a white woman, for one day during that year, I saw a white girl on a street in downtown Kansas City and said, softly, almost reverently, to myself, "When I grow up, I'm going to marry her." What was there about that girl? If she were especially beautiful, I doubt that my young eyes would have perceived it, and I wasn't defying the white world's prohibition of interracial marriages. But, because she was white, she was the unknown, carrying experiences which were not mine and never could be, except through her. (Was the writer in me asserting itself that early?) Black girls were from a world I knew, and with them I could only re-experience the familiar. I needed someone to take me places I could not go on my own.

If that had not been my childhood intuition, my adolescent experiences with black girls would have produced the same result. The girls of my youth were middle-class, judging boys by the kind of house their parents owned, the clothes they wore, and what their father did for a living. I did not want to be so judged, yet through high school and college, I carried one crush after another to the altar of love, only to find the priest always absent. The girls who endured my clumsy attentions were kind and though I was "too intense, too serious, too eccentric" for them to think of me romantically, they accepted me as a friend, and I became one of the "girls," privy to all the gossip, the discussions about their boyfriends, and the only male at one girl's bridal shower. I accepted what they offered, but could never forget their judgment on me as one they could not love.

At Fisk, I met white girls for the first time, and they did not think it odd that I got excited by a paragraph of Spinoza, a line of Verlaine, or the "Emperor" Concerto. Even after the painful experiences with white girls at San Diego State, I was not disillusioned. They rejected me because I was black. Black girls rejected me because I was me. (Even Sylvia ended our relationship because she preferred bourgeois safety to the insecurity of self-realization. Janeice would not marry me, because she told me years later, "I was afraid of you.")

White girls liked me, especially when I told them I wanted a wife who would go out to work and let me stay home and care for the house. They were not perturbed when I showed up for a date in jeans, with only enough money for a quart of beer, if that. (And later it was Anna who told me that my hair, which had always been called "nappy," was beautiful, and though I didn't believe her, I thanked her for the lie. She also said, "I like the color of your body," and years later, in the last months of my marriage, Margaret said, "You have a beautiful body," and I, whose skinniness had been the source of much laughter and many jokes by black girls, hugged her closer.) If I'd married a black woman, no one would've been more surprised than me.

Arlene and I were married three days before Christmas, and on our wedding night, she cried herself to sleep, afraid that she had made a mistake. She had wanted to live alone, to have the time and space in which to know herself, but I needed her, and she, flattered by my need, called it love. We were mere children, afraid of the wolves which materialized at the edge of the forest at dusk. In our efforts to love, we would learn to hurt each other with the finesse of a king's torturer.

3

Marriage protected me from the loneliness, but deprived me of solitude. I was working as a welfare investigator in Harlem, and Arlene was finishing her B. A. at the New School. I came home and wanted only to sit, be quiet, and prepare myself to write. I couldn't, for this person insisted on talking to me and expected me to respond. This person wanted to go to the movies, to a restaurant, to have friends over for dinner. This person expected me to acknowledge her existence and I tried until the inevitable day when I had to acknowledge my own. Thus began the periods of depression, weeks when I communicated only in monosyllables and then only in response to direct questions. Finally, she could endure no more and would cry, yell, rage and threaten to leave. I apologized; she apologized; we declared our love like a Romeo and Juliet in a church production and made frantic, frightened love. A month or two would pass and the cycle would repeat itself.

What had I expected from marriage? I didn't know. I wanted to share my presence with someone, but not my life. It was enough for me that she was there, a visible reminder of the outer world. I tried to make her understand that she made it possible for me to withdraw without becoming hopelessly entangled in myself. She was flattered, but unconvinced. She only loved *me*. She should have loved the writing, too, because I was not separate from it. I had not anticipated sharing every breath of someone's life. I didn't know how and didn't care to learn. (Three months after we were married, she was ill and I hated her for interrupting my work. I loved her, I wrote in my journal, "but I love writing more. To write is more important than anything or anyone. . . . To be a great artist is my dharma. I'll leave being a good person to those who can get outside themselves more completely.")

I tried to learn how to live with another, but I had so tenuous a hold on my identity that I began apologizing for being who I was. "I hope that living with me won't strain you too much," I wrote her. "I feel guilty that I can't love you in the manner that you want to be loved. . . . Nonetheless, I love you. In my own way, which is like a haiku, I guess." But three lines of seventeen-syllable love were not adequate when she wanted a sonnet. I was afraid that she would leave me unless I became the person she wanted me to be, and I knew that if I had to live alone again, I would commit suicide. So, I tried to find a balance between her needs and those of my interior life.

I returned to the pattern of living I'd had in San Diego, staying up after she went to bed ("But a husband and wife are supposed to go to bed at the same time," she said, at first), to read, write, listen to Bach, and then, after four or five hours' sleep, rise and go to Harlem, into the homes of the old, the blind, the women with children. I didn't know what to say to the twenty-one-year-old mentally-ill boy with no friends except those on the screens of the movie theaters where he sat all day, every day, or the sixteen-year-old with her third baby, or the old people waiting to die and wondering why Death moved as slowly as they, or the old man with a severe speech impediment with whom I sat and talked one afternoon, scarcely understanding a word he said, but, finally, as I was leaving, understanding that I was the first person in twenty-one years who had listened to his voice. I walked up and down the stairs of the tenements, stepping over the junkies and winos sleeping in the doorways and on the stairwells, to reach an apartment where I was shown a rat-bitten baby, and I came home and Arlene wondered why I did not want to speak.

After four months I hated myself for having become a paper clip god who was flattered, cajoled and begged for a few extra dollars to make life more palatable. I squeezed the system for whatever extra dollars it would yield but could never forget that my income depended on poverty. (There were a few of us working at the Welfare Department who whispered about a man named Malcolm X, whose voice was then beginning to be heard by the few who dared listen. I stopped wearing a suit and tie to work, and when questioned about it by my supervisor, told him that I could not sit before poor black people dressed like a white boss. "What are you?" he demanded to know. "A follower of this Malcolm X? One of those *Black* Muslims?" I didn't know what I thought of Malcolm or the Muslims, but anything a white man hated that much couldn't be too wrong. "Yes!" I declared firmly.)

I quit, not only because I was unable to live with the impotence, but it was time I gave my life wholly to writing, or stop telling myself that I was a writer. If I was supposed to write, every moment I did something else was a sin. I would write, and if that was what God wanted, He would pay the rent.

4

I began work on a novella, "Catskill Morning." Using Karin as the model for Emily, the central character, I lived what I regretted had not been. (I finished it that summer and nine years later, rewrote and published it in *Two Love Stories*.)

I read, also, and reshaped and redefined my definitions of what was good writing, and who I was as a writer, technically and psychologically.

May 12, 1963
(Journal)

I'm trying to write in as many styles as possible. This obviously goes contrary to the adage that the style is the man. I believe that the style is determined by the subject matter and characters. Thus, I see style in much the same light as I view poetic meters. And the distinctiveness which separates style and imitation of styles comes in the way the writer uses words—the peculiar quality he brings to his arrangement and choice of them. This much of style is the man. I want to avoid having everything I write sound alike, as is the case with most writers. Each subject, even in a book of short stories, should be granted the respect of being approached differently. Just as an artist will draw a bottle at different times of day when the light is different, just as he will use charcoal, pen and ink, water color and oils on one subject, so must the writer show the different aspects of his subject. Nothing is as unilateral as a writer would have us to believe.

Maybe my thinking in this vein isn't worth pursuing. I think it is. I must not be afraid to fail.

May 13, 1963
4 A.M.
(Journal)

Am reading Priestley's *Margin Released* and ran across the following:
". . . in my attitude toward my work I belong to the eighteenth century when professional authors were expected to do anything from sermons to farces."

We went to New Hampshire for the summer. Arlene answered a "House for Rent" ad in *Saturday Review*, and after the owners met us, we found ourselves with a summer house for forty dollars and the promise to paint the house's interior. At a police department auction we bought a 1958 Plymouth for fifteen dollars.

It was the only happy summer of our marriage. She lay in her beloved sun, picked dew-soaked berries along the road, and cooked blueberry pancakes over the wood-burning stove. I delighted in drawing water from the well, chopping dead trees for firewood, and sitting in the outhouse with the door open on chilly evenings, peering at the star-heavy sky. We sat before the fireplace at night, while birch trees shone white in the moonlight, and were very much in love.

Arlene studied French, Russian and black history that summer, and her involvement in the latter led to my first extensive readings in the history of my people. I also read Tolstoy, Dostoievsky, Balzac, Merton, Robinson Jeffers, Emerson, Isaac Singer and Harvey Swados. I wrote a short story, "The Ram's Horn," which was published eight years later in the *Massachusetts Review*, and began "Alabama Boy," a novella about a young black man who comes north to study at Columbia in the late fifties, and on graduating, finds that his new love of ideas and affinity for spiritual matters alienates him from the just-beginning civil rights movement.

Though not autobiographical in its details, "Alabama Boy" was an attempt to describe, and possibly resolve the increasing threat to my identity represented by "the movement." When Dr. King had led demonstrations in Birmingham that spring, I'd wanted to be there to let the police dogs tear my flesh instead of that of black children. I wanted to be in Mississippi working with SNCC, and no matter how often I told myself that writing was important, I was not convinced anymore. My contemporaries went to jail in the struggle for my freedom, while I sat in the mountains of New Hampshire looking at birch trees, watching the clouds and writing.

> Under the grasses
> In the middle of the road,
> The green snake—so still!

5

We returned to New York in September, and my political radicalization accelerated when we were served with an eviction notice. Having moved into the apartment without the landlady's permission, and having had her refuse to cash our checks for a year, we should have anticipated such. I accepted the eviction writ with resignation and was ready to look for another apartment. Arlene was outraged, secured a show cause order against the landlady, and delayed the eviction. Once in court, the landlady's case was dismissed on a technicality.

I had a new respect for Arlene's politics. She could see the class struggle in a bowl of Rice Krispies and lived in anger at a system that forced us to live in a rat-infested tenement, with only intermittent heat in the winter. She made me look at society as something other than a collection of individuals, each responsible for the state of his/her soul. A slow, subtle transformation began inside me, and without knowing exactly when, I forgot Merton and became a part of my times.

One evening in the spring of 1964, I met Ivanhoe Donaldson and John O'Neil, two SNCC organizers, who talked to me about the coming Mississippi Summer Project. SNCC was recruiting a thousand people to come to the state and organize the Mississippi Freedom Democratic Party to challenge the seating of the all-white Mississippi delegation at the Democratic party convention that August. Ivanhoe asked me to join the folk singers' project, as I had been singing at SNCC rallies and benefits in New York for some time. I readily agreed.

I expected Arlene to share the excitement of my conversion to politics, for she had been responsible for it. To my surprise, she was more angry than I'd ever known her, because I had made a decision without discussing it with her. I was bewildered, wondering why I should discuss with her something I was going to do. "But we're married!" she kept repeating. I nodded, but I had never discussed personal decisions with anyone, not even my parents. (They learned that I had left home from a note on the dining room table: "Have gone to New York. Will write.") I heard Arlene's words, but they meant nothing.

After several hours of anger and tears, she gave up trying to make me understand what I had done wrong, smiled, and wanted to know what we would be doing in Mississippi. I didn't know how to say that I was going alone. I could not share the South with Arlene, or any northern white at least. I would be returning to the land of my foreparents for a rebaptism, and she could not walk into that stream with me. I could show her the long roads, the old trees, the cotton fields and plantation shacks, but I was not a tourist guide.

She could go to Mississippi, but not with me. She insisted that we had to go together, for marriage was two people living one life. She refused to act unless it was as part of a couple, and she didn't go to Mississippi that summer, or attend the University of Wisconsin the following year, as she wanted to, or move to Philadelphia the year after that, because I didn't want to. "You go," I would tell her. "But what will become of our marriage?" she wanted to know. A physical separation was an inconvenience, but it could not affect the marriage, I contended, if we were not separate from each other inside ourselves. Marriage was two people sharing as much as they could of their separate lives, I told her. We found each other incomprehensible, for we were living two different relationships.

We were not wholly responsible for what we wanted from the marriage. As a woman, Arlene had been trained to be the satellite orbiting a man's sun, supported by the pull of his gravity. I had been educated to shine. She saw my desire to act independently as a rejection of her. I thought I was treating her as an equal, not an appendage. She wanted to lose herself in marriage; I wanted to use marriage as a springboard to self-realization. We were husband and wife, walking in different directions on roads which never crossed. But the day I left for Mississippi we cried, because for almost two years we'd not been apart more than a few hours. Within two years, however, I would leave to go on trips with more nonchalance than I went to the corner bakery to buy cheese danish.

6

July 5, 1964
Clarksdale, Miss.
10 A.M.
(Journal)

Hot already. Like Grandmother's kitchen on a summer day when she was heating irons in a tub of coals and cooking on the wood-burning stove at the same time. It is what one would expect, however, in the Mississippi delta and in Clarksdale, "the blues capital of the world."

I've been traveling down Highway 61—

Sixty-one highway, Lord, the longest road I know (2x)
Run from Chicago to the Gulf of Mexico.
(Fred McDowell)

Through the country that birthed Robert Johnson, Muddy Waters, Charlie Patton, Eli Green, Son House, and Fred Mc-

Dowell. It's flat, except for the trees protruding from the earth occasionally. All one sees is cotton—from the edge of the highway to the horizon—cotton. Sometimes a shack can be seen from the highway, but it merely looks like a different kind of cotton plant. Nothing takes your awareness away form the Delta. It is sky, land and heat—each one a plane that stretches interminably and relentlessly. Even the highway is the minimum, the essence of a highway. It is narrow and, unlike the superhighways, Highway 61 does not impress itself on the surroundings. Like the blues, the Delta is life in its essentialness. Sky and land. It is one line repeated twice and a rhyming last line—succinct and more than adequate in its expression.

> Here comes that Greyhound, with his tongue hanging out the side (2x)
> I done bought my ticket, gon' get on that bus and ride.
>
> (Tommy McClennon)

July 7, 1964
Hattiesburg, Miss.
Late evening
(Journal)

Officially I came to Mississippi to sing in freedom schools, at mass meetings and to hold workshops on Negro music. Unofficially, though, I came to learn and to be born again. I came to see my family's beginning in this country. I'm on a pilgrimage and it's incidental that I am also involved in the Mississippi civil rights struggle. Even though I am a southerner, my relationship with the "race problem," integration, civil rights or however one thinks of it, has always been tangential. I want to go back to the beginning, to stand in the middle of a country road and feel what my slave great-grandparents felt. I want to see the landscape and the other slaves with their eyes. I want to hear them sing their songs, the songs I sing now. I want to be freed from slavery and feel the confusion and joy that emancipation brought. I want to stand in that road and hear field hollers and work songs change into the blues.

For most Americans only their family past is important, but I have a collective past, a past embracing the history of a nation and the history of a people. My present was shaped by it. Right now, my past and my present are a sketch in chiaroscuro; I was a slave and now I am free. But chiaroscuro omits the gradations . . . the modulations from one key to another, the transition from slave to freedman. So I am here. Mississippi. A pilgrimage to a cathedral of the Black Mass.

July 8, 1964
Laurel, Miss.
11 P.M.
(Journal)

The intensity of emotion with which the people sing freedom songs is almost frightening. This is not the first time I've seen it, but it has never repelled me before. I know, however, that it is only through these songs that they are able to release the frustrations of years and find the courage to face the coming years.

The teenagers are more emotional than the adults. The old people are more resigned. They fight, but the emotion involved is tempered by knowledge and patience, by age and the psychic guerilla warfare they have waged all of their lives against the whites. The young people know nothing except raw emotion.

I found myself leading the singing, but totally removed from the emotions which the songs induced. I believe that "We shall overcome someday." I know that I'm not going to let "nobody turn me 'round," but when I sing these songs I think of my enemy as those things inside—lack of integrity, lack of imagination, callousness, cruelty. Even if I am free, a lack of the basic human attributes will defeat me. If that happens, a picket line won't be of any use. No Congressional legislation can ever overcome that which makes a man a slave to the forces within him.

I can't criticize the emotions which a mass meeting unleashes, however. God only knows that life in these small towns is as close to hell as one can come on this earth. At least the people can sing and pray and hope.

July 10, 1964
Biloxi, Miss.
(Journal)

This is the first time I've lived and been with Negroes in three years, I guess. It amazes me sometimes when I think how much, in a way, I'm out of contact with Negroes. Sometimes I see a young Negro couple walking down the street in New York and I wonder what Negroes are thinking. Yet, in another way, my contact is closer with them than it ever was, because of music. I'm able to realize things about them that I wouldn't without the distance that not living in a Negro ghetto gives. Too, I've never been as concerned with Negroness as I have with plain and simple me-ness. . . .

111

July 11, 1964
Biloxi, Miss.
(Journal)

Has it only been a week since I boarded the bus at Port Authority in New York? Faith alone makes me believe that I have a wife and a "home" there. I do not know it. My knowledge has become limited to heat, to singing freedom songs, to sleeping in a different town each night and to being alone. My knowledge has increased to the degree that I am wary of any car that passes slowly down the street. The backfire of a truck or the loud slam of a screen door are identifiable as such only after I realize that no one has screamed. That, however, is no assurance that the next unnatural sound won't be followed by a scream. And possibly my own. I don't want to die, but I'm sure that no one does. Others, though, are willing to die for freedom. I'm not even willing. Each morning I awake thinking, today I die.

Consciously or not, I think that many awake feeling the same. In some the fear is evident. In others it takes the form of recklessness that verges on insanity at times. Sex, liquor and the speed of an automobile become the outlets for those who get no release at mass meetings. No one can live constantly with death without becoming mutilated or free.

The greatest courage, however, is living in Mississippi. Unfortunately, all you read of and hear of are the harassments, the murders, beatings and jailings. The real stories, though, are of the Mississippi Negroes who walk to the courthouse to register to vote, knowing that loss of job and life may be the consequence. The stories are of the Mississippi Negroes who have opened their homes to white and Negro civil rights workers this summer and are not afraid to sit on their front porch in the evening and talk to the blond girl from Iowa while the traffic goes by. Courage is not a dramatic act; it is not an act easily observed by another, but courage is the norm in Mississippi.

July 13, 1964
Tougaloo, Miss.
Early A.M.
(Journal)

After sleeping most of the day I went over to Hellen's house. She lives in a beautiful white house that made me want to leave that New York apartment more than ever.

I guess it's a mistake for two sad people to spend a day together. Particularly a mouse-gray, rainy day on a lonely road.

"Sometimes I'm sad for months and all I do is drink. I'm either sad or happy, you know. Never in-between. It has to be that way. If you're an intense person, that's the only way it can be."

Hellen is twenty-three and she's from Clarksdale. She is a short, medium-brown-skinned girl with eyes that can't be lied to. In two days she is leaving for McComb, one of the worst towns in the state.

"One time I went down in that area with Casey. We just wanted to get away for a day, so we went down there looking for the Natchez Trace. We didn't find it, but we came up on this ghost house. These two tall white columns standing in the back in some trees. They were just standing there. It was strange. You know? There it was in the middle of all this silence."

Hellen has been in "the movement" since she finished high school. For her it was the natural thing to do.

"I like you because you know a lot of sad songs. I wish I could play the guitar. Could you teach me to play 'Another Man Done Gone'? That's my favorite song. Somebody taught me to play it once, but I never had a guitar to practice on."

It was raining now and night had emerged from the all-day grayness. We were both drinking bourbon as I showed her how to finger an E minor chord. It didn't matter that she wouldn't learn to play it that night. It didn't matter that she had a difficult time carrying a tune when I wasn't singing with her. I don't know if I can say what did matter. Maybe the bourbon. It could do something we couldn't. It could obliterate the thought of half of a man's body draped over a log in the river, found a few days ago while they were searching for the bodies of Goodman, Schwerner and Chaney. It could make me not care about 4000 lynchings and more that have occurred in my native land. It could make me forget how long and empty a Mississippi highway is at night; how few houses there are and how many miles and miles of forests there are with dirt roads disappearing into them.

She is only twenty-three and for three years she has done what should have been unnecessary. How much hate can one individual feel directed at her before her soul fills with a sadness that penetrates even her happy moments?

She is an old woman and I am an old man and the same trees from which so many Negroes were hanged are being washed by the rain tonight. The rain beats on the roofs of the lynched and the lynchers. It soaks into the charred wood of a bombed church and runs down the stained glass windows of another.

The grass is green on the banks of the rivers, but when you go fishing, take along a winding sheet.

Another man done gone.
Another man done gone.
Another man done gone
Another man done gone
Another man done gone.

I didn't know his name, etc.

They killed another man, etc.

Another man done gone, etc.

It is late now and I must sleep. There isn't much any one man can do in this life, but each man should do what he has to and when he has to. Sometimes it is nothing more than making a pilgrimage. Another time it will be nothing more than dying.

I got to keep moving, I got to keep moving,
blues falling down like hail,
blues falling down like hail,
Uunh, blues falling down like hail,
blues falling down like hail,
And the day keeps on 'minding me there's a
hellhound on my trail,
hellhound on my trail,
hellhound on my trail.

(Robert Johnson)

July 14, 1964
Vicksburg, Miss.
(Letter to Arlene)

I feel better today. I was glad to talk to you last nite, but I wish you hadn't said, "I was in a good mood until I called you. I'm sorry I called." You can imagine how that made me feel. I won't say anything more about it, but try to understand that I, too, get terribly lonely, even though I'm constantly surrounded by people, that I'm under a tremendous strain and that it hurts more than anything else to hear your best friend say, "I'm sorry I called."

Before, you seemed here with me. Now, I don't know where you are. Maybe it's because I don't know where I am. It's hard to think now. Living in a transitory way causes it, I think. Maybe if I didn't have a home, I could accept the transitoriness as being permanent, a way of life. The bed I slept in last night was as hard as they come. The night before last I slept on bedsprings. The night before that, a mattress on the floor. The night before that in the back of the car. I've consumed untold quantities of soda pop and beer, water and coffee. I've sweated so much while leading singing in churches and dance halls that the matches in my pocket are too damp to use afterwards. I've thought about living in the cities I've been in and passed through —Mendenhall, Mississippi; D'Lo, Mississippi. It was outside of D'Lo that we saw this old Negro couple hitching a ride. . . . It was a hot day, around noon. We stopped the car and they got in. They were going to town, to D'Lo for a bottle of pop. He was so drunk he could barely stand. She, at least, could do that but not much more. We let them out in front of the grocery store and she borrowed a dime from me and as we drove away we wondered, how does "the movement" affect them? Will the civil rights bill have any effect in D'Lo, Mississippi? Or driving back from Moss Point we saw a young couple sitting beside a car. We stopped. They'd had a flat and they didn't have a spare. The girl was cute in her dirty, torn yellow party dress. Her hand was bleeding and she was holding it in a piece of dirty brown paper. "Where're you from?" we asked. "Chicago," she smiled. Then she laughed. "Collins, Mis'sippi." She bummed a cigarette and asked if we were "freedom riders." As we drove off they resumed their seats by the side of the road after having refused our proffered aid.

Who knows? Maybe they're sitting there now, unperturbed by it all, waiting for Godot. Or there're the houses by the road or the two little boys I saw walking on the wrong side of the road at dusk or the truck filled with white kids who made faces and yelled as we passed them. It all makes you wonder, wonder when will men be men, when will this nonsense cease, when will fear and terror not be the atmosphere in which one walks and talks, eats and sleeps. All of this hurts me because I am impotent. There is nothing that I can do to relieve the injustices, the miseries. Say a kind word, register a voter, sing a song, but there'll always be D'Lo, Mississippi. And simultaneously with this there will be love and laughter, sex and children, dancing and playing, the beauties of mountains and rivers, there will be Bach and Scarlatti, Rembrandt and Malcolm Lowry, there will be you and I and somehow I'm still unable to reconcile the joy and the sorrow. Yes, they are one, a part of a bigger whole. Each is necessary and should not be thought of as just or unjust, beautiful or ugly. Nonetheless, it angers me that beauty has to have ugliness walk beside it, that all that exists does exist and no one person can alleviate it.

These are the sort of things that I can't say over the phone and that I doubt I could say to you directly. I'm not much of a talker, I conclude more and more. I'd much rather say it on paper. . . . It's been frustrating in a way singing here, because I really haven't felt that anyone was ready to hear what I have to say— that death is awful, that you should see that my grave is kept clean, that none of us will ever be free until we love, really love, and understand and sacrifice and be willing to lay down our lives for our brothers, until we aren't clogged up anymore with our own desires and interests, until we aren't concerned anymore with making people like us, but are concerned with knowing another like we know ourselves, to cry when another cries, whether he be in the same room or a million miles away. But I can't say those things because they seem so alien to everyone, so foreign. And so irrelevant.

Do you know what I'm saying? I hope so, though I'm not too sure myself.

7

I had thought I was going to Mississippi because I cared about the political struggle of my people. Once there, I became what I was—an instrument which described and analyzed souls. I envied those who believed in registering people to vote, teaching in freedom schools, and challenging the power structure of the state. They belonged to something larger than their solitary selves; I was a spirit hovering over my body but never entering it. (After I sang at mass meetings, the old people would come up: "Son, I just want to tell you how thankful we are that y'all are here." And I would nod and mutter something appropriate, knowing that I was not one of those she should be thanking. I did not feel what she felt about freedom and did not understand how everyone, except me, could yell, "FREEDOM NOW!" Over and over and over. "FREEDOM NOW! FREEDOM NOW! FREEDOM! NOW!" Silently I would say, "Freedom any ol' time." I knew Spinoza too well to believe in a freedom one called for as if it were a dog that had wandered away from home.)

I could not accept who I was, however, and I had wanted to hide in the willing body of one of the young white volunteers. (I didn't, and for the most absurd reason: I was married.) Unable to play the role of "freedom fighter" and unable to escape from myself, I left, wanting to be with Arlene, and, in talking with her, understand who I was. I knew, too, that my coming home would please her, for she had been lonely without me, and I felt guilty for having left her alone. (I was too young to know that each of us creates the emotional atmosphere we breathe. Unhappiness is a choice and if I had known that, I would have not indulged in the egotism of believing that I would make her happy by returning.)

I was home scarcely an hour before she began punishing me with tears and anger from a bottomless reservoir of resentment. I could only think of the woman I'd refused to sleep with and knew that it was a mistake I would not repeat. (One afternoon during the New Hampshire summer we'd had a mild disagreement and afterward, sat looking through the window toward the mountains. Where five minutes before she had been angry, now she was loving and affectionate, as if one minute of time did not connect with and lead to the next. I was confused by this trait of hers and finally said, "When you get angry, I feel like you don't love me."

"I don't," she returned, matter-of-factly.

"Why not?"

"Because when I'm angry," she continued casually, "I don't feel any love. Sometimes I really hate you."

"I don't understand that," I said, fearfully. "If I ever felt hatred for you, I couldn't live with you."

"That doesn't make sense! Just because I hate you at one particular moment doesn't mean that I'll hate you forever."

I couldn't say it, but I wondered if the same applied to love. "Even though I might not feel love at a particular moment, that doesn't mean that that love has ceased to exist."

"Oh, Julie! That's ridiculous!"

I couldn't say anything more and ended the conversation, not wanting to recognize just how important her words were. She thought love was a feeling.)

I accepted her anger, but looked into her face, hoping to see some shadow of myself. (Love is a mirror in which the lovers experience themselves as beauty.) I saw only hatred. Suddenly, the voice, which had been silent since that September afternoon four years before on Capitol Hill, spoke: "It is over." This time it did not have to repeat itself. It was over, though I would need six years more to fully accept and act on that truth. But with that pronouncement, I ceased to trust my soul with her, separated myself from her internally, but allowed her to believe that I loved her. This was not conscious deception, for to have admitted the truth to myself would have returned me to loneliness. It was better to say, "I love you," a thousand times a day and hope that there was magic in that incantation, and we used "I love you" like a cosmetic, rubbing it into the clefts of our broken marriage so expertly that we looked like the ideal couple to all who knew us.

That fall when Arlene suggested that we have a child, I shrugged internally. I knew that she was resolving the problem of what to do with her life as her Commencement approached. I had urged her to go to graduate school, to write and eventually teach. A publisher had already expressed serious interest in a paper she'd written on the economy of the South. But when she suggested having a child, I knew she had reached that place of fear where I had stood often, and did not want to take up her life and follow it. I should have taken her in my arms and told her that it was not a child she wanted, but a name to know herself by and to call herself, Mother, was not to gain an identity but a function. I should have spun a cocoon of love for her and told her that to love is to be afraid and that fear only withers when one says, "I will live with you." But I did not have the words to say what I had learned, and was not sure that I had the right. Who was I to tell her not to have a child, if that was what she wanted? It was her decision, and although I would, of course, share equally in caring for the child, the instant it threatened my life as a writer, it became hers. I should have said all that, but I didn't, and with dispassionate curiosity, I watched her abdomen swell.

8

Ironically, her pregnancy corresponded with the beginning of my public life, and while she distended into identity, I was published for the first time.

That first appearance in print was an article in *Sing Out* attacking white blues singers, and asserting that white people could not sing the blues.

Though I was attacked by the folk music critic of *The New York Times*, as well as many of the magazine's readers for being a racial chauvinist, *Sing Out*'s editor, Irwin Silber, asked me to join the magazine as an associate editor. He opened the magazine's pages to me, supported me in every controversy I created with my nationalist views on black music, which were unusual in those pre-Black Power days. For the next four years, my essays, reviews, songs, and later, photographs, appeared regularly in the magazine.

That fall I also became a contributing editor to *Broadside*, the topical song magazine, in whose pages the songs of Bob Dylan, Phil Ochs, Tom Paxton, Peter La Farge, Len Chandler, Eric Anderson and others appeared long before their composers became famous. I came to the magazine through two songs I'd written on returning from Mississippi. Singing those songs in a *Broadside* benefit concert at the Village Gate early the following winter led directly to a recording contract with Vanguard Records.

The first record appeared in the autumn of 1965. On its cover was a large photograph of an ex-slave and a small one of me, symbolizing the relationship I felt with the old ones. Of the ten songs on the album, eight were original, most of them blues on contemporary themes, a love song, and an extended version of the classic ballad, "Stagolee," which I recreated as part-song, part-monologue. I wrote the album notes and in them gave a capsule history of black ethnic music as it related to the psycho-history of blacks, and concluded with a definition of myself in the context of that history.

> Although I am not (and will not be) assimilated wholly into Western culture, I am acclimated to it. Thus, a few of the songs here reflect the nights of listening to Bach and Gregorian chants, the nights of reading and painting and writing and dreaming and holding warm coffee cups while talking through the night. Others reflect the evenings leaning against street corner telephone poles, playing the "dozens" and telling "lies," the Sunday mornings in rural and urban churches, listening to my father preach or line out a hymn and hearing the congregation shout and sing. Others reflect the dusty country roads of Arkansas and Tennessee, the confusion of a small boy who couldn't understand why he couldn't sit in the front of the bus, and the anger and shame and fear of being a Negro in the South. All of the songs represent

that conglomeration of my collective and personal past, which is my present.

I could scarcely keep pace with my life. Pete Seeger asked me to work on a book with him, *The Twelve String Guitar as Played by Leadbelly*, which was published in 1965, and I was suddenly catapulted into the folk music Establishment when, in the fall of 1965, I was elected to the Board of Directors of the Newport Folk Foundation. I did not take myself so seriously to believe that I would have been there if I had not been black.

9

Our daughter was born the summer of 1965. Through Arlene's pregnancy I had known she was carrying a girl and so convinced her that we never considered a boy's name. It was impossible that my first child would not be the girl I should've been. I resisted naming her Michele, sensing how incestuous that would be, but she acquired Simone as her middle name, in honor of Michele's idol, Simone de Beauvoir.

I was happy holding her during the first hour of her life, but it was an abstract happiness, flowing around a question mark before which I asked, Who is she? To say that she was my daughter merely described her relationship to me in the world's terms. Who was *she*, I wanted to know. I envied Arlene who had carried the child in her bowels, lain awake at night feeling her kicks, and had experienced the pain of her birth. I began the child's life a stranger, an outsider, essential to begin the process but after that infinitesimal instant, absolutely unnecessary, a disposable needle discarded after the inoculation. (The only other service I performed was allowing only Bach to be played in the apartment throughout Arlene's pregnancy, for I wanted my daughter to be born with absolute pitch. She was.)

Once we brought the child home, however, I knew who she was—a seven-pound tyrant whose never-ending demands could not be ignored. I had most of the responsibility for her, because Arlene had decided to go to graduate school. I did not resent being left alone with the baby, but I could find no love in me for her. I had no talent for fatherhood and no ego needs which becoming a father might have filled. I did not hate the child, either. She was merely foreign matter lodged in my eye which would have to be removed somehow.

In December, the Foundation asked me to go to Mississippi in the spring to collect music and organize festivals in local communities, a program Guy had initiated on the Sea Islands. I accepted without hesitation.

I knew Arlene would be angry and feel deserted, and I felt guilty leaving her alone with the baby. But having grown up in a house where the father was frequently away, I did not consider my absence significant. My mother had managed; I assumed Arlene would, too.

I left, vaguely aware that I was escaping the greatest danger I'd yet encountered—the family. One's life could be consumed in little mouthfuls by the family, and society approved the cannibalism. I was supposed to be gone for two months. I was away for almost two years.

10

Mississippi was quiet that spring of 1966. The tension of two years before was absent, for few civil rights workers were left in the state. I settled in Itta Bena, a small town in the delta north of Greenwood. Willie McGhee, a SNCC organizer with whom I'd be working, lived there and another SNCC organizer, Willie Peacock, lived in Greenwood. I stayed in the home of Miss Laura, an old woman, who had been the first to join "the movement" when McGhee came to organize in Itta Bena.

I awoke each morning, washed my face at the standing faucet in the back yard (one day idly watching while white men, armed with rifles and following bloodhounds, ran through the back yard in pursuit of a convict who'd escaped from the chain gang). By ten A.M. it was hot, but Peacock, McGhee and I started our day's journey through small towns and onto plantations, looking for the old ones who remembered a music older than they.

March 18, 1966
(Letter to Arlene)

Last night I recorded two men on the McIntyre Plantation near here. It was a little cabin, a shotgun cabin, sitting on the edge of the field. The wind swept across the vast delta like the winter winds of the dakotas, rattling the tin roof of the cabin. I hope that fearful wind sound is on the tape, because it provided a perfect background to the religious singing of Jim Bennett and Scott Harris. Bennett is 82 years old and is almost childlike. In him I could see what the plantation system can do to a man. Scott Harris is 47 and is quite a man. He's been a bootlegger, been to the county farm at least three times. He and Mr. Bennett sang "The Old Ship of Zion" and on completion, Scott started talking and I guess I have a good hour or more of him praying and testifying—talking about the time when the plantation boss made his father take off his shoes and walk him barefooted, about his mother's death and the song she sang on her dying bed, about lynchings, about the Klan. The last time he was on the county farm was in 1963. He did fifty-eight days, but it was for demonstrating. He led the march. Scott is a leader if there ever was one, and his speech is filled with the speech of this area. "Molly-dodger" is one of his favorite words. "Your home ain't here, you molly-dodger. Now, you wants to know what a molly-dodger is, huh? Well, I'm got to tell you. Now suppose you was somewhere drinking some corn liquor and the police came. What would you do? You'd try to dodge 'em now, would you? And as you took off cross the field, the police would look out the door and say, 'Yonder go that molly-dodger!' "

Most of the material I recorded was not original, for the old music had virtually died, but we organized festivals in Itta Benna and Issaquena County, where old and young came together for an evening of singing, and occasionally someone would suddenly re-call a song that had not been sung for years, and the air would be alive with the excitement of memory recovered.

My work as a collector might have had better results, however, if I had not been exploring a new medium—photography. On a brief trip to Mississippi the previous December, the early morning fog suspended over the flat, barren cotton fields was so beautiful that I wanted to hold the image on my retina forever. I had wanted to photograph for many years, but resisted the impulse because there were already too many photographers in the world. However, I tired of the white photographers who came south and took photo-graphs of poor, suffering blacks. A white person, unless he/she was unusually sensitive, could see only abstractions in the South—pov-erty, black people. The emotional response was pity and this was what was photographed. I did not see the poverty, having grown up with it, and where whites saw a shack, I saw a person's home, and when I walked in, it was to photograph the life of that home.

My being was visual that spring, as I photographed constantly, fearing that what I saw would disappear if I closed my eyes even to blink, but, at least, I had the instrument to thwart the flow of time, to freeze reality and hug it forever. It was as if I had found the means of conquering Death.

I had been at Miss Laura's for almost a month when she told me one evening: "The white folks come today, son, and told me that they gon' take away my old-age check if I let you stay here. I hates to ask you to go, 'cause you one of my own, but—" I wouldn't let her finish, for there was nothing to be ashamed of. I was powerless to stop the state from suspending her from the welfare rolls, and unable to support her if they did. You didn't ask others to take risks if you couldn't protect them. I moved to Tougaloo, where Bob Fletcher, my college friend from Fisk, and now a SNCC photographer, lived with Marilyn Lowen, a poet and dancer, and one of my closest friends. There I made the final steps toward becoming a revolutionary.

11

In the spring of 1966, revolution was in the air, like ragweed in September. It was the ambiance of the times, the Sirens' melody young sailors set their sextants to find, and even I would not be leashed to the masthead.

That search for identity which I had made in suffocating loneliness in the fifties became a public rite in the sixties. But where I, and the Beat Generation, had viewed our lives as protests against an inhumane society, the generation of the sixties sought to change the society directly. (I could never counter Arlene's trenchant arguments about the "evils of capitalism," "Property is theft," that institutions shape people and to change the institutions is to change the people. I insisted weakly, as I had to Candie during the sit-ins, that real change was spiritual, and Arlene would quote Marx, Lenin and Stalin to show me that the revolutionary's concern was the same as mine. I did not know how to refute her, particularly when we awoke each morning to the smell of rats, and I learned to distinguish the odor of live ones from dead ones. As I groped under radiators and behind walls to find the body of the stinking rat making it difficult for us to breathe, I became less convinced that the system should not be overthrown. And, during that first week our infant daughter was home and I sat up each night to be certain no rats would eat of her, I began wondering if I should not be the one to do it. I knew there was a God, but where was He the Sunday morning four black children were dynamited to heaven in a Birmingham church, and where was He that Sunday morning in February, 1965, when we awoke to the news that the United States was dropping bombs on the people of North Vietnam? I could not find Him.)

That spring I lived with and talked constantly to SNCC workers: Bob Moses, Charlie Cobb, Worth Long, Maria Varela, Bob, Marilyn, Ruth Howard, and so many others. I'd never met so many people who cared and were willing to commit their lives to expressing that caring. And I wondered, what was it that had held me back for so long? Since the New Hampshire summer, I had found it increasingly difficult to live with myself, knowing that I should be in the South. I wondered if I would have remained in 1964 if not for Arlene, and I knew that I would have.

There was no day or particular moment when I decided to join SNCC. I had no alternative, for even if I had not cared, the writer in me would not have allowed me to stand outside history at this time. It wanted to gather impressions and emotions, feel the texture of a political movement and understand the commitment of those involved. So my motives for joining were not pure, and I did not pretend to myself that they were. I simply accepted the inevitable and on the deepest level, I knew that meant surrendering to that weakness in myself which had never made peace with being alone. I wanted to belong to something, to have a secure, uncomplicated identity which would liberate me from uncertainty and the unknown. The revolution accepted all supplicants, gave them a clear and simple *raison d'être*, and if the revolution succeeded, immortality. I had to become a revolutionary to learn that movements, ideologies, and causes can only destroy identity. I joined the revolution and became less than mySelf.

VI

1

Yvonne was one of the most extraordinarily beautiful women I'd ever met. As languid as that Atlanta, Georgia, May night when we were first known by the other, she brought me, gently, to a meeting with the sensual/sexual self I had increasingly sublimated in father-daughter relationships with teenage girls and young women. (They came after I sang at civil rights rallies and hootenannies. It was not sex they wanted, but someone who would listen and care about their search for a way to live and remain fragile. I needed them to remind me that I was not the morose person I was becoming with Arlene, using silence as a shield instead of the stream wherein I was spawned. So I wrote long letters to Connie, a young woman I'd met after a concert in Boston, with whom I could talk about God, and Ellen who wanted to be a writer, and always Laurie, whose low-pitched, dark-shaded voice on the phone was like an embrace.)

Arlene didn't believe these relationships were as platonic as I claimed. She knew what I tried to deny: affairs are first enacted in the imagination. I was afraid to smell the sensuality permeating these relationships, or even acknowledge that I had sexual desires. (Arlene and I had an active sexual life, but she was usually the initiator. Often after we made love, I lay awake, my body staring blankly into the darkness, wondering, is that all there is? A surge of feeling through the penis as brief as the *tick* of a clock? I wondered what it was Arlene seemed to enjoy so much and wanted so

125

frequently, for afterward, I was alone and sleepless on an emptiness so wide, infinity was lost within it.)

Fantasies were the playground for reality, and, in them, I fondled the full-blossomed breasts of my young friends, caressed with my tongue the hidden beauty between their thighs, and afterward lay naked in the silence, shimmering with awe. I made love with women I passed on the street, the women in magazine ads, and always, after our legs untwined, my being loved that of the one beside me. Often, I lived these fantasies masturbating next to Arlene while she was asleep.

My fantasy life was, however, on that mumbling level of consciousness, heard but not listened to by my entire self, existing but unconscious of its existence. (But part of the struggle to be whole is to make conscious the unconscious, to differentiate our idea of our self from the reality.) I thought I was indifferent to sex. Yvonne guided me toward the truth.

I'd met her briefly on the way to Mississippi in March, and when I passed through Atlanta on my return to New York in May, I knew, the moment I saw her, that we would be together that night. It was a repetition of the unconsummated experience with the girl at Four Corners the month before. It was as if we had known each other previously, and the moment of meeting was a continuation of a piece of music, the pages of whose opening movement were lost.

I was amazed that she wanted me. No woman ever had, and most especially, no black woman, not to hold and love with her body. (That was the difference, perhaps. The body is love's tongue and Arlene's spoke only of desire. She wanted me for the gratification of her wants, and masturbation was more satisfying, an *a capella* aria of praise.) Yvonne sang me praises with her body, and for the first time, I dared to think that I might be beautiful. (Three years later, Arlene and I were at a movie theater in Greenwich Village, and Yvonne came in, saw me, and sat down. She was living in New York, too, but we had talked only on the phone. After the movie we chatted briefly, then went our separate ways. Arlene and I walked a half block in silence before she said, "You slept with her, didn't you?" Part of me wanted to tell her a thousand yeses, to take revenge for an affair she'd confessed having while I was in the South, but I would not wound what Yvonne and I had been. She was a small miracle in my life, and to even call it an "affair" was to deprive the memory of its numinosity. I wondered how Arlene had known, but when two people have swum the night sky together, their bodies smile at each other, basking in the firefly glow of summer nights and twisted sheets, grateful for the gift of the other.)

Even if Arlene and I had had a perfect marriage, I would have loved Yvonne. What existed between us had its source in us. I was not looking for what I could not have with Arlene, but for what could be only with Yvonne. We are who we are, and what two people can be to each other is limited. We fail when we try to be everything to the other, and when it cannot be, we accuse ourselves, or the other, of being inadequate. Love is the attempt of finite beings to participate in the infinite. The failure comes when the lovers think they are infinite.

2

I returned to New York to tell Arlene that I was moving to Atlanta to head SNCC's photography department. My announcement was a surprise to her, but that spring I'd written her from Mississippi, trying to prepare her.

> . . . I imagine that when spring comes and the grass pushes its way through the ground, it is painful for the earth to loosen to let these sprouts come through. Having been hard and solid all winter, the earth has to loosen and it is rained upon; it is blown across the world and if we could hear the earth, what shrieks it must make for one flower to bloom. Well, we're growing, too, and what makes it so painful sometimes is that we are the earth and the flower that blooms. It is a difficult thing to be committed to an idea and work to bring it about, because that commitment is all important. It can be a commitment to see that Simone gets outside every day, or it can be a commitment to do what little one can do to fashion one brick for the foundation of the revolution. Neither is more important than the other and to be committed means that the personal, that individual which is so highly spoken of in American ideology, is unimportant. Perhaps the most impressive thing to me in Fanon's book on Algeria was the nature of commitment and what it meant in the lives of the people. Wives going off for months to live away from husbands in caves and what not, with little means of communicating. Husbands leaving wives and chil-

dren in the middle of the night for a day, a week, a month, years, or forever. But the commitment demanded that and in fulfilling that demand new, healthier people were created. Sometimes I wonder if America does not try to keep women enslaved by propounding through movies, magazines and television the image of the woman as nothing without her man. Most popular songs propound the same philosophy and men, of course, feel that it is right and proper. . . . Of course, a woman can be committed to one man and family and it can be beautiful and good, but for most it is not a commitment, but their last hold on life. . . .

Arlene never learned to understand my indirect way of talking, and instead of having prepared herself to accept the consequences of my new political commitment, she reacted as if I was her "last hold on life." I withstood her anger, and with more difficulty, her pleas and tears, and the guilt at leaving her alone with the child. She could not understand my refusal to take her and Simone with me, nor my refusal to say when, if ever, I was coming back. I could not understand her refusal to smile at me and say, "Do what you have to do." We could not see each other for looking at ourselves.

I moved to Atlanta, not knowing if the marriage was finished, but secretly hoping that it was. Yvonne and I lived together through the hot Atlanta summer, making love in the cool of the dawn and the songs of the birds.

3

I worked in the basement darkroom of the SNCC office throughout the summer, poring over contact sheets, making prints and planning propaganda materials. It was an odd way to participate in the most important summer of black America's political history. Stokely Carmichael, SNCC's new chairman, was carrying the cry of Black Power across the country and cities burned in his wake. I lived as if it were happening in some other place, watching with customary dispassion so that I could see that which the more passionate might not see.

From the beginning I had reservations about Black Power and black consciousness, which I had expressed in a letter to Arlene written after I'd visited the Atlanta SNCC office that March.

SNCC is in a mass of confusion. The conversation is of "Whitey" and "black people," "black consciousness," etc. One interesting thing is the addressing of everyone Negro as "brother." The whole "brother" thing is fascinating because Malcolm took it out of the church. It creates a friendly feeling and I must admit that I like it. . . . The other interesting thing is the creation of an African Bureau of SNCC. It came about from the two trips that SNCC people made to Africa. . . . There is definitely a conscious effort to strengthen ties with Africa. Bob Moses and his wife are setting up a conference to discuss how the freedom movement is a part of the African liberation movement. [Bob Moses was one of SNCC's most singular figures. A Harvard graduate, he came to Mississippi in 1961 and because of his courage, his refusal to be projected as a leader, and his humanism, he commanded more respect than anyone in "the movement."] He and several others wrote a report of their plans which disturbed me. It was extremely polemical in nature ("Our glorious African past" bit) and went on to talk about Negroes identifying with Africa and their past as a means of achieving "black consciousness." The most disturbing part of the report was the last section on "Music and the Arts." Two sentences comprised this section and it said, "Music and the arts are very important. Black music should be used through the use of such groups as the Negro folklore troupe." There was a little more to it, but not much. Bob is organizing a conference and nothing but history profs and Negro history experts are being invited as panelists, etc. It is going to be a meeting of black intellectuals. Being alienated from the people, it seems to me imperative that this alienation not be compounded by getting together with each other to discuss "black consciousness," which the people already have! I was also skeptical of Bob's report and black consciousness, because he seemed so unaware of how to go about creating black consciousness. The paper emphasized the Negro's connection with Africa, which is placing the emphasis in the wrong place. It is denying the Negro's uniqueness as an Afro-American. The paper, believe it or not, did not consider identity in this way at all. . . .

. . . I feel the issue is once again being avoided. Yes, identity with Africa, but to the extent of learning African languages, adopting dress, etc., I don't know. Also, there is a woeful lack of basic cultural knowledge in SNCC. An overabundance of emotion, yes, but cultural knowledge, no. And I mean cultural knowledge about themselves as Afro-Americans. . . . I don't disagree with a cultural program, but I wonder about setting up (cultural) centers with such a concentration on Africa. . . . Maybe I can't see what Bob sees because I haven't been to Africa. Well, one interesting feature of all of this is the amazement and consternation Northern white liberals are going to have when they find out what is developing.

SNCC was creating the same black fantasy I'd heard in 1961 on Harlem street corners. The existential fact of black existence was that we were the only people without a known, deep-rooted historical past. No cohesive culture survived the slave trade, which made the story of our ancestors that much more remarkable, because those slaves took fragments of remembered culture and infused them into the European culture they had to learn, and created a new culture. Blacks could only find their racial identity within the context of the experiences in America.

Much of SNCC's leadership was northern, however, and there were profound differences between northern and southern blacks. Those of us from the South had lived outside the perimeter of white culture; northern blacks were infected with it. Their black militancy was so strident that I regarded them as recent converts to the race, and their rage at whites, misdirected self-hatred. White people weren't that important to waste time and energy on.

I wondered why the northern blacks in SNCC had not listened more closely to the old people they'd worked with in Mississippi. (In speaking of her dead husband, Miss Laura said, "Me and the flies was the last to leave that black man." Another day she explained that she didn't eat fish because, "So many colored been thrown in these here rivers for the fish to feed on that to eat a fish would be like eating myself." She had a primal knowledge of the inter-relatedness of all beings, alive and dead. It was a Mississippi black animism.) Northern blacks cried for Africa, because there can be no roots when the soil is the broken linoleum of tenement apartments, or the piled carpets of black suburbia. (My father was born in northern Mississippi and, one day that spring of 1966, I searched out a cousin who lived on the "home place." It was after midnight when I arrived at Cousin Jessie's and knocked on the door of the darkened house. "Whooo?" came the owl-like cry after a long wait. "This is Julius Lester," I called. "I'm Reverend W. D. Lester's youngest boy. I believe I'm your cousin." There was a whoop of joy as the door was flung open, and I was engulfed in the fat arms of a woman who'd never seen me. But I was family, and that was enough. I stayed several days with her and her husband, and one rainy morning walked up the steep muddy hill behind the house, slipping in the mud as a mule eyed me hostilely. He didn't move, however, as I passed him and climbed over the wire fence, crossed a field and came to a sloping hill on whose side my kin were buried. I walked among the graves, telling them who I was and how I carried them in me. I wanted to sprinkle their graves with wine, because I knew the dead got thirsty and lonely and wanted to be remembered. But I had nothing but myself, and I presented that to them as I treaded softly over those pits which were now their homes. Another morning I went into Batesville, the nearest town, and joined the black men sitting near the railroad station. I sat for a long while, until I felt that they had accepted the presence of this young, bearded stranger, and then asked one of the oldest men if he'd ever heard of Square Lester, my slave great-grand-father. "Sho!" he exclaimed. "Square Lester! He been dead a long time." "I'm his great grand-boy," I said, softly. "Lawd today!" the old one exclaimed. "This here is Square Lester's great grand-boy!" After the general noises of exclamation had died, he continued, "Square Lester was famous around here. He was a master carpenter and was the only man I ever knowed what built a house with six fireplaces and all of 'em drew off the same flue. Built it for an ol' white lady. He was a good blues picker, too! Yessuh! Square could make a guitar talk!" I hadn't known just how much of the old one's blood I carried. I sat there throughout the afternoon, where he had undoubtedly sat and, perhaps I felt much of the same deep peace I think he knew, the peace which came when you knew that white people didn't own your soul.) Maybe I would have created an Africa of the mind, too, if I had not had ancestors to talk to.

I did not voice my reservations about Black Power that summer, for if I had, I would have had to ask why I had enlisted. I was so determined to be a revolutionary that I refused to look at anything within me which might contradict who I wanted to be.

So, while Black Power seared America, I designed a wall and desk calendar using photos of black rural life from the SNCC files, prepared a booklet on the rebellion which occurred in Atlanta that summer, another one on the Lowndes County Freedom Organization, a new black political party, and wrote a small book called

Black Folktales, which was illustrated by a SNCC artist and close friend, Jennifer Lawson, and designed by my closest friend in the organization, Maria Varela, whom I'd met in Tougaloo that spring. (*Black Folktales* was later rewritten and expanded and published under that title in 1969 with illustrations by Tom Feelings.)

The most important writing I did that summer was an essay, "The Angry Children of Malcolm X," which was to have been the introduction to Guy and Candie's second collection of freedom songs, *Freedom Is a Constant Struggle.* They did not like the angry tenor of the essay and used it instead as an afterword (preceded by their own introduction politely disavowing my words), but *Sing Out* featured it. That fall I was offered a contract for a book to be based on it, and *Look Out, Whitey! Black Power's Gon' Get Your Mama* came into being.

<h1 style="text-align:center">4</h1>

One evening late in the summer I walked into Yvonne's apartment, and she said, without prelude, "I'm sorry, but you have to go. I can't tell you why, and I'm sorry about that, but you just have to go." I looked at her for a moment, wanting to know why but not asking, because if she could have told me, she would have. I nodded, packed and moved to the basement of the SNCC office where I slept on a dirty mattress for the next six months. (Three years later, shortly after I'd seen Yvonne at the movies, we went out to dinner. Leaving the restaurant she said, suddenly, "You were married." I didn't look at her, afraid that if I did she wouldn't finish what it had taken her so long to say. "I just couldn't get over the feeling that it was wrong to be living with a married man. I never did believe in that kind of stuff and still don't." "But Arlene and I were separated," I argued. "Didn't matter!" Yvonne reprimanded me. "You were still married, and had a child, too. It wasn't right, Julius." Nothing more was said until another evening, two years later. I was divorced now, but she had married. "If you hadn't gotten yourself married, woman," I teased, "I might've come looking for you." "And I might've gone with you," she said, seriously. I hadn't expected that response. "But why didn't you say that then?" I asked, suddenly serious as I tried to fathom what my life would have been. "You were married." "Uh-uh!" I retorted.

"I was living with you. If that piece of paper bothered you so much, why didn't you just tell me that you had to know that things were really over between me and her!" Yvonne shook her head. "Too risky. What if you had chosen her? Ain't no black woman gon' put herself in that position in relation to a white woman!" I sat there, shaking my head and wanting to cry, wanting to scream at her for not having taken the risk. Didn't she know that she wouldn't have lost?)

5

Arlene and I were separated, but in letters and interminable phone calls, continued trying to understand who we were and what, or if, our marriage was. If we had not had a child, perhaps we could have said a joyous farewell, but our daughter was a silent force demanding that we resolve our conflicts. According to Arlene, I was the source of the problem, choosing myself over my family. I acknowledged in one letter that I was, indeed, "supremely selfish. I must fulfill myself, since there is no other reason I was given life." The marriage would succeed only if she separated her destiny from mine, and accepted me as I was.

When she read my letters, she understood, but my presence, in person or on the telephone defied her intellect. And I felt closer to her when there was a thousand miles between us. We were reconciled, however, and pledged ourselves to be more understanding and sensitive to the other's needs. More than that was necessary, for love is the wordless recognition that I am you and you are me. It allows you to become the other person, without losing your own sense of self, without becoming absorbed or dominated by the other. It is a disinterested joy in giving, because the act of love completes you. Arlene sought completion by being loved.

6

The world changed to winter while I lived in the arc of a yellow darkroom safelight, watching reality's faces emerge onto Kodabromide developing papers. The darkroom was like a monastic enclosure, for no one dared intrude, and for twelve to sixteen hours

133

each day, I stayed there, glad for the tedious, precise work of print making, which reduced existence to a manageable scale.

I could not be wholly oblivious to the reality emerging outside, however, for Black Power looked more and more like a scimitar, and I was not certain whose heads lay at whose feet. Politically, Black Power meant black political, economic and cultural control of black communities, but in the SNCC office, on the streets and in the bars of Atlanta, I heard a growing litany of hatred.

If I had not been married to a white woman, perhaps I would not have cared. (I hope that I would have.) But I was, and I did not want her killed by somebody out to get "Whitey." Yet, who was I trying to fool, as I worked on *Look Out, Whitey! Black Power's Gon' Get Your Mama?* I was black and sleeping white, as some people in SNCC made me know in direct and subtle ways. Wasn't that a contradiction? Wasn't my white wife a symbol of a racial self-hatred I refused to admit? ("Every man wants his children to look like him," Muhammad Ali told me pointedly when I interviewed him several years later. And I thought of my daughter and the newly-born son who looked like sun-tanned white children when I looked for them across a crowded playground, and I wondered if there was something wrong with me that I'd never wanted my children to look like anyone except themselves.) Did I hate black women, as my persecutors in SNCC contended? I didn't think so, for there was Yvonne, and Ruth, a majestic, dark-skinned young woman from Spelman College whom I loved that winter. And there would be others. The problem, I finally concluded, was that I refused to love only black women. That refusal, however, prevented my people from wholly accepting me. They wanted my choice of a wife to affirm them, but something so profoundly personal could only affirm the two individual lives and I did not know why it was only with white women that I could share those parts of myself the word *black* did not describe. (Maria. Thin, intense, with sharp features, large, soft eyes, and short brunette hair. I loved her from the moment I met her the spring of 1966 in Tougaloo, but didn't know what to do about it, except write letters and talk on the phone. It was with her that I talked about Arlene and whether my greater responsibility was to myself or the marriage, particularly after Arlene told me, in a dead voice early that winter of 1967 that she was pregnant. Still, I refused to return home, not because I did not feel or care about Arlene's increasing loneliness, or the

134

pressures she endured working, caring for our daughter, and carrying the child I knew would be a son. I could not rationalize my irresponsibility at being away from her, of not having money to send her, of not thinking about returning home, and I hated myself. Yet, a force within me refused to let me do otherwise, and I wrote Maria, "All I can do is say a quiet, 'Thy will be done,' because I try to live in a way that makes me an instrument of God. I've given up trying to understand. I just try to accept and assume that the Lord knows what's better for me than I do. 'Be still and let Him speak,' Thomas Merton once wrote. That's it—all of it." Maria would not support such an explanation, though she understood it. Maria concurred with Arlene: I was a bastard. But she did not condemn me and shared my pain, and I signed my letters to her, "Hawk," and she understood, protecting that identity symbol which expressed my need for interior freedom as I gave my identity to "the revolution." I do not know how I would have survived if Maria had not been there. We did not have a physical relationship, and we should have, for the love was there, but our bodies were too afraid to know it.

I sat beside her during the SNCC staff meeting in December, 1966, when the organization voted to expel whites. I understood the political necessity for the decision, for it established the right of black organizations to determine their membership, a right which had always been allowed whites. However, SNCC did not make a political decision as much as an emotional one, evicting the aliens from the city and stoning them outside the gates. I sat beside Maria, reaching out for my own salvation. She, too, understood the necessity for the decision, but the heart has its own kinds of knowledge which the "correct" political line cannot reorder. She and I held each other's lonely hearts in the palms of our hands, not flinching while the other's blood stained our fingers, but taking that blood to paint our lips. Because I loved her, and she, me, I was saved from being seduced by the hate which was stroking the loins of so many blacks. How luxurious it would have been to let my hatred of the acts of whites slide unnoticed into a hatred for the actors. How secure I would have felt with hatred's thighs clasped around me, for I would have known who I was and what my purpose was. I would have had an unbreakable identity, and I was so weary of feeling my way across unknown terrain on moonless nights. But Maria was there, not as an object of romance, or

135

a body to burrow into when winter came, but as one who cared that, sometimes, I hurt. So I sat beside her while her former black lover sat across the room, his eyes averted as he marched into blackness. I held Maria's hand, knowing that to see through a glass, darkly, was to falsify one's self.

Later, she articulated the essence of who we were, she and I, as we tried to survive in the midst of a black revolution we feared had aborted.

> I've decided to live by my definitions—and not someone else's definitions of me.
>
> I've decided that this is a time in history when those fighting to be individuals and to *really* believe in themselves—have little to say to those fighting to group a splintered, fractured people—our judgments and definitions cannot apply to each other—if we can accept that, we can still love each other—if not—then we—the individuals are left with loving ourselves which is enough to keep one going if you really believe in yourself.
>
> I really feel that God is in every person and that the more you're true to yourself and the more truth you find in yourself the more of Him you find. I think the freedom in His love is so frightening. I think that we are all monks—we have a mission—we are poor—we are or try to be obedient to our ethic—we are or try to be pure about integrating our values into our personal selves and our public selves—those are the vows of poverty, obedience and charity. We are, perhaps, the only true believers.

We knew who we were, ex-Catholic Maria and crypto-Catholic me, but we didn't know that it was impossible to be revolutionaries and live by our definitions. There was scarcely any relationship between the two, and we must have known, because why else did we hide our true selves when others came in the room? When I was told, however, that I should not love white women, I would not hide. To refuse to love was to refuse life.)

7

In March, 1967, Charlie Cobb, a SNCC organizer, and I went to North Vietnam as SNCC's representatives on one of the investigation teams the Bertrand Russell War Crimes Tribunal was sending to document U. S. bombing. We were there a month, touring hospitals, churches and towns bombed by U. S. planes, as well as factories, cultural sites, and agricultural cooperatives.

To the Vietnamese, I was a revolutionary, and I wanted to be that for them. But the artist in me chose this time to assert itself, and I wrote more poetry during the month there than I had in the previous year.

lxvi
Drinking tea,
I listen to the rain.

lxvii
If it were not war-time,
I would smile at the acne-blemished
Kids with rifles on their backs.

lxix
As I dozed off to
Sleep, the sound of
Bombing woke me.

lxx
I sent her a rose
From the bush at
The bombed pagoda.

lxxii
But the birds still sing
in Vietnam.

lxxvi
By the third day,
I hardly noticed the bombing.

When I wasn't writing, I was photographing, for I doubt there are few places on earth more beautiful than North Vietnam. Occasionally, I tried to be the revolutionary I wanted to be, but one afternoon while listening to a group of youths talk about the effects of the war, I looked around the room and my eyes were seized by those of a young woman. For the remainder of the after-noon, there was no war, no revolution, but only us.

8

I left Hanoi on April 15, and after two weeks in Paris, went to Stockholm, Sweden, for the meeting of the War Crimes Tribunal. It was a gathering of American and European intellectuals, writers and radicals which heard the evidence of the investigating teams sent to North Vietnam. Among its members were Jean-Paul Sartre, Simone de Beauvoir, Isaac Deutscher, Tariq Ali, Dave Dellinger, Carl Ogelsby, Vladimir Dedijer, and Courtland Cox, representing SNCC in Stokely's stead.

The Tribunal was dominated by Sartre and De Beauvoir, and Michele was disappointed to see her idol trotting behind Sartre like a newly-found puppy. But Michele did not falter in her love of Simone, for perhaps it was too much to expect one person to write of new ways of being and live them, too. Moses only saw the Promised Land.

I considered the Tribunal an intellectual exercise of no political consequence. (See "Judgement in Stockholm" in *Revolutionary Notes* for the analysis of the Tribunal I wrote after I returned.) I spent little time at Folkets Huts, where the Tribunal was meeting, and explored Stockholm, a beautiful city built on islands. One could not go far without seeing rushing, white water. I felt at home there, as I had not in Paris. (I would love Paris in retrospect, miss it painfully, and hate myself for having been so closed to it. My political self had reasserted itself there and castigated as "bourgeois" and "white" much that I loved, and I didn't go to the Louvre, the Rodin Museum, Père Lachaise, or Notre Dame. But I had walked the streets from morning to night, sat in Luxembourg Gardens, at sidewalk cafes drinking *café au lait* and eating croissants, sensing that at some future time I would return there to live, revolution or no revolution.)

In Sweden, however, my true nature returned in the presence of Swedish women. I had heard that they were God's gift to shy men, but I was not prepared when, first in Stockholm and later, Uppsala, I found myself being asked to spend the night with someone who, in one instance, did not even introduce herself.

My closest friend was Ulla, the woman I stayed with in Uppsala. She was one of the quiet ones, and we sat at her tiny kitchen table, talking or not talking. It didn't matter, because quiet people know how to use words as an extension of silence. We wandered the streets of the college town, stared at the frothing water of rushing streams, and when we went shopping, I pretended that I was her husband.

She gave me the silence in which the experiences of the past year could reach a still point. I had not paused since leaving New

York the previous February for what I had thought would be a two-month trip to Mississippi. The most important change was that I no longer wanted Arlene to call me Julie. At age twenty-seven I had ceased to be the diminutive of myself. During the year I had lived away from her, I had tested myself in the world, finished my first book, exchanged ideas with Pham van Dong, the head of the North Vietnamese government, talked with European intellectuals, and most important, perhaps, experienced myself through other women as someone beautiful. "I am Julius now," I wrote her.

Ulla went away for a weekend, and I lay on the floor in front of her stereo and listened to John Coltrane's "Spiritual" for three days, stopping only to eat and sleep. The music consecrated me and on a chilly Swedish dawn, I was reunited with my ancestors through Coltrane's tenor saxophone speaking of the southern land from which I had come, and somehow, it was linked to God. Those spirituals, whose essence Coltrane stood at the center of, had been sung by the ancestors beneath the midnight skies, and they were lines to another reality, The Reality, and that was prime. The ancestors had known, despite the whips and constant presence of Death. They had known and had sung, "If anybody asks you who I am, tell 'em I'm a child of God," not a nigger, not a slave, but a child of God. I was their child.

However, I could not reconcile this part of me, which I felt to be the true one, with my political life. "I'm still a poet basically," I wrote Arlene. My concern was, "How do you change the soul? A poet is revolutionary because he wants to change people's lives." Whatever I did was "in a continuum from the poet-saint-mystic thing." That was true, but was I mad for trying to be Rimbaud, St. Francis and Che Guevara?

9

At the end of May I returned to New York. Our son was born six weeks prematurely in July, and five days after his birth, I left for Cuba, where I had been invited to participate in a festival of protest songwriters and singers.

The day after I arrived in Havana, however, Stokely flew in unexpectedly from London, where he had been attending a conference on the "Dialectics of Liberation," organized by R. D. Laing.

I moved into his suite on the top floor of the Havana Libre Hotel, and for the next three weeks, played the role of his "comrade-in-arms," making his appointments, writing the speech he delivered to the Organization of Latin-American Solidarity meeting, answering the phone, briefing him before his meetings with the North Vietnamese, the National Liberation Front of South Vietnam, and representatives of various Latin American revolutionary groups, and decided to whom he did and did not give interviews. (It was with great pleasure that I turned down James Reston of *The New York Times*.)

Stokely was that strangest of anomalies, a revolutionary celebrity, and he expected the fact to be acknowledged. He was more than a little annoyed when the North Vietnamese were not, at first, receptive to his request to visit Hanoi when he left Cuba. "They must not know who I am," he commented angrily. They found out, because he made the trip.

Our visit to Cuba coincided with the rebellion in Detroit, and at a press conference in Havana, Stokely hailed it as "the beginning of urban guerrilla warfare," a remark that made headlines in Cuba and the United States, as we found out when we received an angry telephone call from the SNCC Central Committee demanding that Stokely keep his "damned mouth shut." Stokely's pronouncement about the Detroit rebellion was typical, because he elevated rhetorical exaggeration to an art form. Living with him twenty-four hours a day for the three weeks we were in Cuba, I saw, despite my desire not to, that his politics and rhetoric came as much from ego needs as from a sense of caring about the lives of black people. (The first time I remember seeing him was in May, 1966, shortly before he was elected chairman of SNCC. We were in Lowndes County, Alabama, on the primary election day which would decide if enough blacks in the county wanted their own political party. Stokely was surrounded by a group of reporters, and I was disturbed that he did not appear to be unhappy with the attention. I asked Maria if he was enjoying himself as much as it appeared. She sighed and nodded. Two months later, we were sitting in the basement of the SNCC office, and I told him, laughing, that his picture was in the most recent issue of *Jet*, which had described him as having the eyes of a "Near Eastern mystic poet." I was laughing so hard that it was a moment before I realized he wasn't. "Where's the magazine, man? Let me see it." I gave it to him, and watched as he read the story about himself several times before putting my magazine in his back pocket. Soon after that we began calling him Starmichael.) In Cuba, my earlier impressions were sadly confirmed. Stokely fed on attention like a puppy at its mother's teats, and he seemed to think that I'd brought my cameras to Cuba to photograph his every step.

Most distressing, though, were the evenings we were alone in the suite. I was glad for the quiet, but the silence seemed to make Stokely uneasy and he would fill the air with words, as if he were throwing flares to brighten the night. He talked about the tailor-made sharkskin suits he'd bought in London and recounted sexual experiences with women like a white hunter telling tales about a safari. I wanted to talk about the day's events, what direction SNCC should take in view of what we were learning, but he was not interested. He needed an audience, for he knew only how to perform. He talked, drank rum and swallowed pills. "Are you sick?" I asked one night. "Uh-uh. These are painkillers I got from my dentist." "You got a toothache?" I asked, naively. "Naw, homes. I couldn't bring no smoke into Cuba, and I can't sleep if I ain't high, and damn! This rum and these painkillers ain't doing shit!" Eventually, he would manage to swallow enough pills and drink enough socialist rum and would sleep what must have been a frightfully lonely sleep. It was my failure as a human being that I did not know how to tell him not to quake in the limbo hours of the night when there were no crowds to tell him who he was. I think he knew that history had chosen him for a specific role and he could not fulfill it. Not because he wasn't bright, or didn't care about the pain of other people's lives. Stokely cared, but he had allowed himself to become the Mick Jagger of Revolution, who, when the auditorium was empty, wandered across the empty stage wondering who he was. Stokely came, like St. Michael, to slay devils, but his clenched fist, arm thrust high into the air, held no sword.

Being with Stokely, however, gave me an opportunity I would not have had otherwise—meeting and traveling for three days with Fidel Castro. I'd first seen Fidel at the July Twenty-sixth rally in Santiago. Having read in the American press of his two-and-a-half-hour "harangues," I didn't know what to expect and was not prepared for what transpired. Fidel arrived late, which, I learned, was customary, and his appearance on the podium evoked loud cheering and applause from the crowd of a half million. The ovation was quickly and abruptly stopped by the playing of the Cuban National Anthem. The speech which followed lasted for more than two hours and passed like thirty minutes. Having been provided with earphones through which I could hear an English interpreter, I soon let them dangle around my neck, because I wanted to hear Fidel's voice, not a translation of his words. Whatever he might say was secondary to who he was. Though my knowledge of Spanish was poor, it was sufficient to allow me to discern that he was not addressing the people as much as he was conversing with them, sharing his thinking on what it meant to be a revolutionary. He made me feel as if he were talking solely to me, though he did not look in my direction once. But everyone felt that way, I learned. Fidel had the extraordinary capacity to make a crowd of half a million people feel that they were individuals, not part of an undifferentiated mass. Love emanated from the man as I had experienced it in Pierre de Lattre, Janeice, and Ginny Schmitz. He cared and, for the first time, I understood that I was not wrong when I insisted that the revolutionary's only task was the creation of a social order which made loving possible.

At the end of his speech, the response from the crowd was overwhelming, but scarcely had it begun before the Cuban National Anthem was played again, and Fidel left the platform. A leader who refused to allow his words to be applauded, or his person adulated was truly impressive. (Stokely didn't seem to notice.)

The following day, Stokely and I were driven by jeep to a small town in the mountains of Oriente Province where Fidel was to speak that night, and the following morning, we were told, he would talk with Stokely. The speech Fidel gave that night was shorter, an hour or so in length, and was primarily about the artificial insemination of cows. Fidel has said that when he retires, he wants to be a farmer, and that night, he spoke as a peasant to peasants about the problems of increasing cattle production. He talked glowingly about a massive bull the government had recently purchased, of how much semen the bull would produce and how many cows could be impregnated in so many years. He told of CIA efforts to prevent the purchase of the bull and of subsequent CIA efforts to kill it. He pledged that if the artificial insemination project was successful, the Cuban government, once its cattle production needs were met, would give, not sell, semen to any country that needed it. He emphasized the gift aspect, as well he should have, because the idea of a government giving something away, expecting nothing in return, was truly revolutionary.

The following morning, Stokely and I met Fidel briefly at breakfast, he giving me one of his cigars to replace the one I was smoking, which he disparaged as not being Cuba's best. Stokely joined Fidel in the lead jeep, while I rode with the Minister of Labor in another one.

What was supposed to be a three-hour ride back to Santiago turned into a three-day expedition, whose itinerary was created at any junction where Fidel remembered an agricultural cooperative he wanted to visit, a friend he hadn't seen in a while, a hospital he wanted to see, or a youth camp where he wanted to play basketball. Dusk of the first evening found us stuck in a creek bed at the bottom of a mountain in the Sierra Maestras. In the darkness, I could hear Fidel shouting, giving orders, and organizing people to push the jeeps out of the creek. It was to no avail. Then, out of the darkness, a man suddenly appeared carrying a kerosene lantern and leading a bull. He showed no surprise when he saw Fidel, calmly hitched the bull to the front of the jeep, and with a tap on the animal's rump, the jeep was pulled free. Then, with as little ceremony as he had come, he departed, the clanging of the bell around the bull's neck and the tiny light of the kerosene lamp his only accompaniment.

I never learned the gist of Stokely's conversation with Fidel. Stokely was unnaturally quiet when we reached a camp at the top of the mountain. He would only say that Fidel did not understand racism, but from Stokely's sullenness, I had the distinct impression that the meeting had not gone well. If it had, I knew that Stokely would have told me more than I wanted to hear.

When the second morning dawned, Stokely and I were feeling more than a little dirty, having brought no toilet items or clothes with us. As the second day developed into another excursion over dusty mountain roads, I began wondering if I was going to spend the rest of my life following Fidel Castro through the mountains of Cuba. I would not have minded, for to be with Fidel was to be with a man who lived intensely. Whether he was talking about baseball or the Cuban economy, there was a contagious passion about him. Above all, he exemplified more than anyone I've ever met Che s dictum that "the revolutionary is guided by the highest principles of love."

It was mid-August when Stokely and I left Cuba for Moscow. I was there only a few hours before going to Paris and, after an overnight stay, to New York. Stokely would continue on to North Vietnam, China and Africa. I wanted to go, but not with him. He could not be comfortable with someone who retained a self separate from his needs and wants. I liked him, but was tired of being his one-man retinue, personal secretary, and alter ego. I was weary, too, of playing revolutionary emissary, sitting in meetings with serious revolutionaries who believed that I was like them. I knew I was not, no matter how sincere my desire for revolution was. I was a bourgeois intellectual who would return from Cuba to receive a $2500 advance for a book about revolution. The Venezuelan, South Vietnamese, and Mexican revolutionaries I'd met in Cuba went home to be hunted by police and soldiers, jailed, and possibly, killed. Other countries put you in jail for even writing about revolution: America paid you. Stokely could hold the revolutionary banner aloft by himself. My arms were tired.

10

When I returned to New York, it was to stay. While in Cuba I'd decided that, with the birth of my second child, I had to accept the responsibility of having a family, whether I liked it or not. My children had not petitioned for life. They were born and had the right to expect that the generator of their lives assume the responsibility for them.

I wouldn't be any less of a revolutionary, however. In North Vietnam and Cuba, I had seen societies centering themselves in compassion, not materialism. I wanted the same kind of society in America, and filled with Cuban revolutionary fervor, I was convinced that the only way to begin was through "revolutionary armed struggle."

Excerpt

From "Open Letter," *Broadside,* October, 1967:

. . . I love so intensely that I hate everything that frustrates, stifles, destroys . . . beauty and I hate it so much that I will kill to see that it comes into being. To kill is often an act of love. And I learned that from a beautiful, shy young girl who is a guerrilla in South Vietnam. She's killed 25 G. I.'s and I knew when I met her that she knew about a love I haven't experienced yet, and look forward to. I look forward to the day when I will place a person in my rifle sight, squeeze the trigger, hear the explosion and watch that person fall. And after the shooting has stopped, I will continue that act of love that began when I started to hate, by helping others to build a country that will exist for its people and not vice versa.

Those words do not sound like any person to whom I would give my name, or even want to, but they are mine. I cannot re-create, even for myself, a psychological portrait of that person. Maybe he never existed except as a concept created by the ethos of the historical moment.

Underlining

From Frantz Fanon's *Wretched of the Earth*:

> For the native, life can only spring up again out of the rotting corpses of the settler. . . . For the colonised people this violence, because it constitutes their only work, invests their characters with positive and creative qualities. The practice of violence binds them together as a whole, since each individual forms a violent link in the great chain, a part of the great organism of violence which has surged upwards in reaction to the settler's violence in the beginning. . . . The armed struggle mobilises the people . . . it . . . introduces into each man's consciousness the ideas of a common cause, of a national destiny and of a collective history.

But Julius Lester never used books as the sole source of his knowledge, and he had been in the streets of Atlanta and Newark during the rebellions there, and had experienced a vengeful redemption in the taunting of policemen, the sound of gunfire, and the heat of hellish flames. Part of him still wanted to apply for the job of pulling the switch on the "cracker." (The blue-velvet sea was at our backs. Stokely and I lay on the ground, firing AK-47 rifles at targets on a Cuban hillside. I didn't know why, except it was the time of revolution. I had never fired a gun, or even held anything resembling one since the day in my tenth year when I playfully fired my BB gun at a cardinal. It had not occurred to me that I might hit it, and even as I saw it stop in its feathered flight and plummet to the ground, I could not believe that had any relationship to my casual pull of the trigger. I waited for it to rise from the Arkansas dust, and when it didn't, I walked over, reluctantly, convinced that it had flown away without my having seen it. It was as red as a bloodstain and still as only death is. Twenty summers later, I was a revolutionary and the labor pains of revolution were violence. I fitted the AK-47 to my right shoulder and quickly forgot that I was holding a conveyor of death and concentrated on learning to shoot, as if it were a skill like playing the guitar. Before long, I was hitting the target with regularity, and then, bull's-eye! I smiled. Soon I tired of shooting at the target and my mind transformed it into "enemies." I imagined myself on the rooftop of a Harlem tenement and across the street, on another rooftop, were U. S. soldiers. BANG! Bull's-eye. BANG! BANG! Bull's-eye again. And with the sea shimmering behind me like a mirage, I continued firing, and "they" fell with each gentle squeeze of the trigger. It was fun! You simply had to forget that you were depriving someone of his life. That was easy.)

It was remarkably easy if he did not think, if he did not look at the mystic in his soul, if he let himself believe that historical necessity was more important than haiku. (One day in Hanoi as I walked toward a bomb shelter during an air raid, I saw the waitress from the hotel dining room run past me with a rifle in one hand, a helmet in the other. Each morning we flirted playfully with each other, and I had never thought of her as more than a shy young woman. She must have noticed me staring in amazement at her as the air raid sirens screamed a fearful urgency, but I stopped to gaze at her, and she stopped, too, looked at me, blushed, and then ran on to her assigned position. How dare she blush in the middle of a war while antiaircraft guns filled the clear blue of the afternoon with tiny white clouds.)

Underlining

From Fanon's *Wretched of the Earth*:

> Violence is a cleansing force. It frees the native from his inferiority complex and from his despair and inaction; it makes him fearless and restores his self-respect.

Was it the redemptive nature of violence, Julius wondered, which allowed North Vietnamese women to carry rifles and retain the looks of virgins? Maybe that was what allowed the male soldiers to walk the streets of Hanoi in the evenings, rifles in one hand, bouquets of flowers in the other, and not look incongruous. Maybe, he thought, there were two kinds of violence: one which ravaged the face of Lyndon Johnson, and another which made Ho Chi Minh look like a Taoist sage. Perhaps the former was a violence which engaged one's ego and conferred identity, while the latter was simply accepting an unfortunate necessity.

Underlinings

From Hemingway's *For Whom the Bell Tolls*:

. . . you mustn't believe in killing. . . . You must do it as a necessity, but you must not believe it. If you believe in it the whole thing is wrong.

From Julius Lester's *Revolutionary Notes*:

The revolutionary is he who cries for the one he has killed.

Julius knew, however, that if he ever raised a rifle to his shoulder and centered a person in its sights, he could not squeeze the trigger. He could kill rats, roaches and flies, but how often he'd hated walking in the woods because each footstep crushed unseen insects. But that was his problem, a vestige of bourgeois sentimentality he had to purge from his soul. The days of blood were at hand, and he had to find the way to articulate a concept of violence as a cleansing force so that his people would not become executioners. He was St. Bernard preaching to the knights of the Crusade. But how could the man of Clear Light, who had written about the love which "loves because it loves" have helped organize a war against "infidels"? The monk knew better, didn't he?

(The fall of 1967 after I returned from Cuba, I began writing a weekly column of political analysis for *The Guardian*, the leading radical newsweekly. [Many of these columns written between the fall of 1967 and the winter of 1969 were collected and published in 1969 in my third book, *Revolutionary Notes*.] I assigned myself the task of being the caretaker of the "movement's" soul, criticizing its weaknesses, excesses, and sounding warnings of potential errors. I also saw myself as a bridge between the black radical movement and the white New Left.)

Whoever or whatever Julius Lester was inside himself, he told himself and others, that he was a revolutionary. Yet, he belonged

147

to no revolutionary group, having drifted away from SNCC in the spring of 1968 because the organization had ceased to be viable. He did not go to demonstrations or rallies, or involve himself in the organizing efforts undertaken by people in the housing project where he and his family moved that spring. He went through each day as he always had, i.e., trying to be alone with himself. With the advance money from his first book, he rented a studio on East Seventeenth Street where he set up a darkroom. He worked little there, but it was a place, his place, a small, square room where no one could touch him. Late that spring, he finished his second book, *To Be a Slave*, and repaid a portion of the debt he owed his great-grandparents. He observed the vernal equinox in the way he'd always observed it in New York—sitting by the fountain in Greenwich Village's Washington Square Park, drinking red wine at a sidewalk table at The Riviera on Sheridan Square. Sometimes, after his wife had been forced to make his life unbearable, he took his children to the playground.

What was revolutionary about his life? Nothing, but no one seemed to notice. However, the distance between his daily life and his political identity was obvious in his writings, for he wrote as if he were observing birds through binoculars, noting their coloring and migratory habits in a diary. The next year he was wryly amused when he read a review of *Revolutionary Notes* in which the reviewer, Mary Reinholz, wrote that "Julius Lester emerges as the monkish kind—serious, solemn, highly moralistic, given to making *ex cathedra* pronouncements on the nature of the revolutionary in priestly, faintly pompous prose." She ended her critical and insightful review by saying that Julius Lester might become "a highly effective critic of the Left" if he could "leap over the monastic wall." But Julius' problem was that he was perched on that wall, looking into the cloister with one self, watching the life outside with another, and living nowhere.

In the early summer of 1968, his first book, *Look Out, Whitey! Black Power's Gon' Get Your Mama*, was published. The book jacket showed the hard, unsmiling face of what critics and readers took to be a "black militant," as he read that he was. "Who, me?" He laughed to himself. But he looked at that photograph and saw that, yes, the expression was not one designed to make people feel friendly toward him. (The photograph was taken on a bitterly cold day after Arlene and I had had an argument. My anger was directed at her, the cold, and the photographer, my close friend David Gahr, who kept shouting, "One more! Just one more!")

Julius Lester had written and published a book and for him, the dream of the college senior had been realized. Or had it? He had wanted to be James Joyce, the fearless, inexhaustible explorer of the Unconscious. *Time* magazine said that he represented the "black tone of voice at its angriest tone." But that wasn't true, was it? He'd written a book delineating the historical roots of Black Power and its contemporary meaning. He'd fitted style to subject matter and written a conscious polemic, filled with invective, satiric thrusts, rhetoric and generalizations. He had written a book of 152 pages. Why did everyone think the book represented the totality of his being? Did others really think that he, or any human personality, could be wholly contained in one brief work?

He knew that writers are observers and he had trained himself to be able to do anything "from sermons to farces," as Priestley had written about the eighteenth-century scribes. But the twentieth century wanted its writers to be more than practitioners of their craft. This century looked to its writers for some kind of moral leadership. God help it. (February, 1972. I had completed a talk on children's literature in Vancouver, British Columbia, and Joanne and I were hurrying to the airport to catch a chartered plane to Seattle. "Mr. Lester!" a voice called as I got in the car. I stopped and turned. "Can I ask you a question?" the young man said, nervously. I nodded, trying to hide my impatience. "Do you still believe what you wrote in *Revolutionary Notes*?" The need in his voice demanded an affirmative answer and I gave it. He sighed. "That makes me feel a lot better, because that book changed my life." I shuddered, trying to remember what I had written, but I had not read the book in the three years it had been in print. Yet, words I had written and forgotten had transformed his life, and a few minutes later, sitting in the two-seater plane and peering into the darkness, I wondered if I was now responsible for that life. Like Montaigne, all I had written had been "by way of discourse, and nothing by way of advice." And truly I agreed with him when he went on to say that "I should not speak so boldly if it were my due to be believed." Or was I playing games with myself? Didn't I want people to believe what I wrote? Yes, but not to the extent of involving me, if they chose to believe what I believed. I did write "by way of discourse" and often, when people expressed to me some disagreement with something I'd written, they would be taken aback when my only response was a shrug of the shoulders. I didn't care if they disagreed or agreed. I did not write to gain converts; I wrote because—well, because.

I envied Montaigne who wrote during a time when the young entered apprenticeships instead of going in search of themselves, and parents they never had. Montaigne did not have to play surrogate father to adolescents who wanted to take his life to feast upon, a necessary component in their diets. But I could not use Montaigne as my authority and so easily evade the fact that I was responsible when someone told me that I had changed their life. Typeset words remain as they are placed, while their author goes his merry way, but the words remain, a form of sorcery affecting lives. Why must people confuse the writer with his words? Ah, yes, Tolstoy! Now I understood. I would have repudiated *War and Peace,* too, because for the author, each book is really a tombstone marking the burying hole of a self now dead. For the reader, it is a new book, the midwife to their souls. There was nothing to be done, except write truly when I sat down to write. I had in *Revolutionary Notes,* as much as I could have at the time, but knowing that did not expunge the guilt I felt sitting in that little plane, wondering how the pilot knew where Seattle was in the darkness. And, I would always bear the guilt, for *Revolutionary Notes* and all subsequent books, because no matter how truly I wrote, I was the only one who would ever know that I am more than the sum of my words.)

11

The same summer that *Look Out, Whitey!* was published, my public life intensified with the inception of a new career, a radio show. That spring, New York's Pacifica station, WBAI-FM, invited me to do a half-hour weekly show interviewing political radicals. It was successful and, that summer, I substituted for Bob Fass and Steve Post, hosts of all-night shows during the week and on the weekend, respectively, and found myself on the air seven nights a week, playing jazz and taking calls on the air from listeners.

The audience response was surprising, for in that summer when

Black Power and radicalism reached its apex, I was the only black person on the air, it seemed, who was willing to talk to whites without using them as whipping posts. I was, also, the only black person on New York City's airwaves who represented the black radical political viewpoint.

That fall I was given a two-hour live show on Thursday evenings, which I called, self-mockingly, "The Great Proletarian Cultural Revolution." On it I interviewed black writers, musicians, nationalists, and others who did not have access to the media. That was my responsibility as a black in the media at that time. Typically, it did not occur to me that listeners would assume that the show represented me wholly.

In the late autumn and early winter of 1968–69, New York City was tortured by racial tensions exceeding any since I'd been there. They began that fall when the United Federation of Teachers went on strike to protest the firing of nine teachers from the black, community-controlled Ocean Hill-Brownsville school district in Brooklyn. The issue was to what extent the newly-formed community school boards were to be able to hire and fire personnel. It quickly became a racial issue, because a black school board sought to dismiss nine white teachers. (The fact that the majority of the teachers in the Ocean Hill-Brownsville school district were white and were not fired was quickly overlooked by opponents to community control.) Albert Shanker, president of the UFT, accused the local school board of anti-Semitism, and, with that charge, any hope of a rational resolution of the matter was killed. (The majority of the white teachers in the school district were Jewish and many supported the community board's action. It was of no avail.) Jewish organizations began issuing statements about black anti-Semitism; white teachers on picket lines screamed epithets at black and Puerto Rican children who went to school. The schools were eventually closed and parent groups broke in and opened them. In addition, the Metropolitan Museum of Art opened an exhibit, "Harlem on my Mind," and in the show's catalogue, a reference was found to "Jewish" storekeepers and landlords. The writer of the catalogue's introduction was a black high school student, and the charges of black anti-Semitism reached a new high.

I was one of those reporting the strike for WBAI, and in the course of that assignment, met Les Campbell, a black teacher in the Ocean Hill-Brownsville district, who had been singled out by UFT president Shanker as anti-Semitic, among other things. I found Les to be gentle, soft-spoken, sensitive, and a remarkable teacher. I invited him on my show to talk at length about his politics and the school situation.

He appeared on the evening of December twenty-sixth, and before we went on the air, he showed me several poems written by one of his students which he wanted to read. One of them began, "Hey, there, Jew-boy! You with the yarmulke on your head! Hey, there, Jew-boy! I wish you were dead!" Les was uncertain about reading it, but I wanted him to, because it was indicative of the racial tensions engendered by the strike, and I wanted others to know how the strike was affecting black youth.

He read the poem that night, one among several by his student. I'd explained why I'd asked him to read it, and during the week, received no mail objecting to the show. On the next show, I played the tape of Campbell reading the poem, and took phone calls on the air about it. Listener response was serious and concerned, but not hysterical. No one said that the poem should not have been aired.

It would have ended there if *The New York Times* of January 16 had not carried a front page story that the UFT was filing a complaint with the Federal Communications Commission protesting the airing of the poem and requesting that WBAI's license be revoked. (If such a complaint had been filed, WBAI would have been sent a copy by the FCC and asked to respond. No such complaint was ever received by the station. The UFT used the station as a pawn in its efforts to stop community control of schools in black districts.)

For the next two weeks, WBAI received thousands of hate letters; Jewish organizations, and particularly the newly-organized Jewish Defense League, demanded that the station fire me, something which was never considered. I received a number of threats on my life, including one left with my answering service. The FBI called one afternoon and told me that they had uncovered a plot to kidnap me. When I asked what they were going to do about it, they said it was out of their jurisdiction until I was kidnaped and carried across a state line. They suggested I call the local police. I decided to risk abduction. The Jewish Defense League distributed leaflets throughout the city bearing my picture, and the caption: "Cancel out Julius, or he may cancel out you!" They also threatened to picket the New School for Social Research, where, that fall, I had begun teaching a course on black history. (The school wanted to cancel my class the night of the threatened demonstration. I would not agree. Class was held; there was no demonstration.)

I did not like being regarded as the black Hitler, but said nothing in my defense, not even when reporters asked me if I were anti-Semitic. "What do you think?" was always my response. A denial would have been meaningless, for I was being attacked by people who had not heard the shows on which the poem was aired, but had read about it in the distorted *Times* story.

On the night of January twenty-third, three black high-school students appeared on the show, and during the course of it, one of them remarked, offhandedly, "Hitler didn't make enough lampshades out of them." I found the remark obscene and personally offensive, but I lacked the maturity to know how to dissociate myself from it while upholding the student's First Amendment right to make it. However, after the show, I knew that I could not be silent any longer. My silence had simply encouraged one black, at least, to think that my show was a platform for anti-Semitism.

The Jewish Defense League called for a demonstration at the station for the next Thursday night to demand my dismissal. The afternoon of the show, I secluded myself in my new, skylighted studio on East Twentieth Street, trying to clarify my thinking about anti-Semitism. What was it, exactly? *Was* I one? What would my great-grandfather, Adolf Altschul, think of me? I also needed to be alone with my fear, for the Jewish Defense League was determined to eradicate the image of Jews as the eternal victim. I could understand that, but did not particularly care to be a victim of Jewish manliness. I considered going to the station before the demonstrators arrived and avoiding the possibility of being beaten or killed. I decided not to. Those people hated me, albeit for reasons having nothing to do with me. Nonetheless, it was my obligation, to them and to myself, to receive that hate, regardless of the consequences.

I did not feel courageous. Nor did I feel guilty for having allowed the poem to be aired. I remained (and remain) convinced that I had done what had to be done. Now what had to be done was to accept whatever happened as a result. The prospect of dying wasn't as disturbing as the thought of doing so because of a bad poem.

I usually rode the bus to the station, but that evening I walked alone up Park Avenue, wanting to give anyone who so desired the opportunity to do me violence. Nothing happened. When I turned onto Thirty-ninth Street where the station was located, and saw the angry, yelling crowd of demonstrators, I knew that I could not walk down that block alone. The street was blocked off and I asked the policeman standing guard there if he would accompany me down the block. He refused, even after I explained that I was the one for whom they were waiting and I was not the Messiah. "Sorry, buddy. I can't leave my post."

Slowly, I started down the block, my head lowered. If death were going to come, I did not want to see it. Ironically, no one recognized me as I walked past the mass of the demonstrators. For an instant, I wanted to yell, "Hey, y'all! It's me!" Not in defiance or as an act of bravado, but I couldn't help feeling that it was a pity that they were expending all that energy and hate and the object of it was now before their eyes, and they didn't see him. Reason prevailed, however, and I made it to the front of the station and looked up into the surprised face of Steve Post, who hurriedly assembled a police guard around me before the demonstrators realized that I had arrived. The flash of photographers' bulbs accompanied the outcry of rage from the demonstrators and I was thankful for the seventy-five policemen standing between me and them.

Inside the station, I learned that the police had arrested several people on the roof, where they had been trying to loosen the elevator cable, as well as people with chains and clubs.

(TRANSCRIPT of remarks on WBAI-FM, January 30, 1969)

This is a wonderful time to be alive. Very rarely does anyone have the opportunity to be alive at a time when history is so obviously changing. It brings an added intensity to living, as well as an added responsibility. But it also brings a certain joy.

We're involved in history and never has that seemed more obvious than in the sixties. At times it feels as if we're being pushed along, unable to control or even direct the way we'd like to go because the roots of what's coming out now are so fantastically deep, so fantastically old.

When the teachers' strike began last fall, I thought that the issue involved was community control of schools and that the racism which was exemplified by the teachers' strike and in the teachers' strike was a part of that. Now I realize that when you roll away one layer, there's another one, more vicious, more ugly, and then you roll away that one, and, lo and behold, there's another one. And you begin to wonder, where does it all end? I have no answer because I wasn't here when it began. But I'm here now, which means that I do have a responsibility to do what I can to see that it does end.

It's been very interesting to watch how things have gone from community control to black anti-Semitism, to Should WBAI be allowed to exist? to Should Julius Lester be on the air? The only real issue involved is the one of community control, but that has been totally obscured by the manufacture of so-called "issues" such as black anti-Semitism. So one must address himself to that and, hopefully, lay it to rest before minds can return to that which is relevant—community control of schools for blacks.

Perhaps I should explain what I see as my function on the air. My primary job is to relate to and speak as a member of the black community. Everybody in New York City has more than enough outlets for whatever they might want to say, however they might want to say it. Black people do not. So I'm here two hours a week, trying to serve as a forum for the black community. Secondly, I'm here to allow those nonblacks who are interested an opportunity to listen and to talk with me, in the hope that they will come to some understanding of the black frame of reference, the black psyche, the black mind. This is not to say that I expect them to agree. They may not and I accept that. They should, however, have the opportunity to listen. In this light, there can be no question as to whether or not WBAI is serving a valuable function. It seems, however, that white people believe in free speech only as long as they agree with what is being said. A black man in the communications media is generally there as a representative of the Establishment, not as a member of the black community. There are a few exceptions and I am one of them, and I think that that may be why so many people are upset. There's a black person on the air talking to black people, not trying to mollify white people. Thus, there was pressure on me to disavow Les Campbell, Tyrone Woods,* and what they said, and that pressure came from nonblacks, Jews, and Anglo-Saxons. They looked upon me as an individual, while I have no choice but to look upon myself as a black, who as an individual has certain skills that he is trying to make available to blacks.

You see, I know that anti-Semitism is a vile phenomenon. It's a phenomenon which has caused millions upon millions of Jews to lose their lives. However, it is a mistake, and a major mistake, to equate black

* Tyrone Woods was the student who made the reference to Hitler and lampshades.

anti-Semitism, a phrase I will use for the sake of convenience only, with the anti-Semitism which exists in Germany and Eastern Europe. If black people had the capability of organizing and carrying out a pogrom against the Jews, then there would be quite a bit to fear. It should be obvious to anyone that blacks do not have that capability. Not only do blacks not have the capability, I doubt very seriously if blacks even have the desire. But Jews have not bothered to try and see that black anti-Semitism is different. It is different because the power relationships which exist in this country are different. In Germany, the Jews were the minority surrounded by a majority which carried out heinous crimes against them. In America, it is we who are the Jews. It is we who are surrounded by a hostile majority. It is we who are constantly under attack. There is no need for black people to wear yellow Stars of David on their sleeves; that Star of David is all over us. And the greatest irony of all is that it is the Jews who are in the position of being Germans.

In the city of New York, a situation exists in which black people, being powerless, are seeking to gain a degree of power over their lives and over the institutions which affect their lives. It so happens that in many of those institutions, the people who hold the power are Jews. In the attempt to gain power, if there is resistance by Jews, then, of course, blacks are going to respond. And they're not going to respond by saying "it's the merchants who are holding us down," or "it's the schoolteachers who are holding us down"—not as long as they're being attacked as blacks. In the school strike, Rhody McCoy * always talked about teachers, not Jewish teachers. Yet, the response of Albert Shanker and the UFT was to accuse blacks of anti-Semitism. A good percentage of New York City policemen are Irish. When demonstrators call them "pigs," they do not respond by saying "you're anti-Irish." Yet, when blacks consistently attacked the political position of the UFT, their response was to accuse blacks of being anti-Semitic and to point to their liberal record on race relations and the fact that Shanker marched in Selma. Indeed, Jews tend to be a little self-righteous about their liberal record, always jumping to point out that they have been in the forefront of the fight for racial equality. Yes, they have played a prominent role and blacks always thought it was because they believed in certain principles. When they remind us continually of this role, then we realize that they were pitying us and wanted our gratitude, not the realization of the principles of justice and humanity.

Maybe that's where the problem comes now. Jews consider themselves liberals. Blacks consider them paternalistic. Blacks do not accept the Jews' definition of either the problem or the claim that Jews have

* Rhody McCoy was principal of one of the schools in the Ocean Hill-Brownsville district and the chief spokesman for black community control .

been in the forefront. And what can only be called Jewish contempt for blacks reaches its epitome when Jews continually go to the graveyard and dig up Michael Schwerner and Andrew Goodman * "who died for you." That Schwerner and Goodman paid the ultimate price cannot and will not be denied, but blacks pay a high price every day of every week of every year, and every day some of them pay the ultimate price. When you're powerless, you reach a point where you realize that you're all alone. You have no one but each other. Those who said that they were your friends were never your friends, because they unilaterally defined the relationship. Nonetheless, you had a certain sympathy from them, and having that sympathy, you expected that it would remain. But we have learned that sympathy exists only when it is a question of morals. When it was a moral issue, a question of integration in the South, for example, blacks had nonblack friends. But we have learned, in the rivers of blood from thousands of black bodies, that America does not run on morals. America articulates moral principles. It has articulated moral principles in relationship to black people since we have been here, but when it comes to acting, America acts on the basis of power. Power, and power alone. When black people reached the point of correctly analyzing that it was not a question of morals, but a question of power, then it meant that they had to attack those who held the power.

Many people have written me and said that "Jews are not your enemy because they don't hold the real power. There are others, back of them, who hold the real power." And that's true. However, a colonized people, which blacks are, cannot make fine distinctions as to who holds the power. Everyone else, the nonblacks, are the colonizers, and Jews are no exception because they hold only a measure of that power. It is power, and the Establishment maintains its powers partially through Jews. When a powerless people, a colonized people, begin to fight for power, then the first thing they will do is to lash out verbally at the most immediate enemy. In this particular instance, that hurt, the articulation, the demand that the colonizer listen, is accomplished in a violent manner, like the language of the poem. In this particular instance, the language set off a historical response which has no relationship to what black people are talking about.

Many people were very distressed by the remark of Tyrone Woods that Hitler should've made more Jews into lampshades. And people

---

* Michael Schwerner and Andrew Goodman were two civil rights workers killed in Mississippi in 1964. Andrew Goodman's father, Bob Goodman, was head of the New York board of the Pacifica Foundation, which operates WBAI, and remained staunch in his support of the station, and was particularly kind to me throughout this whole period. The Schwerner family had been personal friends for many years and offered to come to my defense during this time. I refused. The offer was sufficient.

157

were doubly distressed when I did not disassociate myself from that remark. And I've been asked many times this week whether or not I am anti-Semitic. To the question of whether or not I am anti-Semitic, I won't answer, because it's not a relevant question to me. The relevant question is changing the structure of this country, because that's the only way black people will achieve the necessary power. The question of anti-Semitism is not a relevant one for the black community. The remark that Tyrone Woods made is not one I would have made. It's not my style. I didn't say anything against the remark because I think I understood what he was trying to say. I was aware that he was speaking symbolically, not literally. And I was also aware that he was defending himself. He was also seeking, in a very direct way, to escape the definition of this controversy which others have put on it. Because what we have seen has been a moral response to a political problem.

We've reached a point where the stage is set now. I think that black people have destroyed the previous relationship which they had with the Jewish community, in which we were the victims of a kind of paternalism, which is only a benevolent racism. It is oppressive, no matter how gentle its touch. That old relationship has been destroyed and the stage is set now for a real relationship where *our* feelings, *our* view of America and how to operate has to be given serious consideration.

When I began I talked about living in an age when the processes of history rest upon our very brows, and who we are as individuals becomes, perhaps, totally irrelevant. I recognize that there are Jews who are exceptions to what I say. I recognize that there are blacks who do not agree with what I say. I recognize that there are good Jews, if you want to put it that way, and bad. However, I believe that everybody's good. They have difficulty expressing it sometimes, in fact, all the time, which is what the struggle's all about. If there's going to be any resolution of the problem that will not mean the total obliteration of America, and afterward silence, then it means that Jews and Anglo-Saxons are going to have to examine themselves. They are going to have to relinquish the security which comes from the definition which the society has given them. They're going to have to question themselves and they're going to have to open up, to be, at the least, receptive to what blacks are trying to say.

Yet, sometimes, I get filled with despair. We talk, and we talk, and we talk, and nothing changes. Perhaps there's only so much that words can do. Perhaps it is an illusion to think that words can do anything. Today I was reading James Baldwin's *The Fire Next Time*, which came out in 1962, and I was astounded when I read it. The truths which he spoke in 1962 are so relevant in 1969. The book was a bestseller, read, by, I'm sure, many more liberals and intellectuals, Anglo-Saxon and

Jewish, than it was by blacks. And yet, Anglo-Saxons and Jews still don't understand. Baldwin says in there, I quote,

. . . the social treatment accorded even the most successful Negroes proved that one needed in order to be free something more than a bank account. One needed a handle, a lever, a means of inspiring fear. It was absolutely clear that the police would whip you and take you in as long as they could get away with it, and that everyone else—housewives, taxi drivers, elevator boys, dish washers, bartenders, lawyers, judges, doctors, and grocers—would never, by the operation of any generous human feeling, cease to use you as an outlet for his frustrations and hostilities. Neither civilized reason nor Christian love would cause any of those people to treat you as they presumably wanted to be treated; only the fear of your power to retaliate would cause them to do that, or to seem to do it, which was (and is) good enough. There appears to be a vast amount of confusion on this point. But I do not know many Negroes who are eager to be accepted by white people, still less to be loved by them; they, the blacks, simply don't wish to be beaten over the head by the whites every instant of our brief passage on this planet. White people in this country will have quite enough to do in learning how to accept and love themselves and each other, and when they have achieved this—which will not be tomorrow, and may very well be never —the Negro problem will no longer exist, for it will no longer be needed.

12

The anti-Semitic poem controversy forced me to acknowledge that the distance between who I knew as me and who others knew by my name had become too great. There was scarcely a relationship between the private and public selves anymore. (I was a name equated with a political viewpoint—black revolution—and when I spoke on college campuses, I was aware, in those minutes before I was introduced, that the black students waited eagerly to hear the author of *Look Out, Whitey!*, and the white students waited in eager dread to be punished for their racist sins. I wondered if I should be who the black students thought I was, and invariably, I chose not to. I did not speak in anger, curse white society, or disparage whites. The black students were disappointed; the white students were elated. I was depressed, because the black students rejected me, and the white students assumed that I was unlike the black students who spurned their hopes for interracial

159

coalitions. Neither group understood that I was both of them.)

I stopped writing and publishing, resigning my *Guardian* column in February, 1969. I had nothing more to say, and I was also increasingly disturbed by the direction the radical movement seemed to be taking. During the autumn of 1968, I had tried to warn against this.

Excerpt

From *Revolutionary Notes*:

The feeling that revolution is a necessity is the mere beginning and is really nothing to compliment oneself for feeling. Anyone who is not afraid to feel his humanity feels the necessity for the creation of a society in which man can truly be man and women can truly be women. . . . We say that we are involved in a revolution because we feel better about ourselves. A revolutionary, however, does not exist for himself. In fact, it is his own self which exists least for him, because at the same time that he feels revolutionized within, he feels the pain of the selves that have not been revolutionized. . . .

. . . Rap Brown says, "In revolution one either walks off the battlefield victorious or is left lying there." At least, if we are left lying there, let it not be because we committed suicide.

October 6, 1968

It is difficult to be a revolutionary, for to be a revolutionary means to believe in the innate goodness of man, to know that man in this environment has been programmed into nonman. Our job is to change the environment so that man can be man. . . .

November 2, 1968

The revolution proceeds not by steps of a league at a time, but slowly —painfully slowly—and its steps are often so small as to be unnoticeable. The revolution proceeds not by the speeches at the barricades, but from one person to another person, in conversation and in work. The revolution proceeds not at the pace of our desires, but by its own laws. To break down the old and build the new is not a task accomplished in one generation or several, or by one individual more than another. It is accomplished only when each feels as responsible for the other as he does himself and acts in accordance with that responsibility.

February 1, 1969

As Students for a Democratic Society changed into the guerrilla cadre, Weathermen, as the Black Panther Party indulged in an orgy of violent rhetoric, I became frightened. As people raised clenched fists into the air and shouted, "Power to the People," my mind saw outstretched arms and flattened hands and heard, "Sieg

Heil!" If this was what the revolution was going to be, we were in more trouble than we realized.

I had thought it possible to inject the radical political movement with a spiritual essence. "The revolutionary knows that to change the institutions he must change himself," I'd written in the introduction to *Revolutionary Notes*. "He and his comrades must become new men, for it is from new men that the new institutions will come which, in turn, will create the new society." The revolution I wrote about had only one purpose: to transform humanity into vehicles for God. By the spring of 1969, it was evident, even to me, that any revolution the Panthers or SDS might make would force me to lead the counterrevolution.

I resumed my *Guardian* column in the spring to criticize the Panthers and SDS, was attacked by Kathleen Cleaver as a "punk, sissy and coward," and found that one of my closest friends agreed with her, though not her choice of words. I heard rumors that the Panthers were "out to get me," and I wanted to take bets on whether they or the Jewish Defense League would kill me first. (I put my money on the JDL.)

Spring came, but I did not notice. Each morning I went to my studio to work on a new book, *Search for the New Land,* a semipersonal history of the radical sixties, and, as I wrote, it became my farewell to the revolution. When friendships cannot withstand political and personal differences, there can be no significant change. The revolution was supposed to carry the embryo of the new society, new ways of being. The embryo had calcified in our wombs. (Another close friend surprised me one afternoon while sitting in my apartment, when he blurted, "I don't think you should be married to a white woman." We had been friends for three years; he knew Arlene, had played with our children, and I shared my children with very few. I looked at him, shock visible on my face, but before I could think of a response, he continued, almost apologetically, "Well, I guess you say that's my problem, huh?" "You're right," I responded coldly. I never saw him again.)

I sat before the typewriter and, almost blinded by the migraines which have always accompanied writing, began the long process of merging my private and public selves.

Excerpt

From *Search for the New Land*:
It is so hard not to hate and it is unreasonable to ask one to love those

who are trying to kill you, isn't it? So one hates, but unless that hate is continually transformed into energy and that energy into action, the hate has nowhere to go and it eventually fills every organ of the body with its lethal radiation. If you're black, it is all too easy to hate white people. . . . He who hates whites, however, may only be hating the whiteness in himself, thereby not loving black people, but loving black hatred of whiteness. . . . One hates injustice, loves humanity and kills only because the killing is forced upon him.

I often visit the graveyard in the woods back of the base camp to remember those whose intense desire to love was so thwarted that their love hardened and turned to hate. They were buried there, on the edge of the camp, and I took it upon myself to see that their graves were kept clean, for they had so taken the pain of others into themselves, that they were only more angered as they learned that revolution wasn't instant, that they could not, by the sheer strength of their wills, bring it into being. . . .

It is difficult and I sit among the graves and weep for those who saw the Promised Land and did not know that even the birds cannot fly there. Even they must leap from limb through the forests, jungles and swamps. Even they must walk over the desert sands, through the air which holds the heat like a lion holds the flesh of a running gazelle in its claws.

. . . We are victims, all of us now making our way through the wilderness. We are victims before we were born and sometimes our hatred of what was done to us threatens to destroy all that we want to be, all that we can be. If we hate the past more than we love the future, we will succeed in bringing the past into the future and those who come afterward will find our bones on the desert sand. . . .

We aren't what we know we can be, but we must not let despair immobilize us. More than anything, perhaps, the revolutionary needs faith, the faith of the Old Testament prophets, the faith of Meister Eckhart and the desert mystics. . . .

There is no human endeavor more difficult than the search for the New Land. Well, we shall try. We may not succeed, but we must do what we can.

Our humanity demands it of us.

13

Late that spring I received an invitation from James Holloway of Berea College in Berea, Kentucky, to speak at the school. I accepted. Holloway and I had spoken several times on the phone, initially when he called to ask permission to reprint one of my *Guardian* columns in *Katallagete,* the magazine he edited under the auspices of the Committee of Southern Churchmen. Subsequently, I had written an essay for the magazine on the 1968 election.

It was an overcast day when I arrived, and as we drove from the Lexington, Kentucky, airport, I slumped in the seat and let the Kentucky hills wrap me in their quiet. Perhaps it was the peace at seeing the hills that caused me to remember that the Abbey of Gethsemani, where Thomas Merton had lived, was nearby. A few questions, and Jim revealed that he had known Merton and had attended his funeral the previous December. Talking of Merton for the first time in years brought faint whiffs of something I'd once loved to partake of, and a wistfulness for the person I had been.

When we arrived on campus, I was put in the care of some black students, who closed around me like dogs at the sight of a fox. I didn't know what to do, because I wanted to talk to the white students also. I have a special affection for southern whites, particularly the young, because I share a history with them, which I want to know as they experienced it. But the black students surrounded me. They were like Secret Service agents, but instead of protecting me from assassination, they were unconscious agents of the act.

That evening as they escorted me to the chapel where I was to speak, a white girl approached me. She hugged her arms tightly around her, as if she had no one to hold her but herself. When she spoke to me, her eyes fluttered up to mine and down to the ground quickly. There was a slight quaver in her voice, which was not shyness but fear. Her eyes brimmed with the same fright as she looked at me and saw a black man phalanxed by unsmiling, hard-eyed young blacks, and her look told me that she thought I was one of them. I didn't know what to do, not wanting to make the black students feel that I was rejecting them: They were my people. Yet, I wanted to let that girl know that who she saw was not me. I wanted to ask her to unclasp her arms and hold me, so that I could cry for what was happening to me.

She asked me a question. I don't remember what, but it was not something which could be answered glibly, and I made a gentle joke, hoping to make her laugh. The joke bounced against her fear and plopped at my feet like a dead fish. She looked at me, bewildered, muttered something and hurried away.

I spoke that evening, masking the pain at not having been able to communicate with her, and hoped she could sense that my words were directed to her. But afterward, she left without speaking to me. I resolved that night that I would never allow myself to be the captive of blacks again, or let them use me as a club in their battle against anguish. It would be far better if they hated me, because what they called love was denying me life.

The test of my resolution came almost immediately, because a few weeks later I spoke in Harlem before Barbara Ann Teer's National Black Theatre. I had fantasized many times about what I would say if someone ever asked me publicly, "How do you rationalize being black and having a white wife?" I was unprepared, however, when that was the first question that Saturday afternoon. For two hours I sat on the stage and responded to the questions, all of which followed from that explosive first one. I didn't defend myself or try to justify my marriage, saying that if it was a contradiction, it was a contradiction. Some in the audience responded by rejecting me, saying they would never read another word I wrote. Surprisingly, however, the black women seemed to accept me and what I said, and afterward, a small group invited me to dinner with them. The subject of white women did not come up once.

Later, however, I was angry that I had responded to the initial question about my marriage. I had allowed myself to be cross-examined about the most personal aspect of my life by people who didn't know me. I shouldn't have. Yet I knew that I would do the same the next time the question was asked. There was nothing else to do.

Summer approached. I hated what I had become—a dummy for a revolutionary ventriloquist, an actor in a bad play. I had to find the way back to my Self, but I no longer knew where to look. The only thought that sustained me was immersing myself in the sky.

VII

1

June 21, 1969
(Journal)
Martha's Vineyard. The water a few yards away. In the distance the revolving beams of lighthouses. I sit in this house, glad, yet feeling a little guilty. After all, I'm a "revolutionary," I tell myself. Do revolutionaries rent houses for $2500 on Martha's Vineyard? Yet, I'm not certain that it is a contradiction. Perhaps the contradiction comes in trying to live your life in terms of some "outside" image instead of living it in terms of your self. What am I? A poet who wishes to change the soul of Man. Thus, in terms of that definition, anything which helps me to be a better poet is good. And, of course, Man's capacity for self-deception is infinite and I have to face the fact that I may be deceiving myself.

I'm thirty now. Five books behind me . . . no financial worries. . . . I'm thirty and I feel it, i.e., the young no longer represent me. I don't quite understand the campus rebellions. There's a lot I don't understand now. I have very tenuous connections with "the movement" now. Hardly any at all. Yet, publicly I represent something to a lot of people that I'm not anymore. At least I don't feel it. Maybe I have come as far as I can come at this point.

I guess what I must do is what I have always done—follow the sound of that inner voice and not be afraid to go where it says I must go.

165

The wind is high this morning and the waters of Vineyard Sound are white-capped. The sea gulls struggle against the wind.

I feel a strange coming together of something in being here— (1) the new contact with Thomas Merton this spring through Jim Holloway; (2) working on the Du Bois book and his grappling with the duality of being black in a white world; (3) Du Bois first came here in 1883. How strange to come to Martha's Vineyard and come into contact with him. So, in being here, there is some sort of strange reason, pattern, design, it seems.

Martha's Vineyard is an island six miles off the Cape Cod coast of Massachusetts, and for almost a century, has been the summer resort home of intellectuals, artists, writers, and the wealthy. (On various summer days I saw Mia Farrow, Andre Previn, James Taylor, McGeorge Bundy, Senator Edward Brooke, William Styron, James Reston, and Jules Feiffer, who, to my delighted surprise, recognized me.)

Though I wanted to believe there was no contradiction in being a revolutionary and summering on the Vineyard, I couldn't delude myself. My revolutionary writings paid for the house on the beach and the weekly air fare to New York for my radio show, on which I talked about revolution, of course. I could have used my increased earnings to finance a revolutionary press, a people's store, or any of a hundred projects, and although I gave large sums to individuals whose work I respected, my financial success released latent bourgeois aspirations rather than increased revolutionary fervor. We are the dreams of our youths, and those dreams must be fulfilled for us to be free of them. I had to live mine of summers by the ocean, a skylighted studio, and meals at restaurants chosen by me, not my income. I had to see myself in the eyes of others as a successful writer (and, perhaps, that meant more to me than being a revolutionary), writing reviews for and being reviewed in the *Sunday Times Book Review*, meeting Norman Mailer and hearing him say, "Oh, yes!" at the mention of my name. I did not, however, confuse myself with the dreams of that college boy who wanted to be a writer. I was flattered that Norman Mailer recognized my name, but that was not a substitute for being fully revealed to myself. Indeed, having great numbers of people know your name could take you so far away from your self that if you weren't vigilant, you became nothing more than an appellation, a canapé others passed through their lips and into their gullets, exclaiming, "Oh, yes!" while reaching for the next one.

Moving to Martha's Vineyard was the only way I knew to separate myself from my public identity. The necessary first act of returning to myself was being physically apart from the revolution. Living on an island, and that particular island, I was as isolated from my contemporaries as that place was from the mainland, and it was strangely reassuring to have my aloneness visible at every point on the horizon.

We lived in a house on Lobsterville Beach at the tip of the island in Gay Head. Through the large living-room window, I looked out onto sand dunes, the water and the sky. and they were the only reality I could trust. (At dusk each day I walked alone over the dunes to squat beside the water, listening for the sound of a distant drum, looking for a sea gull to bring me a leafed twig from some unseen shore whose beach I doubted I would ever reach. Only when the fog blew in from the ocean side, however, did I know a measure of peace, for all evidence of human existence was then obliterated, and no one could reach through the moist gauze of the fog and harm me.)

My only friend that summer was a black kite shaped like a bat's wings. I would stand on the beach, send the kite into the ocean-charged air, and while it rode the sky, I did, too.

Arlene and I limited conversation to the only subject not covered with scabs—the children. It was the first time in our marriage we were unable to talk, and with the word-bindings of our love fraying, we were left flinging silence at each other.

In the two years since I'd returned from the South, we had had periods of calm and even happiness, but they were merely respites, giving us time to whirl our horses around and prepare for the next charge. Our life together looked like a splatter painting done with blood.

She seethed with unacknowledged hatred for a husband who had written five books and almost a hundred essays and reviews in the previous three years, taught black history at her alma mater, had his own radio show, flew off regularly to speak at colleges throughout the country, and increasingly preferred to sleep by himself on the day bed in the living room. The markers of her achievements were turds in the potty and not the diaper. That

167

spring before we moved to Martha's Vineyard, her resentment intensified. I understood it, but it was not enough to open myself to her pain, to listen as she described in excruciating detail what it was to live day after monotonous day with two small children, to have her sit on my lap and hug me so tightly that I felt like a raft being clung to in white water.

We tried to find a solution, and put Simone in nursery school; I hired one of my New School students to care for Coltrane one afternoon a week. I agreed to care for the children in the evenings. But a cotton swab cannot staunch internal hemorrhaging. She needed me to *feel* that the children were my responsibility. I had enough responsibilities, and home had to be the one place where there were none. It wasn't.

Her resentment of my life was so forceful that I was afraid to go to bed before her, and one rare night when I did, I awoke in terror when she came into the room, certain that she had a knife in her hand. I seldom came home without expecting to find my manuscripts burned, my books cut up and records shattered, though I knew rationally she would not have done that.

One afternoon a few months before we went to Martha's Vineyard, we sat at the round oak table in the kitchen, and she spoke her desperation in a whisper: "Julie, don't you see that I want the same chance that you have? I'm a brilliant woman, but I'm stuck with two kids. I want to be out in the world like you, meeting exciting people and doing things." She talked for some time, and when she finished, I said what I had hoped she would have realized by herself, what I should have said when the first child had only an invisible hold on the wall of her womb. She had chosen motherhood instead of the terrors of self-realization, and now wanted me to sacrifice part of my life to give her another chance. I wouldn't. She needed me to do that, but we can only give to another who we are, and they can only receive it. We must tend to our own needs. Arlene and I began our lives together, brave young children wearing the thin armor of hope and idealism. How fortunate I'd thought I was to find her, and I'd encouraged her to study, write, and be her brilliant self. I didn't ask her to become a mother, for I had married a *woman*, someone to march beside through the valley of dry bones. Now, she wanted to hold me responsible for what her life had become. I refused to stand trial. It was she who had betrayed me by wearing the sandals of a gladiator and running when the lions charged into the arena. I spoke the words dispassionately, for there was nothing I could do to save her. (And what if she had, one morning, awakened and said that she was leaving to live her life and I could have the children? I would have nodded, then, after she closed the door, cried, raged, writhed in pain, lost my sanity for a while, but I would have persevered and triumphed. There was no other alternative.) Far beneath the surface of myself, there are hand-hewn, hand-laid slabs of stone, placed there by my parents, teachers, and the black communities of Kansas City and Nashville, and it was a foundation which did not allow me to curse life as unfair, or expect it to be kind, just, or even happy. I resented her complaints about how hard it was being a woman, for I had never imposed my black tribulations on her. Life is and you are and you sail as well as you can through the maelstrom. You don't, however, blame the storm if you never learned to sail. I would do all I could to help her, except give her my life. However, I feared that in lieu of one of her own, she would not be satisfied with less than mine.

My real life was with other women, who did not want or expect me to give their lives meaning. It seemed that I carried a polygamy gene from some African ancestor, for these relationships were not affairs as much as they were other marriages, with their own problems, joys, struggles. I was not seeking refuge from Arlene, but trying to illuminate shadowed corners of my self, for each woman and each relationship was different, and so was I. (Romantic love is narcissistic, for it is the experiencing of one's self through another that we love as much, if not more than the other. To know myself as a procreator of joy rather than the angel of pestilence and famine was a unique experience. I liked who I was with every woman I loved, except my wife.)

I still could not believe that there were women who wanted to lie with me, and with my thin body stretched beneath theirs, I wished that I were truly Michele, with breasts to thrust into their mouths, with a body to give to them as pregnant with wonder as I found theirs. How could a woman love the monotonous plane of the male body? I thought of myself as a male lesbian and learned that sex was not an act to be performed, judged, and a blue ribbon affixed to the buttocks of the best performer, but a way of telling the other that he/she is holy, made in the image of God and loved by Him. Sex was not a procession to orgasm, but an aimless exploration of the infinite in the finite personhood of another, and I, who, unknown to Arlene (maybe), suffered premature ejaculations with her, sailed the sea of night with other women. (I did not recognize that my sexual dissatisfaction with Arlene was a commentary on our relationship, and I also failed to comprehend what she was trying to tell me when, for almost a year after the birth of our son, her Bartholin glands would not function. We thought she was suffering from some odd form of postpartum depression, but the body speaks what the mind refuses to form into words, and only after we were divorced did I realize that her dry, unyielding vagina was a seal against me.)

I was so ecstatic in the flourishing of my sexuality that I decided to have a sexual relationship with a different woman to atone for every year of marriage. Not only would that be conclusive proof of my sexual desirability, but it would rewrite my personal history, superimposing another woman's face on each year of pain. (Did I hate Arlene so much? I had no intention of telling her of these other relationships. It was necessary to keep them secret, for my revenge was in pretending to participate and believe in our marriage, the only reality she had, and sometimes, when she was attempting to load my soul with her misery, I caressed the scratches one woman left on my body and smiled inwardly. No, I did not hate her, for hate is a relationship. I was indifferent, caring about her only when she expressed her pain, or, more accurately, perhaps, I allowed myself to receive that pain as punishment for my sins.)

It would have been less cruel to leave her, and we'd discussed separation frequently, as well as the idea of living in separate apartments but continuing our marriage. I was willing; she was not. I should have left anyway, but I would look at my thousands of books and records, think about how hard it would be to find a new apartment, and it was easier to stay. Habit was security, and by the summer of 1969, the marriage was the only certainty in my life. As untenable as it had become, it was a shelter.

So I stayed, afraid of being scorched by the loneliness I saw when I peeked outside. Having run to the cave of matrimony to escape that loneliness, I was even less able, seven years later, to stand unprotected before the world. Thus, we lived in silence, waiting.

2

I began work that summer on my sixth book, a collection of the writings of the preeminent black intellectual, W. E. B. Du Bois. As I researched the book, one quality which had characterized his life and work impressed itself on me—integrity. In a career which spanned eighty years, he changed his opinions, contradicted himself from one period to another, but never failed to tell the whole truth as he knew it.

I realized that I had allowed myself to become a spokesman, a shill who stood outside the carnival tent enticing strangers to come inside and see the the two-headed baby about whom I had doubts. It was an error I had to rectify. But how could I cease my revolutionary role-playing without becoming an embittered and disillusioned ex-radical, cursing the god which had failed me? How did one continue to believe, when the ikon lay at one's feet like shattered glass from a wrecked car?

(ARTICLE: "Reflections on Reaching the Age of Thirty," *Katallagete*, October, 1969)

I am growing old. Every day I look at my children and their growing is the yardstick of my aging. When my daughter is fourteen, I will be forty. When she is twenty-four, I will be fifty. I am growing old. The bills which come in the mail are now addressed to me and it is I, not my father, who looks in the checkbook to see which ones can be paid immediately and which must wait. I read the paper and my eye skips the article about a demonstration and comes to rest on one about the six per cent increase in prices last year and I understand why I spend more and more money to bring home the same amount of food. I read the paper and I am not as interested in Congressional debates on troop withdrawals from Vietnam as I am in debates on extension of the surtax and tax reform.

I am growing old and I become aware of it when I talk to the young who say they are revolutionary. I do not disbelieve them, but I am reluctant to trust them completely. I look at them and wonder, will they still be talking about revolution when it is their time to earn the dollars to pay the bills? Or will these years of their youth merely be a pleasant interlude affording them nostalgic pleasures on quiet evenings in the days of their aging.

The young have said, "Don't trust anyone over thirty" and there is truth in that. It is those over thirty who have betrayed the moral principles in which the young believe and fight for and which the revolution will make real for every man. Yet, I can say with equal truth, "Don't trust anyone under thirty." It is easy for them to talk revolution, because they have little to risk. Their revolutionary commitment has not been tested by rising prices, increasing taxes and low wages. They can be pure revolutionaries because they do not have to worry about losing jobs because of their political beliefs and activities.

I am haunted by a statement of Robert Frost's: "I was never a radical in my youth because I didn't want to be a conservative in my old age." And what a shock it is to realize that there is life after twenty-five. In fact, most of it. (As adolescents all of us were certain that we would die beautiful tragic deaths by the time we were twenty-five. When we don't, it is horrifying to realize that we have fifty years, more or less, in front of us that we have to do something with.) It is at that point that the revolutionary commitment of our youth is tested to its utmost, for revolutions are not lived in the grand parades of the masses down broad boulevards, nor in the columns of the guerrilla band, with its fixed purpose, making its way through the forest. Revolutions are lived day-by-God-awful-day, like the drops of water from a slow-dripping faucet. When we are young, we want wrongs to be righted instantly. We have no time to wait. "We want the world and we want it NOW!" sings Jim Morrison of The Doors. But what if we don't get it NOW? (There is no doubt that we deserve it NOW, but whenever the dispossessed take control of the world, there is every probability that those of us now alive will have provided sustenance for the worms and will be smiling vacant smiles toward a sky we cannot see.)

You reach the age of thirty and you slowly understand that you may not even be a memory in anyone's mind "when the revolution comes." Some never recover from the shock and with the knowledge that they will probably not be around to benefit personally from the new society, they decide to get all they can out of this one and let the new take care of itself. And they become good liberals. Others become disillusioned and bitter. Others, however, face the challenge of being thirty and revolutionary, of being committed to and working for total change in the society, while making a living from and raising one's children in that society. And challenge is not an adequate word to describe trying to live such a life. An agony of agonies it is. (I remember the months preceding the publication of my first book, *Look Out, Whitey! Black Power's Gon' Get Your Mama.* I wanted it to be read, to be sold, of course, yet if it were, I would make money from it. America is the only country that ever existed in which you can make a living talking and writing about the destruction of the country. What kind of revolutionary am I, I wondered, who gets semiannual royalty statements on his latest book about revolution? What kind of revolutionary am I who can get $500 for giving a 1½ hour talk on revolution at a college? What kind of revolution is this? One must accept and live with the contradictions. Only the monk and the nun can live pure lives in this society. The rest of us have to live impure lives even as we work for the pure society. It is like a woman with tuberculosis getting pregnant.)

There are those who have decided that the demands of the revolution are such that they must be monks without monasteries—no marriage, no family, no long-term romantic involvements. They will spend 100% of their time and their lives working for the revolution. That is good and necessary. But there are those of us who married before revolution meant something more than what happened in Russia in 1917. There are those of us who considered ourselves revolutionary, but wanted our lives, too. (I first met Nancy when she was 14. It was the same summer I met Arlene, whom I married six months later. We were at a camp and Nancy was the most beautiful girl there—blonde, blue-eyed, rosy-cheeked, nubile as only 14-year-old girls are and totally apolitical. She was the image of Miss Junior America and at the time, I thought her mental capacity didn't exceed her image. She wrote me off and on after camp and when she entered Barnard three years later, we would talk on the phone occasionally. She said she had changed, that she was involved in SDS, had been on demonstrations and considered herself a revolutionary. I remember the morning the black students took over Hamilton Hall at Columbia the spring of '67, I was roused from my bed at 6 A.M. and asked to come up and give them some advice seeing as how I had all this experience in "the movement." All my experience told me that the best advice was for everybody to get some sleep like I was trying to do and take over the building later. That was my first thought and I commented to myself that, yes, I was getting old, but revolutionary commitment was stronger than common sense and I got out of my warm bed beside my warm wife and ventured out into the morning up to Columbia University which I didn't give a good goddam about. If they didn't want to set it on fire, I would come home and go back to bed, which is exactly what happened. And as I came out of Hamilton Hall, who should I see standing out front in the rain, but Nancy. A week later, as I followed events at Columbia in the pages of *Newsweek*, there was a picture of her making a picket sign and I couldn't believe that this was the same girl I had known when she was fourteen. It was and we went out several times and I learned that she was serious, one of the most serious of the young I've ever met. Revolution for her was synonymous with life. But one evening that summer she said to me, "I know that I'm a revolutionary, but I want to have

173

kids." She laughed. "I know what you're going to say, but my life will not be complete if I don't. I really don't think I can be a complete revolutionary otherwise." I sipped my beer and told her about sick children who cry for eight hours, about diapers that always need changing, about baby-sitters you can't trust, about having children and finding that it isn't like the pictures in the Ivory soap ads. She said she knew. A few weeks ago she called to invite me and Arlene to her wedding. I'm glad that she is going to do both.)

It is not easy and the older one gets, the more difficult it becomes. I am so afraid that when I am forty, my daughter will have for a father a man who does not understand, who does not listen and who does not learn from her. She may have for a father a man who unconsciously sold his idealism and commitment for the security of a bank account, a home and a little comfort. She may have for a father a man whose love of humanity has turned to hatred because humanity did not respond with a resounding YES when he cried, "We want the world and we want it NOW!" Her father may be a man whose bitterness is so pervasive that he will be loath to see her generation succeed where his failed.

Being a revolutionary means not only fighting to bring about that change, but it means maintaining a constant vigil on one's self, searching for the weaknesses and faults within which must be destroyed if he is not to betray the dreams of his youth. The jazz musician and revolutionary, the late John Coltrane, wrote a composition called "Vigil," of which he said: "(Vigil) implies watchfulness. Anyone trying to attain perfection is faced with various obstacles in life which tend to sidetrack him. Here, therefore, I mean watchfulness against elements that might be destructive—from within or without." Just as the monk keeps God at the center of his being, I must keep the necessity for revolution at the center of mine. (Is there any difference between the two?) I must fight to keep it there, no matter how large the royalty checks may get, no matter how many "good" reviews my books may get. (Rosie was twenty-six and the mother of four girls. She, her husband and children lived in a three-room railroad flat. He worked at a wrought-iron furniture plant two hours away from our block. When he came home from work, it was only long enough to eat, shower, dress and go out. Three rooms filled with furniture and children is no solace after four hours travelling to and from work and eight hours on the job. Rosie had no place to go, except to seances once a month where she talked to the dead. And when it is easier to communicate with the dead, there is no word to describe what living has become. She had wanted children, but her husband had wanted a son. A man who has a son has a future. A woman has only the present. She hadn't minded the first two children, even though they were girls. However, when the third child was also a girl, she lived in dread of the fourth pregnancy. And she wanted nothing less than death when the doctor congratulated her on the birth of her fourth girl. What kind of woman was she that she could not give birth to a boy? No one had ever told Rosie that the male determines the sex of the child. The fifth child was a boy, but Rosie couldn't care. She could only wonder why it had taken so long. Her pregnancies were over, but there were too many clothes to wash, too much food to cook, too little money to do anything with and too many children. There was no energy to care for them. There was no time to care. There could not be even any desire to care.)

I must fight to remember, now that I am thirty, that the revolution is Rosie. Rosie must be freed so that she can be Rosie and no matter how much pain living with the contradictions creates in me, it is nothing to the pain of Rosie, who will not even have the opportunity to fight for her life as I fight for mine. Thus, I become responsible not only for me, but for Rosie.

I am growing old and I never thought I would. When you are twenty, it is impossible to imagine being thirty. When you're thirty, it is not only easy to imagine forty, you can feel the inevitability of fifty. And feeling it, I am so afraid, sometimes, that when I am fifty, I will have forgotten that Rosie's life is in my hands, for I am a revolutionary. I will have forgotten that the beat of my heart does not belong to me. I must keep a constant vigil to see that this does not happen, for if it does, I will have betrayed my birthright and negated my reason for being and my children, in the fullness of their youth, will have no choice but to kill me as I lie sleeping.

While writing the essay, however, I knew that I was trying to evade a confession of guilt. I had been wrong to become a political revolutionary. I had always known who I was, an unfrocked monk, but I had not trusted that self-knowledge. I had allowed the historical ephemera of headlines and ideologies to persuade me to ring my tonsured skull with the laurel of some distant revolutionary victory. Rereading my journals that summer, I found a seven-year-old entry which commemorated the turning toward the light of a star I did not know had been dead for years.

January 20, 1963
1 A.M.

Working for the Welfare Department and living with Arlene has forced into my mind with more force than ever before that I, Julius Lester, must do something—action away from the type-

175

writer. That all the monks in the world haven't changed a Harlem or an Auschwitz. I'm not totally convinced that this active involvement I am contemplating is totally right, but I am dissatisfied with everything else I've tried—that it's not enough. And I'm unable to delude myself any longer. Thus, I must try direct involvement and simply see what happens. This way I will *know*, whereas now, I don't. And I must know. . . .

Eventually I grabbed a pike and marched to the barricades.

Excerpt

From Interview with Julius Lester: "The Arts and the Black Revolution" *Arts in Society*, The University of Wisconsin, 1968:

Q. Do you think the Negro artist has any degree of responsibility to commit his art to the fight for Negro equality? If so, in what way?

A. If the black artist does not commit his art to the liberation movement (not the fight for Negro equality as you have it), he is not fulfilling his responsibility. The artist is a privileged person, having the ability to communicate the feelings and thoughts of a group of people. It is his responsibility to do this. At this point in history, the black artist has no other responsibility. For too long have black artists spoken to whites and left their own people to be lied to by whites. No more.

I had believed that. To put one's talents at the service of the masses of people was a noble ideal, and thus I had written *Look Out, Whitey!* But had I truly served them, or a phantasmagoria at dusk when silhouetted bushes look like spirits from the unknown world? (I think I better served my people in *To Be a Slave* and *Black Folktales*, books in which my racial voice sang truly.)

However, my personal aesthetic included not only what I said in the interview, but what I consciously omitted; the black artist's ultimate responsibility is to his/her vision of reality. If that particular vision should conflict with the needs and demands of "the people," so be it. It was the artist's responsibility to die rather than capitulate. I had started out to be the black James Joyce and had almost become a revolutionary hack writer.

On the morning of September 3, 1969, when I awoke to the news that Ho Chi Minh was dying, the private self immediately began mumbling the lines of a poem. I tried not to listen, but the voice of the interior self can never be ignored, and sometimes, it demands to be heard. All that day I worked at deciphering the mumbling and when I submitted the poem as my regular *Guardian* column, I should have known that it would mark the end of the revolutionary self's dominance of my being.

(POEM: "The Third of September," *The Guardian*, September 20, 1969)

Half awakened by the light of morning
choking in the greyness
of a third of September Wednesday,
I reached out for the
roundness
softness
fullness
allness of her
and she, awakened,
began to move,
softly,
silently,
gently,
and my hand found that place,
that hidden place,
that secret place,
that
won-
der-
ful place
and in the quiescent light of
a third of September Wednesday morning,
I felt my penis being taken into the
salty
thick
fluidity
of her swirling movement
easily
softly
gently
(as the children were waking).

Afterwards,
my penis, moist and warm,
resting on my thigh like some
fish washed onto the beach by full moontide,

177

I turned on the radio
and we heard that
Ho Chi Minh lay dying.
(The fog covered the seagulls that
sit on the rocky beach when the tide is out.)

I retreated from her,
not talking that day as the radio told us
(every hour on the hour)
that Ho Chi Minh lay dying.
Finally, when night had covered the fog,
we heard that
Ho Chi Minh was dead
and I came back to her.
Ho Chi Minh was dead.
I wanted her again.
The softness
the roundness
the fullness
the allness.

Ho Chi Minh was dead.

The poem was supposed to have appeared in *The Guardian* of September 13, but in its stead, a poem of Ho Chi Minh's was substituted in the space on the editorial page where my column always appeared. When the poem was published the following week, the paper's editors appended a note: "The Guardian staff decided to postpone publication a week . . . because it believed the nature of the above poem in proximity with the news of Ho's death might not be understood to be the appreciation of the Vietnamese leader that it actually is. Julius Lester disagrees with this decision and maintains that by delaying the poem a week the Guardian in effect practiced censorship over his column." I could not see what else it could be, particularly when the decision to postpone publication had been made without consulting me before or informing me afterward. The political commissars had become poetry critics. The revolution was over.

(ARTICLE: "The Other Side of the Tracks," *The Guardian*, September 27, 1969)

I was in Cuba that August of 1967 when George Best was killed. It was on the front page of Granma and I read the article several times to be sure that I was not being misinformed by my poor knowledge of Spanish. But the next day a telegram came from the Atlanta SNCC office and it confirmed George's death in West Point, Mississippi.

I hadn't seen George for some months. He was in college in Florida and would drive up to Atlanta on weekends and during school holidays to work around the office, to talk, to stay in touch. He had worked full time for the organization once, but had decided to go back to school. He couldn't stay away though. In the early hours of basement mornings I would hear the distant ring of the doorbell in the emptiness of the old warehouse which was the SNCC office and with a certain fatalism I would go to the door, expecting this ring of the bell to be the raid we constantly expected, or some cracker full of liquor and hateful politics with a gun in his hand. It was always some SNCC person, though, coming back to the office to ask if I'd seen so-and-so that night. Sometimes, it would be George I'd unlock the door for. "I had to get away from there for a few days, man. See what's going on." The summer of '67 he saw something "going on" in West Point and went there to help organize.

When I went back to Atlanta from Cuba, I tried to learn what I could about his death. Those who had gone to West Point to investigate it said that it was an accident. He had driven off a bridge and drowned in the little creek. Others, however, were convinced that he had been forced off the bridge and then killed. There wasn't enough water in the creek to get a drink of water. Maybe I wanted to believe that George had been murdered. Maybe I needed to believe that because a twenty-one-year-old brother as beautiful as George couldn't die in something as stupid and ridiculous as a car accident. Whatever the reason, I, too, came to believe that he had been murdered.

Then, I learned that SNCC had not sent flowers to his funeral. When I asked about it, I was told that there wasn't any money for flowers. For the first time I began to wonder what was happening to us. (Others had begun to wonder long before.) SNCC was George's life and it was while working for SNCC that he died. Was it too much to think that money could have been gotten from somewhere to send flowers, even one long-stemmed rose in all of its crimson fragility? But I wasn't sure. Maybe there was something I didn't understand. I had been away for four months, been with people who were in the process of realizing a revolution—the Vietnamese and the Cubans—and perhaps I was trying so hard to live the new vision I had seen that I was becoming unmindful of human frailty. Would I have sent flowers had I been there? I couldn't answer.

But I never forget that those with whom George had worked didn't send flowers to his funeral. It was a while after that before I left the organization. Almost a year. But I finally left. It became too much to have to fight the enemy and those with whom I was working. We had been through too much, I guess. The burdens had gotten too heavy and the frustrations had become so painful that we could no longer give each other the personal support each of us needed to do our job— make the revolution. Our love for black people was overwhelmed by our inability to do everything to make that love manifest and after a while we could not even love each other. We got so involved in the day-to-day functioning of an organization, so enmeshed in fixing the mimeograph machine, writing leaflets, raising money, sitting in interminable meetings where we said what we were going to do and had forgotten what we were going to do by the time the meeting was over and eventually we forget, can't even remember that the revolution is an "embryonic journey" and that we are the embryos inside society. If we cannot be human to each other, the revolution will be stillborn.

During the two years that this column has appeared in the Guardian, it has been published without question, whether it expressed the views of the staff or not. When I turned in my column two weeks ago (the poem on the death of Ho Chi Minh which appeared belatedly in last week's Guardian), I knew that few, if any, of the staff or readers would consider it appropriate for the occasion. However, because of the relationship which had existed between the Guardian and myself, it never occurred to me that publication of the column would be delayed and particularly without my being informed of the fact. I first learned that it had not been printed when I saw the paper and no explanation was printed as to why the column was missing. The Guardian, of course, has the right not to print what I or anyone else writes, but when it exercises that right, it also has the responsibility to inform me or anyone else that that right has been exercised. If one cannot expect total honesty in his dealings with his "revolutionary comrades," then one cannot expect it anywhere. Being no longer able to expect that honesty from the Guardian, I can no longer write for the paper.

Through it all I haven't been able to rid myself of the feeling that the Guardian would be too busy meeting its deadline, too busy "making the revolution" to send flowers to my funeral. But I don't like flowers anyway.

Somehow, though, it matters.

My break with *The Guardian* was a lesson in bitter irony, because I recalled that when I had written about killing people, which revolutionary violence was a subtle justification for, no one cared. Yet, when I wrote about sex, *The Guardian* staff held a long meeting and decided that the poem "might not be understood." I'd thought that the revolution was supposed to create a society where some power elite did not arbitrarily determine what "the people" might and might not understand. In fact, the revolution was supposed to give "power to the people." Well, it was my mistake. I should have known that the revolution wouldn't be erotic.

3

We remained on Martha's Vineyard that fall, moving from the house on the beach to one on Lighthouse Road above it. I finished the Du Bois volumes and entered what was to be an intensive two-year period of writing, interrupted only by the weekly trips to New York, where I continued teaching at the New School and producing the radio show.

The published essays of this period became a journal of self-transformation, of the merging of the public and private selves. Because my name was now a public possession, I could no longer allow it to represent someone who did not really exist. Who I was in the interior chambers of my heart had to be exposed for all to see its pulsations. There was no other way to reclaim my self.

The previous spring, *Evergreen Review* had offered me a position as a contributing editor, paying me a monthly retainer for six articles a year. That fall the first two appeared. Ostensibly they were interviews with a racially-mixed couple, David and Susan Williams. In actuality, the "interviews" were fictionalized accounts of my marriage. Susan's biography was Arlene's, except for details of occupation, birthplace, etc. The only other conscious inaccuracy was in characterizing Susan as a solitary person who accepted her husband's separatedness. That was not Arlene, but the advantage of being a writer was that if I could not have the woman I wanted, I could create her on paper. David Williams was, of course, me, though his speaking voice in the "interview" was not mine, nor did I drink as much as I portrayed him.

When the "interviews" appeared, even my closest friends were unsure if they were autobiographical. I was particularly pleased when the *Amsterdam News*, New York's black newspaper, carried a story based on the "interviews" headlined: HOSTILITY GROWS TO MIXED MARRIAGES.

(ARTICLES: "White Woman–Black Man," *Evergreen Review,*
September, 1969

"White Woman–Black Man (Part II)," *Evergreen
Review,* October, 1969)

Perhaps nothing strikes the emotional core of white America more
than the idea, thought, and (God forbid!) sight of a white woman and
black man together. America's ultimate opinion on the subject is
summed up in the rhetorical question: "Would you want your daughter
to marry one?" This was the southerner's reply to school integration and
former President Harry Truman's reply to a reporter's question about
the sit-in movement of the early sixties. It is a strange statement, for it
expresses the utmost contempt, not for blacks, but for black men and
white women. In essence, it is a statement of white male superiority,
and its by-products are racism and female oppression. (Racism is based
on race. Sexism is based on sex. The two differ only in particulars.) In
that simple statement are found the stereotypes of the black male and
white female. It is a statement which immediately brings to mind the
image of a black, hairy beast permeating the atmosphere with the heavy
smell of lust, and the white female, as lovely and fair and gentle a
creature as ever the sun had the good fortune to shine its rays upon.
She sees the beast, and though repelled (but attracted also?), being
a woman she lacks the strength of mind to resist, and thus is ravished
and forever defiled. In Shakespeare's *Othello* (which is more a study of
the white male mind than of a black man), Desdemona's father spoke
for all white men in attempting to explain why Desdemona professed
love for the Moorish general:

> A maiden never bold;
> *Of spirit so still and quiet that her motion*
> *Blush'd at herself; and she—in spite of nature,*
> *Of years, of country, credit, everything—*
> *To fall in love with what she fear'd to look on!*
> It is a judgement maim'd and most imperfect
> That will confess *perfection so could err*
> *Against all rules of nature,* and must be driven
> To find out practices of cunning hell
> Why this should be. *I therefore vouch again*
> *That with some mixtures pow'rful o'er the blood,*
> *Or with some dram, conjur'd to this effect,*
> *He wrought upon her.* [Italics mine.]

The white male–black female relationship evokes no similar response
from white America. In the rural South it is still more the norm than
the exception that a white man who wants to be considered "a man"

182

has to get some "black pussy" every now and then. In the large southern cities it is common to see white men at night cruising through the black sub-city or parked at the curbs waiting for solitary black women to come walking down the street. It is a sign of manhood for a white man to sleep with a black woman. It is a sign of depravity for a white woman to sleep with a black man.

In the past couple of years, the interracial relationship has been the subject of several motion pictures. Written, directed, and produced by white men, these films have invariably concerned themselves with the white woman–black man. (A motion picture about a white man and black woman, would, in all probability, be a box office flop, though Lena Horne, Dionne Warwick, and Donayale Luna have recently appeared in motion pictures opposite white men. And, interestingly enough, each of them has played the role of a mistress.) *Guess Who's Coming to Dinner* was the most serious, being in the good liberal tradition of *Gentleman's Agreement*. It is a sympathetic film. The Jim Brown–Raquel Welch fleshtravaganza *100 Rifles* is merely an attempt to exploit the skeleton in the closet. It is a film for the voyeur, a peek through the keyhole, allowing white women and black men to accept and act out their fantasies without any subsequent guilt feelings. Other films, such as *Joanna* and *Three-Day Pass* (directed by a black man, Melvin Van Peebles), have put the white female–black male on the screen sympathetically, but as yet no film has done more than brush very lightly over the surface. None has had the power of the rape scene in Griffith's *Birth of a Nation*, nor the impact of that film and that particular scene. (That scene alone can be considered responsible for a wave of lynchings and riots that seemed to follow in whatever town it played.)

White men have always been antagonistic to the white female–black male relationship, white women less so except when the social pressures coming from white men have forced an attitude of active antagonism. Blacks have always had ambivalent feelings. The black male is totally hostile to the white male–black female relationship, not only because of the personal affront he sees in a black woman choosing a white man, but also because of the all too recent history of white men taking black women at their whimsy and, if necessary, killing any black man or woman who objected or resisted. The black male attitude toward the white female is more ambivalent. Until recently, she represented status in the eyes of many blacks. At the same time, she represented a means of getting revenge on the white man and white society. Black women have looked upon the white male with much the same attitude as that of the black male toward the white woman, but the attitude is not as widespread or as intense. Being a woman, her opportunities for meet-

183

ing white men are decidedly limited, if not nonexistent. She cannot "pick up" a man as the black male can a woman. More important, the white man has been the traditional rapist preying upon black women. (The black man may have the reputation but he is merely being given the "credit" for what the white man has done and what the white man's morality cannot accept. In one sense, blacks exist as a repository for what white society considers immoral or evil. In those societies without large black populations the poor become that repository.) The black woman, therefore, grows up with a negative image of white men.

Where the black male feels rejected by the black woman–white man relationship, this feeling of rejection is intensified in black women when confronted with the white female–black male. Because the white female is projected by the society as the embodiment and perfect manifestation of womanhood, the black female has to compete. Thus she has learned to straighten her hair and shape it into whatever style white women happen to be wearing (a style created by white men). She has learned to wear the advertisement fashions (created by white men). She has tried to be a white woman, because this is what black men could not help but want, seeing no other images around them. This situation has been changing radically in the past three years, as the black community becomes increasingly conscious of its ethnic values. And, as more and more begin to accept that "black is beautiful," the attitudes toward interracial relationships are also changing. Many young black men now consider it a matter of virtue not to "give a white woman the honor of sleeping with me." Many young blacks harshly criticize those whom they consider to be "talking black and sleeping white." Black women, with their Afros, have achieved for the first time a place of distinction in the black male mind.

While society still disapproves of the white woman–black man, that disapproval is more and more expressed in private and not in its mores, at least in the large metropolitan areas outside the South. In addition, practically every large American city has within its confines a "liberated zone" set up by the young. These "liberated zones" have always existed, but they are becoming increasingly larger and more populated. Forty years ago, it was only in literary, artistic circles that one might occasionally see a "mixed" couple. In the thirties, the Communist Party was another circle. With the beat generation, the civil rights movement, and the hippies each following the other in rapid succession, the "liberated zone" is now quite large. While attitudes against interracial couples intensify within the black community, one sees more and more interracial couples in the "liberated zones" of New York's Greenwich and East Villages.

One such couple is Susan and David Williams (the names are fictitious). Susan is a thirty-one-year-old blonde, blue-eyed violinist, the mother of three and the wife of David, an artist. They have been married nine years and most of her time now is given to the raising of the children, though she still practices the violin and performs, generally with chamber groups, in small concerts several times a year. She is an attractive woman and because she looks nineteen, she is often mistaken for the babysitter when she is seen on the street with her three children (ages seven, five, and three). At least, people want to believe that she's the babysitter.

SCENE: The Williams' apartment. A loft in lower Manhattan. It is furnished in the style of the New York intellectual-artistic young, i.e., a little of this and a little of that. The living room is a combination of small, hand-carved Spanish statues, African sculpture and masks. David's painting of a lynching dominates the room. Posters of Che, a Vietnamese woman, and Mao are affixed on other walls. Bookshelves. Books. Children's toys. Straight-back chairs. A small bed for a divan. It is a winter afternoon. The cold sunlight comes through the kitchen windows where we are sitting at a long oak table. Susan, looking like a young Greenwich Village matron, a piece of bright yellow yarn holding her blonde hair in a pony tail. She wears no make-up, but the light reflecting on the deep orange of her blouse adds color to her face. The prospect of being interviewed frightens her, yet she is curious to know what she might learn about herself and her relationship with David. Except for one of the Bach French Suites on the stereo, the loft is quiet. The children are at school. David is in the studio at the front of the loft. Coffee cups fingered nervously. Cigarettes. I speak with Susan.

JULIUS LESTER: *Well, let's start at the beginning. How did you and David meet?*

SUSAN WILLIAMS: We met at one of those so-called progressive camps. You know the kind. If they have one black, they think they're setting the world on fire. I don't know how it is now, but that's the way it was in 1960. The civil rights movement had just started and Negroes were becoming fashionable. David calls it the age of "We're having a party. You bring the guitar, I'll bring the Negro." And David was the perfect person to invite. He was black and he played guitar. He was the guitar teacher at the camp and I was a counselor.

JL: *Had you had much contact with blacks before you met him?*

SW: Not black men. I'm from a small town in California. And I do mean small. I don't think it's even on the map. There were a couple of black kids in my high school, but I never came in contact with them.

JL: *Why not?*

SW: I don't know. That's just the way it happened. We used to wonder about them, and looking back now I can see that we should've made some effort to make friends with them. I've often wondered since if they were lonely because they never took part in anything at school. But I didn't know then what I know now. None of us did. My parents were liberal. My father's a teacher, so I knew a little about the so-called race problem or whatever you want to call it. But it didn't mean that much to me. I knew you weren't supposed to say "nigger" and that kind of thing. But I can't recall ever talking to a black person until I got to college and I never dated a black man before I met David. At the same time, I didn't try to avoid blacks. I wasn't where they were and they weren't where I was.

JL: *That sounds like the typical liberal cop-out answer.*

SW: Maybe it is, but I'm not saying it as an excuse. It's merely an explanation. The cop-out comes if a white person tries to escape responsibility for that. It's a fact, I think, that it's impossible to grow up white in this country and not be infected with racism. I wonder if it isn't impossible for blacks not to grow up infected with racism, too. Anyway, I grew up with what I would call a small dosage rather than a large one. There were some kids who really hated blacks and let you know it at every opportunity. And while I didn't fight them, I at least knew they were wrong.

JL: *What kind of person were you then?*

SW: Oh, I was pretty wild, believe it or not. I would cut school for weeks at a time and go drag-racing with the boys and that kind of thing. When I went to college, I made sure it was to one of those schools that didn't have rules. And I spent my college years riding motorcycles and smoking pot, and that was at a time when only a daring few smoked. This was in the late fifties and the beat generation was the thing. Long hair, no make-up, and oh-so intellectual. I was a kind of middle-class, arty Hell's Angel.

JL: *This was the age of what Mailer calls the "white Negro." Would you put yourself in that category?*

SW: Not consciously. I mean, I wasn't trying to be black. There were a few kids on campus who were. They would work hard at listening to jazz and smoking pot and wearing sunglasses, using slang and things like that. That wasn't me. Even though I described myself as being wild, no matter how high I was, I still practiced violin four hours a day.

JL: *You mentioned that the first blacks you knew were in college?*

SW: There was one black girl that I became close friends with and we still see each other occasionally. We used to have political discussions all the time. We talked a lot about race, and one spring vacation I went home with her. That was my first contact inside the black community and it was really strange . . . the food, the way her parents and her friends talked. I found out that blacks weren't white people who just came out the wrong color. And I think she had a lot of conflicts about going to a white school and yet wanting to come back after school and relate to where she grew up. And she was really determined not to marry a white man. She dated a lot of white guys, because that was practically all there was at the school. But she was determined to marry black and she did.

JL: *Outside of her, you didn't know any other blacks?*

SW: I had acquaintances, but nothing like the relationship I had with her.

JL: *What did you do when you finished school?*

SW: Well, I didn't finish. At least not then. I dropped out at the end of my junior year. I guess I was the typical bright young girl who goes to college and doesn't have the slightest idea what she wants to do. I was a good violinist, but I really wasn't interested in entering competitions and trying to be a full-time professional. I enjoyed playing and would've been just as happy settling down to fourth chair in some reasonably good orchestra. But what you have to go through to get fourth chair was more than I wanted to contend with. And I didn't want to teach music. On the other hand, I wasn't particularly anxious to get married. So, there I was, caught in the female dilemma, you might say. A college woman is almost forced to choose between dim job prospects or marriage. She really can't compete with a man for a job. They would take a male violinist before they'd take me, even if I were better. Men don't like female competition and men have the power. They really do. So what does a woman do? She does what she doesn't want to do and gets married, and one day, between the diaper pail and the stove, she goes quietly insane and her husband never knows. The alternative is to disappear into that underground of young "swinging chicks" out for a good time. A sophisticated good time, of course, but by the time you're twenty-three, you've gone quietly insane, too. And it happened one day when you woke up and couldn't remember the name of the guy you found yourself in bed with and couldn't remember the name of the one who was there the night before.

I guess I was headed in the latter direction, so I quit school, came to New York and started working for an insurance company. At night I would walk up and down the streets of the Village until I met someone who was less obnoxious than the others and it was home to bed. So often sex is nothing more than an attempt to establish a beachhead against loneliness. After a semester of that I went back to school to get a teaching certificate. I mean, a woman can always teach and go quietly insane at the blackboard one day.

JL: *Is being a woman that grim?*

SW: Painful. Painful's the word. I mean, beneath all the beautiful faces and beautiful figures is despair, and you dress it up in a miniskirt and fishnet stockings and tell yourself you're free because your legs are showing. But I knew I wasn't free. Sleeping with one man forever is considered slavery by some. Sleeping with ten is another kind of slavery. I could probably have written a comparative study of mattresses, but I knew something was wrong. Then I met David the summer after I finished school and I found out what had been wrong. I wasn't a *thing* to him. God, it took him a month to get around to kissing me. I had seldom dated a guy who hadn't tried to touch me the first night. David and I could talk about Bach, politics, art, you name it.

JL: *Was that all there was to it?*

SW: Do you mean did his being black have anything to do with it?

JL: *Yes.*

SW: Probably. That would be unavoidable. It's not talked about as much, but I think white women have as much, if not more, curiosity about black men as black men are supposed to have about white women. That's unavoidable growing up in the Western world. But I didn't fall in love with him because he was black. If blackness had been the attraction, I would've gone to bed with some of those blacks who were plentiful on those nights when I left work and went down to the Village.

JL: *Why didn't you let any of them pick you up?*

SW: I think I was afraid of them. They would sit on the benches in the park and yell at you as you went by, "Hey, bitch!" That's just not the way to approach me. I was terrified as it was and never got used to picking up men. I was a scared little girl and all I knew was that I didn't want to go home alone to a dark, empty apartment. So as soon as I found a man who I thought would at least be gentle, be a little bit warm, that was enough. The black guys who approached me never struck me as being like that.

JL: *What were the exact circumstances under which you met David?*

SW: Oh, God! Do I have to tell you? I mean, I will, but it's embarrassing. We were at the camp and it was one of the pre-camp orientation sessions for counselors only. Well, after dinner the first night, I came out of the dining room into the rec hall and he was sitting in a corner playing the guitar. I went over to him and asked him if he knew any blues.

JL: *What did he say?*

SW: This is where it gets funny. He said yes, and started singing something. I don't remember what now. After we were married he told me that he had never sung the blues before I asked him, but he figured I didn't know any more about the blues than he did and he was right.

JL: *So because he was black, you expected a certain thing of him?*

SW: Yes. That's that unconscious racism. I just thought any black person with a guitar could sing the blues. As it turned out, David played and still plays a very fine classical guitar and hasn't played the blues since we got married. I can't stand to think about it now and I just wonder why he didn't slap me.

JL: *Were there other incidents like that?*

SW: Not that I can remember. And if he hadn't had the guitar I wouldn't have expected anything of him. I sure didn't expect him to be the noble savage or anything like that.

JL: *Did you expect anything of him sexually?*

SW: If I had, I sure would've been disappointed because it took him so long to get around to sex. I was ready the first night.

JL: *I guess you know what's coming next.*

SW: Is it true what they say about black men, right?

JL: *Something like that.*

SW: I guess if I had believed that his being black was supposed to give him some sort of fantastic sexual powers, that's the way it would've been. I enjoy sleeping with him, but I don't lie there thinking that this is a black man fucking me. But that's what everybody wants to know. How big is it? How long is it? Is it really better? Sometimes I feel that every white man whom David and I pass on the street wants to get me into bed to prove that he, a white man, is better than David. And every black woman wants to get David away from me to prove that she, a black woman, is better than me. White men see us and the foundations of Western civilization are at stake. Black women see us and the essence of black culture is at stake. David and I go to bed and it's an historical event. Now Jim Brown and Raquel Welch are in a movie—the bodies of the Western world—and everybody has his fantasies made manifest. Both of them are probably impotent.

JL: *You sound a little bitter.*

SW: No. Just a little resentful. Why should others have the power to project their images and their perverted fantasies upon a private relationship? Yet this society gives them that power. I see it in terms of the kids a lot. I go to the doctor and he wants to know if my husband is Italian. I mean, he can't relate to them as children. Their darkness bothers him. Their darkness contrasts with my all-American whiteness and he has to know. He has to classify them.

JL: *Do you get that kind of thing often?*

SW: This morning I was taking Michele, the three-year-old, to nursery school. We're walking down the street minding our own business and this woman stops, looks, and says, "She isn't. . . ." Her voice just kind of trailed off. I decided I wouldn't help her one damn bit. "Isn't what?" I asked. She wouldn't say it, though. She just shook her head and wandered off.

JL: *How do the children react?*

SW: By the time they were three they knew that they were black and they knew that anyone who thought there was something wrong with that was not too well. They've had to understand a lot earlier than most kids. They still don't understand why white people feel the way they do. If you ever want to know how ridiculous prejudice is, try explaining to a black child why a white person he doesn't know and has never seen before hates him. There is no explanation, but you have to teach your child how to handle it. So you tell him that these people are crazy, which, as I think about it, is perhaps literally true. It's amazing what passes for sanity in this country.

Sometimes it has its amusing side though. One day Michele and I were in a cab and the conversation with the driver turned, as it always does, to race. And it goes without saying that the cab driver didn't think too highly of blacks. He couldn't see too well into the back seat, but even I was a little surprised when he came out with, "Lady, now tell the truth, you wouldn't want your daughter to marry one, would you?" He had hardly seen Michele, but the natural, unquestioned assumption was that Michele was white. Well, I took great pride in saying, "Oh, I wouldn't mind. She is one." He almost had a wreck he turned around so far. The amazing thing to me, though, was his utter refusal to believe it. Michele is light and in New York she's mistaken for Puerto Rican sometimes, but never for white. But he wouldn't accept it. He just kept saying, "Aw, lady. You're putting me on." It ended the conversation though.

JL: *Did you anticipate any of these kinds of problems before you got married? Did you have any doubts about marrying a black man?*

SW: No. I used to feel uncomfortable at first whenever we went out. People stared so much. But David told me not to stare back and that way I wouldn't notice it. Outside of that, I had more doubts about getting married, period.

JL: *How did your parents react to your marrying David?*

SW: Like Spencer Tracy and Katharine Hepburn. They didn't like it one bit. About a year before David and I got married, a cousin of mine had been going out with a black man, but she'd broken the relationship off before it got serious. My mother told me that she thought my cousin had been sensible. This was before I met David. Well, when I told them we were getting married, they flipped. They knew we were living together and that didn't bother them. Like I said, they're liberal. David and I could've fucked in the subway and they would've found some libertarian ground on which to defend me. I could've slept with a different black man every night for a year and wrote and told them about each one. That wouldn't have bothered them. But marriage! We'd been living together for six months and they hadn't minded. I couldn't understand them. Be a whore, but don't get married.

Well, they flew into town and tried every trick in the book. First they told me to "think of the children," how miserable they would be and what problems they would have. Well, I thought of the children and thought, what better way to show your little liberal belief in an egalitarian society than a child who would be an amalgam of African, Indian, and white blood on David's side and Scotch-Irish-German on mine. They couldn't quite see that. Then they got personal and dug up my past and told me I was crazy and this really proved it. I felt I was doing the first sensible thing I'd ever done. At that juncture, my mother started crying and my father threatened to commit suicide. My father went so far as to tell David how much money he gave to CORE each year. That remark really did it. We would've gotten married then if we had had to file for divorce the next day.

JL: *Have your parents changed?*

SW: Oh, yes. It took them about six months, but I think what really did it was those children they said we shouldn't bring into the world. When David, Jr., was born, my mother broke all records getting here to see him. It was her first grandchild and that was all she cared about. I never said anything to her or my father, but I couldn't help but wonder if they had forgotten all they had said about why we shouldn't have children. David hadn't forgotten. My father wanted to take a picture of David, Jr., and David wouldn't let him. He said the flashbulbs would hurt his eyes. David knew that a week-old baby can hardly see, so the flash wouldn't have bothered him. But David would've broken my father's camera to keep him from getting those pictures. My father was very hurt, too. I think maybe he understood.

JL: *From all that you've said, it seems that you were pretty naive about what it meant to be black when you and David got married. You seem to have gone into it with a sort of open-eyed innocence.*

SW: Well, I guess that's true. Maybe if David had raised some objections or shown some fear, then I would've reacted differently. But he didn't. In fact, we hardly discussed race before we got married.

JL: *Why?*

SW: It just never came up. That may sound strange, but it's true. And remember, that was in 1960. We would wonder vaguely if we would have problems, but we figured that if we did we could solve them. The minister who married us gave us this little lecture on what a difficult thing it was we were doing. We didn't know what he was talking about and still don't really. Marriage is an act of faith anyway. I mean, when you sit down and think about it, it's ridiculous. You pledge to love one person for the rest of your life. Wow! You've got to be open-eyed and innocent to do that.

JL: *I guess if you anticipate problems before you marry somebody, you don't marry them.*

SW: The problems we have had couldn't have been anticipated. They've been problems brought about by events in the world which, of course, we couldn't predict or control.

JL: *Like what?*

SW: Well, let me come at it this way. When we married, 1 could only see blackness from a white point of view. You know, segregation, prejudice, discrimination. I couldn't see it from David's. When we started living together, I saw his drawings, paintings, etchings and even then, in 1960, he was concerned with black people in his work. And for some reason that seemed perfectly natural to me. The first time a problem came up was after we'd been married a couple of months. He was going to Harlem to sketch one afternoon and I asked him if I could come along. He said no, not with him. He said I didn't fit in Harlem and that he knew how black people would feel seeing the two of us walk down the street together and he didn't want to inflict that pain on them. Well, I was pretty upset. It didn't make any sense to me. It seemed as if he were trying to deny me, to deliberately cut me out of a part of his life.

JL: *Why did you feel that way?*

SW: Well, I'd been brought up on the American Dream, where a husband and wife are supposed to share everything. You know, the family gets into the Ford station wagon together and faces life. So, I just couldn't understand why I couldn't go with him. Naturally, I wondered if there was some black woman he was going to see. It wouldn't have been the problem it became if it hadn't fed so directly into all of my insecurities, and I have a warehouse full of them. It took me a long time to understand why I couldn't share a lot of things with him. Now we lead two separate lives in many respects and it's OK most of the time.

JL: *Most of the time?*

SW: I have fewer insecurities now about our relationship, and myself. But I still have some which can rise to the surface every now and then.

JL: *Has this separateness in your life and David's made a difference in your relationship?*

SW: Yes, but it's been good, I think. I guess it would be different if we didn't have a common viewpoint about most things. David's pretty much of a loner and being who he is, an artist and an intellectual, what goes on in his head is his reality. And the same is true for me. If either of us were a social person, a person who likes to go to parties or have people around all the time, then there wouldn't be much of a life we could share. I mean, if David really had to be among people all the time, then he couldn't be married to me. He has friends who hate whites, but they accept him because they never see me. He sees them away from the house and everything's fine. He has a whole existence in the black community about which I know only what he tells me. It's taken me almost nine years to really accept that and not feel threatened by it. David spends a part of each year in the South, sketching. That's been very hard to accept. I can't go because I'm white. He says that he can't share the South with me. He grew up there and that's really home to him. He said that if I came he would feel that he was a guide and I was a tourist and he claims there's really no reason why I have to go South with him each year. Well, believe you me, we've had many a fight over that. Once he left and stayed away for two years.

JL: *Two years!*

SW: Two years. Oh, he'd come home once a month and we'd fight and he'd go back. Not so much because we'd fought, but because the South was where he had to be then. It was the most miserable two years of my life. Crying myself to sleep every night, hating him and yet not being able to call it quits.

JL: *Why did he stay away so long?*

SW: Well, like I said before, he'd been drawing and painting black people ever since I had known him. At the same time he felt isolated, because he wasn't participating in the civil rights movement. They didn't need artists. They needed organizers and he didn't feel that was his role. The civil rights movement expanded conceptually with black power and David saw that this was his opportunity to become totally involved. The movement could use his abilities at that point.

JL: *I'm amazed, in a way, that your marriage survived. I know several mixed couples whose relationships rapidly degenerated into nigger-baiting and honky-baiting with the advent of black power.*

SW: I can see how that could happen. But couldn't that only happen if the black person in the relationship hadn't realized he was black before black power? I remember David telling me about one couple who didn't make it past 1966. The guy became blinded by her whiteness. Or maybe he loved her because she was white, and all of a sudden loving a white woman wasn't the surest way to fame and fortune. I guess our relationship would've ended very quickly if he had married me because I'm white or I him because he's black. He didn't discover his blackness with black power. He merely found the political framework he needed.

JL: *I'm sure, however, that his blackness became intensified. Did you feel threatened by this?*

SW: Our marriage was threatened, but more because he wasn't here. I'm one of those women who always has to have the man they love physically around. I just can't take being away from him. I want him here even if he doesn't talk for two weeks, which isn't unusual for him. At least he's here. The intensification of his blackness, as you put it, wasn't threatening to me, because I could grasp that intellectually. When we married, I was the one who talked revolution. David didn't want to hear about it. I was always more involved in politics than he was. So black power made good political sense to me and I could even understand David's involvement. I just wanted him to stay at home and be involved, or take me and the children South with him. But intellectually I knew why neither of those was realistic. But I still have difficulty with it emotionally.

JL: *Does it make you wish you were black?*

SW: Not really. If I had been black, I'm not sure that David would've taken me South with him. And you have to know David to really understand that.

JL: *You really don't know what he would've done if you were black, do you? I mean, it's safer to think that he wouldn't have taken you if you had been black.*

SW: Well, like I said, you have to know David. Sure, I guess what I said sounds like a rationalization. OK. Maybe it is. But I don't think so. It's really irrelevant, though. I mean, it's irrelevant to whether or not I wish I were black. It's really impossible for me to wish that I were black, because I don't feel white. That probably doesn't make any sense.

JL: *Not yet.*

SW: OK. To say the obvious, I'm white. But I don't identify with whiteness. I have no culture and no country, which is the Anglo-Saxon dilemma. If I were Jewish, I'd have a culture and a country. If my background were Italian or Polish or Greek, it would be the same. But I'm not even a WASP, since my parents were agnostics. So I don't identify with whiteness. The only thing with which I can identify is womanness and that brings me into a relationship with blackness. As a woman, I can identify with the prejudice that blacks have to fight. Whites are prejudiced against blacks. They have a set of rules, of generalizations about blacks which they impose upon every black person to such an ex-

195

tent that individual blacks don't exist in the white mind. It's the same way with women. We aren't people. We are things. "A woman's place is in the home" is definition number one and we're accepted as long as we know our place. And that place is at the typewriter typing somebody else's letters, term papers, books. Or at the stove and in bed. We're called "broads," "chicks," "sweetie," "doll," and "baby." We get into a serious discussion with a man and he will eventually try to put us down with "Only a woman would say something like that." So I sometimes wonder how much of the white woman–black man thing in this society is because white women suffer at the hands of white men just as blacks have.

JL: *Many blacks would say that they have suffered equally as much at the hands of white women. Black women would definitely say that.*

SW: That's true, but the root of it, I think, is in the fact that this is a society dominated and controlled by the white male. They define the roles of women, too.

JL: *I think it's a little more complicated than that.*

SW: Oh, I would agree, but I was saying all that to try and show you why I wouldn't wish I were a black woman.

JL: *What you're saying is that because you have a heightened consciousness as a woman, David's blackness has helped you illuminate your own experience.*

SW: To a degree. I can't identify with David culturally and I've never tried. I'm not "hip." I don't use slang. I don't even try to dance. I don't try to talk like he does. In other words, I don't try to live black. Politically, however, there is a commonness between blacks and women in how they've been oppressed. And it's on this level that I can identify and not feel personally threatened by black power or anything else black.

JL: *Well, it seems to me that you're leaving out one important thing.*

SW: Only one?

JL: *Well, it's a key one. How do black women fit into your analysis? I mean, if there's this natural coalition between white women and black men, what's the black woman supposed to do?*

SW: I've thought of that and I just don't know. If I were a black woman, I would hate white women. And I guess that's why I don't feel comfortable with black women. I feel like they hate me and they have every right to.

Of course, there wouldn't be any problem if most white women weren't so obnoxious. You talk to a white man and you're talking to the preserver of Western civilization. You see a white man walking down the street and you're looking at a 2,000-year-old ego. White men are raised to identify with and uphold whiteness. White women are brought up to support that, but they don't carry the burden. Blacks are supposed to fall in line too. But they don't and a lot of white women don't. Let me qualify that. Some white women don't. But what do white women have to thank Western civilization for? Virginia Slim cigarettes? You've come a long way, baby, from cooking over an open fire to cooking on a gas stove.

JL: I'm just not sure I can agree with what you say about white women. The white man has raised the white woman to believe that she is the Queen of the World and I think you underestimate the number of white women who wear the crown proudly and consider it their obligation to defend it. White women set the beauty standard for women all over the world and you have women in Japan going to clinics to get their eyes widened. Maybe you've never noticed those white women walking down the street who let a black man know that he should jump at the opportunity to sleep with her, that he should consider himself blessed. I guess you've never been to one of those parties and watched the white girls try to get the black men away from the black women. It's an ugly, vicious scene. The black woman threatens the white woman's right to sit on the throne. Maybe you're right, but I don't think too many white women see themselves emotionally aligned with black men because of a common oppression. Black men are toys to most white women.

SW: Maybe you're right. I sometimes tend to try and generalize on the basis of my relationship with David. I shouldn't do that. If what you say is true then I guess all white people have to go.

JL: You can accept that? You can include yourself in that?

SW: As long as I can kill a few whites before some black person gets me, yes.

JL: You said a little while ago that if you were a black woman, you would hate white women. I take it that you don't feel bad enough to leave David though.

SW: What can I say? I was lucky enough to marry the man I felt I needed. He is black and it's a bad time historically for a white woman and a black man to love each other. So I try as best I can to live with the pain of history. I mean, I'm not an individual anymore. No one is.

So my individual happiness may have to take a back seat because a race of people are trying to weld themselves into a nation.

JL: *Does that mean you may have to give up David to that nation?*

SW: I guess that's the implication and I get the feeling from David that that is what a lot of his black friends tell him.

JL: *Would you give him up?*

SW: Ask me to kill myself. I want David, and I want that nation to come into being. And I'm going to try and have both.

JL: *And what if you can't?*

SW: Right now, I just can't accept that. I just can't. And frankly, I hope that I die before I have to make such a decision, if that time ever comes.

JL: *Do you feel funny having three black children?*

SW: No.

JL: *Muhammad Ali says that any person wants children that look like them.*

SW: That's too narrow for me. My children are black, but that's their historical definition. They also have individual definitions. It's like me and David. I look at him and I see David, not a black man. I'm aware of his individuality. I'm Susan and he's David and nobody can look at us and really know what that means. They can only see a white woman and a black man.

JL: *Suppose something happened to David. Would you marry another black man?*

SW: Well, if I remarried, I probably would. I guess the first considera-tion would be the children, who are black. I would want them to have a black father. Secondly, after almost ten years, I've become a part of a particular atmosphere, a way of looking at things, which comes partly from the kind of person David is and partly from the fact that David is black, which can't be separated from the person he is. At the same time, I wouldn't marry a black man per se, if you follow me. I would marry the man who most made me feel like me, but I would do my looking, probably, among black men, because I think that's where I would find somebody who would make me feel as David makes me feel.

198

JL: *Are you saying that black men are better than white men?*

SW: I don't like that kind of question. You're asking me to generalize and I'm afraid to do that with a question which I don't understand. Whatever I said, it wouldn't mean anything.

JL: *A lot of young blacks would say that because David married you, he isn't black.*

SW: I know.

JL: *Yet David is black for you. Does it bother you that many blacks might not think so?*

SW: Well, isn't it simply that we see this black man from different angles, from different points of view? And because I don't see him as you do, you want me to deny the validity of what I see. I guess if the definition of blackness is to hate me, then David isn't black. And maybe that's what the problem is: whose definition is valid.

JL: *And?*

SW: I don't know. I want mine to be, but history is with blacks. So I can't know. After all, Julius, I'm one of the questions, aren't I?

David Williams is a thirty-four-year-old black artist. He is of average height, medium-brown-skinned, with intense brown eyes and black hair, which he wears cut close to his head. He dresses casually, affecting no identifiable style of dress. David Williams (the name is fictitious) is a painter, who in the last three years has concentrated more and more on illustrations, cartoons, and posters. For the past nine years he has been married to a white woman, who is a musician and the mother of their three children. (See *Evergreen Review* No. 70 for an interview with his wife, Susan.)

The interview took place in David's studio, which is in the front of the Williams' loft in lower Manhattan. The studio is a huge room, with bare white walls. A drawing board sits in one corner. Next to it is a long table which extends for ten feet along the wall. At the end of the table are a series of file cabinets. Behind a partition at the opposite corner of the room is a bed, a two-burner gas stove with refrigerator underneath. Thus the studio is a self-contained unit, enabling David to "drop out of sight for weeks at a time." The only other items in the studio are a stereo system and bookshelves filled with records and books.

Throughout the interview David sits in a rocking chair facing the windows through which the skyline of midtown Manhattan looms. A small lamp over his drawing board is the only light in the room.

DAVID WILLIAMS: Before you get started I just thought I should let you know that I have mixed feelings about doing this interview.

JULIUS LESTER: *What do you mean?*

DW: Well, anybody in America can get married and they aren't given a second thought. A black man marries a white woman and everybody thinks they have a right to an opinion on it. So, to some degree I can't help but resent doing an interview about my personal life.

JL: *So why are you letting yourself be interviewed?*

DW: I don't know. As much as I feel that no one has the right to know about me and Susan, that doesn't mean I'm right. I'm right in an absolute sense, but the fact remains that there's a world out there that impinges on us every day and Susan and I exist in relation to that world. So I swallow my pride and sit through this interview to satisfy the world's curiosity.

JL: *Does the world impinge on you a lot?*

DW: Every day in each and every way, jim. Being black means you carry the world on your back twenty-four hours a day. Being black and married to a white woman means you carry it forty-eight hours a day. I'm overstating it a little, but sometimes it feels that way. Like the ol' folks used to say, "Sometimes my cotton sack gets so heavy." You know what I mean? Every time we leave the house together, which is at least once a day, I can feel the people looking at us. Some are hostile and that you can deal with. That's no problem. But we walk into a restaurant in the Village and the stares are the curious kind. "Wonder what their story is? How did they get together? What's she like? What's he like?" That kind of thing, you know. And I'd just like to walk in and not be noticed by anyone except the waiter. And, of course, the waiter is the last one to notice you.

JL: *How do you raise three black children to be black when their mother is white?*

DW: Well, you don't tell them black is beautiful. That's the first thing you *don't* do. What you try to do is make sure they never get the idea in their heads that black is ugly.

JL: *How do you do that?*

DW: Well, I think that a lot of it has to do with the atmosphere that exists in the house. If kids feel secure inside the home, then when they start school and have to deal with the world on their own, they have their roots in some kind of firm base. So that I don't go around the house preaching blackness or anything like that. But I make sure that they have books to look at in which there are black people and things to look at on the wall which deal with black people and that they know, as well as they can, that they are black. It's a hard thing to talk about, because so much of it involves being, not talking. You know what I mean?

JL: *What do you tell them about white people?*

DW: To be wary. Don't trust too quickly. I mean, it's tricky. I want them to be prepared to deal with "the man." I don't want them to be alienated from their mother. It's tricky and, once again, I can't lay out a program for you in terms of how you can do it.

JL: *Do you really think you can do that successfully?*

DW: Sure. After all, I'm married to their mother. Susan's not white to me or them. She's Susan. She's mommy. White is not her definition to us. That's the world's definition. So it's only when you start seeing things through the world's eyes that it becomes a serious problem.

JL: *Haven't you ever gotten mad at Susan and called her or thought of her as a honky bitch?*

DW: Uh-uh. If I get mad at Susan and want to hurt her, well, I'll talk about some of her habits or something about her personality. The fact that Susan is white is not uppermost in my mind. That's important in everybody else's mind. I'm not even sure I know what white means in relation to her. She doesn't communicate whiteness. She communicates Susan-ness, or womanness-as-Susan-ness, if that makes any sense.

JL: *Was she the first white girl you ever dated?*

DW: No. I dated a couple in college.

JL: *Where was that?*

DW: A black school down South. It's one of those schools where the cream of the black bourgeoisie crop go to get white. At least that's what it was in the fifties when I was there. A lot of the girls had been debutantes in their home towns and stuff like that. They had wardrobes worth more than a Mississippi sharecropper makes in two years. Most of them came to school to join a sorority and get a husband and, naturally, he had to be a doctor or a lawyer or something like that. Somebody who was going to buy them a house and keep them in clothes. Their minds were like blank checks and the guy who could write in the biggest figures became their husband.

That was the kind of school it was and I guess I was the nigger in the woodpile, so to speak. My background isn't poor. I mean, I never had to eat fatback and cornbread every day for a month or anything like that. We were never hard up for money, but my father didn't have a lot of black middle-class attitudes. He's a Baptist preacher and he had a Cadillac. You know them Baptist church people take care of their preachers. Ain't no doubt about that! And my daddy knows which side his bread is buttered on. He knows that if he starts acting too educated or too high-fallutin', as the old folks say, he ain't gon' have no church. So daddy keeps in good with the brothers and sisters of the community. He'll split a verb quicker than a rooster will jump on a hen. He goes possum hunting a couple of times a year with some of the deacons and things like that. And it's not phony with him. He feels more comfortable with poor people and he hates middle-class people. He can always get the church rocking when he starts talking about "these Negroes who go around here with their noses in the air and forget that their mama is still on her knees scrubbing the white folks' floors!" He's a good cat, very earthy, and I take after him. And nothing brings out the bona-fide nigger in me like a bunch of middle-class niggers. I go out of my way to be offensive when I'm around them and as a result, I wasn't the most popular cat on campus. I didn't shine any shoes or wear a suit and tie, or talk proper or learn how to hold my teacup. Hell, I was the only dude on campus who'd bring his wine bottle to class.

Now the really funny thing about all this is that in high school and college I was always falling head over heels in love with the most middle-class, bourgeois, tight-ass chicks on the scene. But them bitches were fine, jim! My freshman year in college I fell in love with a girl I would've given both arms for. Man, she was so fine the sun used to rise two hours early just so he could see her before anybody else. I ain't lying! She was the kind of chick you'd eat a mile of her shit just to see where it came from. She was fine! And I wanted that girl. I really did. Now see, I knew that if I showed up on campus in my old man's Cadillac and with a suit and tie on, talked real nice, that chick would've followed me wherever I went. And you know what? To this day I can't drive because I didn't want a girl digging me because of my old man's car. I'm so perverse that sometimes I don't understand me. Everything I shouldn't have done to get that girl, I did. Every time I was around her I'd go out of my way to be uncouth and loud and country and vulgar. I'd go up to her and pull out my wine bottle and ask her if she wanted a little taste. Man, that chick hated me worse than LBJ hated Bobby Kennedy.

It was a weird thing. I was attracted to them, but I hated them. I'd take a girl out and the first thing she wanted to know was what my daddy did, what kind of car he had, and what was I studying to be. I'd tell her my daddy was a crap-shooter and he had a motorcycle until the finance company came and got it and I was studying pussy, hers in particular. Well, I need not tell you what kind of reaction I got. I just couldn't stand those phony bitches, but there wasn't anything else around.

My sophomore year I met my first real love. She sure did justice to a pair of high heels, too. She was from New York, an art major, and she had a big influence on me. She'd been exposed to a lot of things I'd never even heard of. In my home town the only resource I had was the colored library and you know where that was at. So she turned me on to a lot of things. But after one year she couldn't cut it anymore and went on back to New York and left me to make it on my own. She was a sweet woman, too.

But in thinking about it, I guess the reason I acted so contrary around those girls was because I wanted them to accept *me*. You know? Not my clothes, or my car, or my daddy's status, or anything like that. So I would just make myself so repulsive that if they loved me I knew it was for real and then I could drop the act. But I had to be accepted on my terms. That was it. I didn't want to be what they wanted me to be. And they wanted me to be their imitation of white.

Now, the whole irony of the situation is that we had this exchange program with some white colleges from up North. They would send some white kids down for a semester and we'd send some black kids up to their schools. It was supposed to be culturally enriching or some bullshit like that. Well, when these white kids came down, they were like me. I mean, not as loud or vulgar or anything like that, but they'd go around barefooted and were pretty bohemian. And these same bourgeois bitches who put me down would be digging and accepting the white kids. Why? They were white! I guess the biggest irony of all was that the white kids were the ones who accepted me on my terms. So my junior year I found myself in love with a white girl.

JL: *Was your relationship with her any different from your relationship with the black girl from New York? The one you went with your sophomore year?*

DW: In essence, no. They both dug me for being me. But there were differences. If you think it can be rough walking down the street with a white girl in New York, do it down South. You keep one eye on the girl and one eye keeps a lookout for the lynch rope. My old man didn't spare any words about white women when I was growing up. "Stay away from white women. Don't look at white women. Don't go near light-skinned colored girls because white people might think they're white." I got all that stuff, but it obviously didn't have much effect on me.

JL: *Why not?*

DW: It just didn't make any sense. I just couldn't understand why I shouldn't look at a good-looking girl no matter if she was white. Just like I couldn't understand why I had to ride in the back of the bus. It just didn't make good sense. Only thing my old man said about white women that made sense was that I could get lynched for messing with one. Lynching I had no difficulty understanding.

JL: *Did your father's preaching against white women make them more attractive to you?*

DW: Probably. If I want my kids to do something, I tell them not to. I guess the more my old man talked about stay away from white women, the more I thought that if white folks didn't like it, it must be good.

JL: *So when you started dating the exchange student, did you feel that you had accomplished something? That you'd gotten a white woman?*

DW: There was a little bit of pride involved. I was defying white folks. Sure, that was an element, but it wasn't the motivation. I wasn't like this one friend of mine who hit on everything white that wore a skirt. If it was white, he wanted it. That wasn't me. If she hadn't been a person that I could talk to and communicate with, there wouldn't have been a relationship.

The really weird thing for me was to find out that I got from whites what I didn't get from blacks. I felt comfortable with the white girls who came down because they didn't demand anything of me except that I be me. And, slowly, I became increasingly afraid of black girls, because they rejected me.

And there's one other thing, which is perhaps the most important. I'm an artist. An intellectual. I was one of those kinds of cats who took a girl out and wanted to discuss concepts of time and shit like that. I was trying to figure out whether God existed. The black girls would look at me like I was stone cold crazy. They couldn't relate to any of that. And then, some little white girl from up North would come down and she'd just recovered from swallowing a bottle of aspirin because she couldn't figure out whether or not life had any meaning. So, like I had some very beautiful, nonromantic relationships with the exchange students.

I wasn't attracted to them because they were white. However, in another sense, I was, if you accept my definition of what white meant in the context I've been trying to lay down. For me it was a liberal, intellectual background. I mean, I came into contact with two kinds of whites. I grew up with hostile crackers to whom I was a nigger. I go to college and I met whites who treated me like a human being, were interested in what I was thinking and I could talk to them and that was because we were both intellectuals. White as white skin, blonde hair, and blue eyes didn't have any meaning to me. But the only people I met at that stage in my life to whom I could relate as an artist and an intellectual were white.

JL: *So, in a sense, you wanted to be accepted by these white kids.*

DW: If by "accepted" you mean get their approval, definitely not. But they were what I measured myself against. I had to prove to myself that I was as smart and talented as they were. You grow up black and whitey sets the standard. Your parents drum it into your head: "If you want to get any place in the world, son, you got to be as good as the white man." That kind of stuff. Well, I knew I was as good as whites. In fact, I knew I was a helluva lot better, but I had to prove it. In my high school in North Carolina, I knew I was the best artist in the school but that didn't mean anything to me. The battle was when you had to tangle with white folks. So the exchange students and the white girl I was in love with did for me what my relationship with Doris, the black girl from New York, did. I learned. I was constantly challenged.

In a real sense, I came alive. When I would tell black people that I wanted to be an artist, they'd smile and say, "That's mighty nice. The race needs good art teachers." Man, you can put some shade on that shit. But that was everyone's assumption. I was going to be an art teacher. I even had one mothafucka tell me, "You may think you're going to be an artist, but you'll end up teaching school like the rest of us." A cat actually said that to me! And I was walking around campus looking at all those blank walls in the buildings and thinking about being the black Diego Rivera and this dude come trying to kill my dream. I walked around thinking about all those faces on the old people and wanting to put that down so everybody could look at their grandfather and stop calling him Uncle Tom. It has never once crossed my mind to be an art teacher. So, like there was no place for me in the black community. Black people had no need of me and white folks didn't want me. So when I finished college, my program was to go to New York, work for a year, and then cut on across the pond and do my thing in Paris or Rome.

JL: *So you felt totally rejected by the black community?*

DW: They didn't encourage me to be me. They were concerned about how I was going to make a living.

JL: *You sound like it's made you bitter.*

DW: To a degree it has. They did everything they could to try and destroy me and I was lucky. They didn't do it, but I know a whole lot of people who weren't so lucky. Like Doris. The black girl from New York? Wiped out, jim. She went back home and people didn't want to hear her dreams. And she didn't fight 'em like I did. She gave in. You ought to see the split-level living room in her house and her neat little kids and then look at her face. She's walking death. Doris was a beautiful woman.

JL: *So if you feel that bitter, how have you maintained a black orientation? I've seen your art and you deal exclusively with black people and quite sympathetically.*

DW: I don't know if I can explain it. I have a love-hate relationship with blacks. Any black person does. The love comes out in my art. The hate comes out in my conversation. A lot of that love comes through my father. He's been one of the strongest figures in my life and he instilled in me a real love for black people, particularly southern, rural blacks. I guess another part of it came through my relationship with Marlene. She was the white girl I went with my junior year. She helped to make me consciously aware of my blackness. Let me qualify that. She didn't do it totally. Becoming aware of your blackness, knowing it, understanding it, is an ongoing thing. But Marlene brought a lot of things to the surface for the first time.

JL: *How?*

DW: Well I guess, number one, just being with her made me consciously fight to maintain my identity. Some cats go out with white women because it brings them as close as they're ever going to get to being white. That couldn't happen to me, because that wasn't my motivation for entering the relationship. But being with her made me aware of so much that I'd never thought about. Too, there was the whole experience of seeing the black world through her eyes. She was seeing it for the first time, so everything was new and exciting to her. And that way I became aware of a lot of stuff that I'd just never thought about. And she was the first girl who ever told me my hair was beautiful. That blew my mind! When she said it I thought she was coming down with some of that deep racist stuff and I jumped bad. "Bitch, you making fun of me? I'll kick your ass!" But she wasn't making fun of me. She didn't know what I was talking about. It took me a while to see that she was right. My hair is beautiful.

It kinda hurts, you know. No black girl ever told me my hair was beautiful. I was always a "nappy-headed nigger" or "a kinky-headed black son-of-a-bitch." Chicks telling me my hair was like steel wool and shit like that. No black chick ever looked at my body and said it was a beautiful color. I had to find all that out from a white girl.

JL: *Do you hate black women because of that?*

DW: You've seen my drawings and things of black women. You know that's not true. I understand now why they said those things. Hell, no black man ever told them they were beautiful. But that's the way it went down. It's different now. Now you got black poets writing poems about how beautiful black women are and black women talking about how together their men are. I don't hate black women, but it's hard to forget those I went to school with.

JL: *How long did your relationship with Marlene last?*

DW: The spring semester of my junior year and through the summer. It just sorta petered out because she went back to her school in Ohio and I went back to mine. But we spent that summer together in New York. She had some kind of job and I just lay around and practiced my guitar and enjoyed life. That's something else. She didn't mind working and supporting me. No black woman would've done that and not resented it. But it was no hang-up for Marlene. And I didn't feel like I was prostituting myself. Hell, I didn't want to work. She did. And it's been the same with me and Susan.

JL: *How did you meet Susan?*

DW: At a summer camp. I was the guitar teacher.

JL: *Why not the art counselor?*

DW: When I said I'd never teach art, I meant it. I had picked up a little classical guitar from Doris and just kept on with it. I used to court

Marlene with Bach preludes. And I enjoy classical guitar, even though I don't play much anymore.

JL: *But why classical guitar?*

DW: The implication being I'm black and I'm not supposed to like classical music. That's bullshit! I also dig Aretha, but I play better Bach than I do blues. It's just that simple. White people stereotype blacks. Blacks stereotype blacks. I try to avoid having anything to do with either.

But back to me and Susan. We were at this camp together. This was the summer after my first year in New York. I was living in Harlem and working in the garment district, trying to save my money to cut out for Europe. But I didn't make enough to save anything because after I bought art supplies each week I was almost broke. I'd walk down the streets and look at everything, man. Everything. Then at night I'd stay up and draw. I was training myself to see, so that I could draw from memory. And that's about all I did.

JL: *No women?*

DW: I saw Doris occasionally. But, like I said, she'd lost the dream and I couldn't respect her. Outside of her, there were a few little things here and there, but they didn't mean anything. It was me, the wine bottle, and a sketchpad. I'd pick up a girl to take home every now and then, but nothing serious. I stayed high so much. I mean, New York's a cruel place, man. Everybody's got a hustle. And everybody's out to do you in. So I spent my season in hell. Then I just happened to see this ad in the *Sunday Times* for a classical guitar teacher at a camp and I got the job. It got me out of the city, because I was on the brink of flipping out completely.

JL: *Was it difficult for you to decide to marry Susan?*

DW: If I hadn't married Susan, I would probably be back home teaching art. I had been so beaten that year that I was close to giving up. Working eight hours a day and then coming home and trying to do what I considered my real work. Loneliness, pain, the whole bit. I was almost ready to give up and I met her, and like my prayers had been answered. She was the one I had been looking for. I know that sounds corny and straight out of Hollywood, but it's true.

JL: *So the fact that she was white didn't give you any reason to hesitate?*

DW: No, it really didn't.

JL: *What was the reaction of your parents?*

DW: Well, I wrote and told them that I was going to marry a white girl and that if they couldn't say anything that would help us, please don't say anything that would hurt us. And that took care of it. I'm sure they weren't overjoyed, but they called and gave me their blessing.

JL: *I know I'm going to sound a little redundant, but I don't believe you when you say you didn't have any doubts about marrying Susan.*

DW: Well, maybe it's semantics. I didn't agonize over it. I wanted to marry her and that was that. I knew that marrying her was different than marrying a black woman. I knew that I would be cutting myself off from black people to a certain extent. But that was one of the consequences I had to accept. It was something I would have to learn to live with.

JL: *Was it important to you that Susan was white?*

DW: Here we go with that again. I don't define Susan as white.

JL: *But she is.*

DW: Right. And here I sit with my definition of Susan defying the world with its definition. When you say she's white, all that means to me is the way her hair looks when the sun comes through the window in the morning. It means the subtle hues her skin takes on depending on the color of what she's wearing. It means her eyes, which are blue, and blue eyes are so weird. They're really fantastic. But all this is aesthetics. Her being white did not qualify her to be my wife.

JL: *Have blacks rejected you because of her?*

DW: Well, black people have never accepted interracial relationships. Never. And now they're saying it, loud and clear. So there has been a lot of rejection. Some find it downright impossible to accept me once they find out that I'm married to Susan. My attitude is that if somebody doesn't dig the fact that I'm married to her, that's their problem. I can respect that, as long as they don't try to tell me that I *shouldn't* be married to her.

But it gets all involved. Some people feel that my marrying a white woman means approval of white people and rejection of blacks. I mean, if you're black in America, it means you aren't an individual. I believe it was Apollinaire, or one of them French poets, who put a crab on a string and went walking down the street. Everybody looked and said, "What's that fool doing?" If he'd been black and done that, they would've said, "What's that nigger doing?" Then they would've called the cops. Like when I was growing up, my mother wouldn't let me get on the bus looking dirty. That's cool. But her reason was not that it's disgusting to be dirty. Uh-uh. Her reason was that white people would think all black people were dirty because I was dirty.

Well, fuck that shit, but that's the way it is. Black people demanded a certain kind of behavior from me because of white folks. Now black people are demanding a certain kind of behavior from me because of black folks. On one level it's progress, but on another level, it has some very bad vibrations. Like young kids saying that Fanon and Frederick Douglass are not relevant to them and they will not read their works because they were married to white women. And nobody challenging that kind of thinking. I had one cat tell me that the reason LeRoi Jones was a revolutionary was because he left his white wife. Well, the implication is that one of the primary qualifications to be a black revolutionary is to have a black woman. And I can't relate to that.

JL: *Do you feel as if you lose anything being married to a white woman?*

DW: I can't live black. You know what I mean? In that life-style sense, because you can only live black with other blacks. OK. I accepted that when I was in love with Marlene.

JL: *I've seen your drawings of black women, like you said, and they are fantastic. How do you think black women feel when they find out you're married to a white woman?*

DW: Oh, they'd like to cut my dick off for a starter. I know how they feel, but my being married to a white woman does not deny the validity of my work. If anything, they should be in awe of my work, that I could be married to a white woman and still be able to see the strength and beauty in black women.

JL: *But how can you totally explore the black experience, the black psyche, to the fullest and be married to a white woman?*

DW: Susan's not a barrier. If she were, I'd split. I mean, I lead a schizophrenic existence. Coming back to what I was just saying about not being able to live black. I can't be around Susan like I am around black people. She wouldn't know how to relate to me. Once I told her that she should look at me as if I were a foreigner and she'd understand a lot more. So I'm schizoid. At those times when I have to, just have to be among black people, I split. I go south for a month, two months or even two years. That's how long it lasted one time.

At the same time, I don't want to stay totally in the black community. I get a different something from hanging out in the Village. I'm schizoid and live on the borderline between the two worlds. Unable to be a part of either, totally, and in a way, not wanting to be. There's pain in the schizophrenia, but most of the time I can live with it. When I can't, I go get some wine.

JL: *During the two-year period when you were away, what happened to your marriage?*

DW: Well, it almost got destroyed. But if I ever have to choose between my marriage and my work, then my marriage has to go and Susan knows that.

JL: *What were you doing while you were away?*

DW: Looking. I had an old, beat-up car, and me and Comrade Wine Bottle were steady on the move. Mississippi to Georgia, up to the Carolinas, across to Virginia, down to Tennessee and back to Mississippi. That's when I started doing posters and cartoons, because I realized that an oil painting was of no use to black people. They needed good art that was functional. Editorial cartoons are functional. Posters are functional. I got rid of a lot of middle-class ideas about art. I became a real black artist. Before my subject matter had always been black, but my way of using it had been Western. Art galleries, museums and like that. Book illustrations are much more relevant. And posters are the best as far as I'm concerned.

JL: *Going back to the schizophrenia for a minute, the implication seems to be that you don't feel whole married to Susan.*

DW: On a personal level, I do. On a racial level, I can't.

JL: *So isn't it hard to be married to her?*

DW: Sometimes. It's hard and it isn't hard. I think part of my problem is words. You know? I mean, it's really weird to try and take what is essentially nonintellectual, our relationship, and lay it out in nice, linear terms, to try and deal with it in words. That's why music and sculpture exist. But the way people use words, and I guess it's in the nature of words, too, everything has to hang together logically. Sentences have a structure.

After my break with *The Guardian*, I was invited to contribute a monthly column to *Liberation*, a radical magazine edited by

Dave Dellinger. Although I was unable to write without some echoes of my now dysfunctional political identity resounding from the page, I called the column "Aquarian Notebook," a tribute not only to my astrological sun-sign but my way of openly identifying with the "hippie" counterculture.

(ARTICLE: "Aquarian Notebook," *Liberation,* December, 1969)

The sixties are coming to an end and it is the time for the writing of eulogies—eulogies for William Moore, Medgar Evers, Chaney, Goodman and Schwerner, James Reeb, Viola Liuzzo, Jonathan Daniels, Jimmie Lee Jackson, Malcolm X, Lee Harvey Oswald, Sammy Younge, Jr., Vernon Dahmer, Bobby Hutton, George Best, Ruby Doris Robinson, Martin Luther King, Jr., those blacks who died in the rebellions of Newark, Detroit, Harlem, Watts, Cleveland and countless other cities and yes, even for Robert Francis Kennedy. (Dying is hard regardless of the political ideology of the deceased.)

It is time to inscribe eulogies on the heart for it is the all-powerful, inexorable image of Death which defines Life. Every minute of every day, Death is there, though when one turns to look at him, he changes into the beautiful face of a friend, or the bright dancing colors of a passing girl's head scarf, or the autumn colors of elm and maple and oak. But Death is always there and occasionally, when feeling forgotten, he will reveal himself suddenly, laughing all the while. (We were sitting in the kitchen that Sunday afternoon in those now dim years before we had children. Friends were coming for dinner and food was cooking on the stove. The radio was on, as it constantly is, and the music stopped abruptly: "We interrupt this broadcast to bring you the following bulletin. Extremist black nationalist leader, Malcolm X, has been shot and seriously wounded as he addressed a small gathering of his followers at the Audubon Ballroom in upper Manhattan. We repeat—" The repetition was unnecessary. I had walked with Death too long to ever doubt or disbelieve him.)

It is the time for the writing of eulogies, particularly this autumn when church bells in small Midwestern towns tolled every four seconds, nailing the reality of death in Vietnam into the hearts of all who heard, when the church congregations in old New England towns listened to the reading of the names of American war dead, when a youth in Washington, D.C., read aloud the names of the war dead at a vigil and could read no more when he heard himself pronounce the name of one of his closest friends of whose death he had not known.

It is time for writing the eulogy of Joan Fox and Craig Badiali. Particularly them, because they chose death on Moratorium Day in the front seat of Craig's father's blue 1962 Ford Falcon. They were seventeen and lived in Blackwood, New Jersey, and chose death because through their dying they hoped that others would gain life. "It seems that people are only touched by death," began one of the notes they left behind. "Maybe people will be touched enough to do something constructive and peaceful with their lives. Then, maybe, our death was worth it." They knew of no other way to communicate the essence of Being to their friends except through the ultimate fact of Non-Being. "Why?" began another note. "Because we love our fellow man enough to sacrifice our lives so that they will try to find the ecstasy in just being alive." It was an act of redemptive love, an act which most Americans have been educated not to understand or respond to. "They were searching for something," one of Joan's friends was quoted as saying, "and when they found it didn't exist they gave up." "The kids had no records," a local policeman commented. "They weren't hippies or anything like that. They were just like everybody else. We're confused. Why did they do it?" And in a local bar, someone wrote what must not be their final epitaph: "They wanted peace? Well, they got peace."

At seventeen they knew of that greater love which leads a man to give his life for others. They knew that and they were only seventeen. They didn't consider themselves "revolutionaries", which is good, considering what passes for "revolutionary" these days. Yet, they knew the truth which led Che, Inti Peredo, Camilo Torres and thousands of others to their deaths. (I never quite understood the symbolism of the crucifixion in Christianity until I read of the deaths of Joan Fox and Craig Badiali. I never liked sitting in church and looking at the crucifix which inevitably hangs where everyone has to see it and maybe I didn't understand because the ministers always said, "Christ died for your sins" and never added that you must die, first within yourself and to yourself and in that act you will gain life everlasting. Once you die to yourself, your physical dying, whenever and however it comes, will not be the termination, but the inception, the resurrection, the beginning.) Joan Fox and Craig Badiali died, so that I might have more life.

Americans are so ill-equipped to understand Death, however. When Norman Morrison immolated himself at the Pentagon, so many, regardless of political beliefs, agreed that he could've been of more "service" if he had stayed alive and worked to end the war. And the same was said about Roger La Porte and Alice Herz. To consciously and willfully and deliberately (with love aforethought) take one's life does not make sense in the American context, which means that there is something wrong with the American context and not with taking one's life as an act of love. Indeed, it is the American context which makes General MacArthur a hero and Roger La Porte some kind of "nut."

October was the month for dying, it seemed. Six days after Joan and Craig died, Jack Kerouac concluded a three-day drinking spree with his death. There are two kinds of loving deaths—the conscious act of Joan and Craig's and the unconscious, but no less deliberate dying of Jack Kerouac. He knew, he had to know, that he was going to die because he lived with such intensity. It was no accident. It simply took Kerouac forty-seven years to complete the process which Joan and Craig finished in seventeen. (He who remembers Kerouac as a force in his life is acknowledging that he is from another generation, a generation that knew no student movements and no political action. Those who would've been the political activists of that day were lonely, spectral figures on campus, travelling many miles through the backyards of their souls. Kerouac was the Che of my coming of age. He was the one who told me that there was another way, a better way, a way that had meaning and I fused the vision he and Allen Ginsberg and Gary Snyder gave me with the knowledge of blackness bequeathed me by my father and thus was born.) Jack Kerouac was a revolutionary, because he made us see, feel and live in a manner counter to that which everyone told us was the only way to live. But to say that he was a revolutionary is to define him in terms which were foreign to him. He was a human being. He was not anti-capitalist, anti-racist, anti-imperialist and would not have understood what that might mean or why people who call themselves revolutionaries would define themselves negatively. If a man tells you what he is for, you know what he is against. But let him tell you what he is against, you still don't know what he is for. Those of us who were a part of that distant piece of American history called the "beat generation" knew what Kerouac was for and there would be less of a radical political movement today if he had not revolutionized the consciousness of so many of us.

Now he is buried in Lowell, Massachusetts, where he was born a French-Canadian-American-Catholic and he died the same. He was one of the truly *American* figures of the last half of the twentieth century. No other country could have produced him, just as no other country but Cuba could have produced Fidel. He was not the America of New York literary cocktail parties, of lunches with editors, of tete-a-tetes with figures of the literary Establishment. His America was of truck stops on midnight Nebraska highways, of cheap liquor and trailer courts, of Horn & Hardarts at closing time. He was the America of William Faulkner and Oxford, Mississippi, of Thomas Wolfe and North Carolina, of Dreiser, Sherwood Anderson and even, Eugene O'Neill. Now he is dead and even those who don't know that he ever lived are better because he chose to kill himself in the act of living and in the act of writing.

(It was one of those sun-filled, sun-laughing days which only exist in California. It was early morning when the plane began its descent to the San Francisco airport. I looked through the window and could see the city poised on its hills.

Kris was waiting for me as I walked into the terminal and in a few moments, we were driving toward the City of St. Francis. She had dropped out of "the movement," having been turned off by everything which was happening. "The movement doesn't have any relationship to anything except itself anymore," she said quietly. "I try to read 'movement' publications and just can't do it. I don't know who they're written for, but it sure isn't me."

We drove into San Francisco and she asked me if there was anything I wanted to do there before we went to her place in Berkeley. There was nothing, except that I did want to see North Beach again, where I had lived in 1959. We drove up Grant Street and it looked little different that August of 1969 than it had when I, in the pain of my twenty years of living, had come to be a part of the "beat generation" and in a small room in a building on the corner of Grant and Columbus, I finished my first novel before going back to the South to be plunged into the sixties. Grant Street looked the same, except there were no familiar faces. The statue of St. Francis was no longer in front of the little Catholic church which was around the corner from where I had seriously contemplated going into a monastery. The statue now stood in front of the Longshoreman's Hall, because the church had wanted to be rid of it. Perhaps it made the priest too aware of his hypocrisy. One could ignore the statue, but if he made the mistake of letting it affect him, it either dominated his life and goaded him into the continual act of trying to be human or one was forced to destroy the statue. The Church appropriated Francis of Assisi for its pantheon, but Francis has never belonged to the Church. It would be different if he did.

We drove down Fisherman's Wharf and I remembered those mornings of ten years before which had been spent there beside the water, looking toward Alcatraz and always toward the Golden Gate Bridge which linked the chasm between the city and Marin County. I could hardly see the bridge that morning. The smog obliterated it and suddenly, I wanted to get away, away from the city of St. Francis, because it was still a city and it was becoming increasingly difficult for me to feel myself in cities. I looked around for some reflection of my Being and all I saw was buildings and grit and dirt and cars and smog and none of it said anything about the Good which I knew was within.

"You feel like driving up the Coast?" I asked her, quietly, but with a feeling of desperation.

"Sure."

In a few minutes we were speeding across the Golden Gate, through Marin County and up into the mountains. Instantly I felt that Good return when I saw the mountains rising above me and heard the quiet in which they were saturated. Curve after curve the road ascended, descended, and ascended yet once again. Kris was driving fast and I gave myself up to the sensuality of motion.

We talked quietly about our lives, particularly about our private pains. She asked me about the exchange which had taken place between Kathleen Cleaver and myself in the Guardian. I wasn't sure that I yet understood what had transpired or why, but I told her what I thought, remarking that 1969 had been my year for losing friends and making enemies because of my political views.

"You aren't the only one," she said. "It's the same out here. People not speaking to each other because they have political differences."

I asked her about friends we had in common and she saw none of them anymore, which meant that there was little point in my trying to see any of them. "I don't understand friendships that are based on politics," she added. "You know? If politics separates you from people, there must be something wrong with your politics."

I slumped down in the seat, letting my knees rest against the dashboard. "I get the feeling that there are thousands of people like us around the country. People who aren't involved in organizations or anything else, but who are still very political, still very concerned, still very involved, but just can't relate anymore to what's called 'the movement.' I just wish I could put my finger on what exactly happened. I mean, why is all this in-fighting and name-calling going on now?" I laughed. "Maybe we're just getting old, Kris."

The ocean was to our left now and the mountains strained toward the sky on the right. Higher and higher we went, curve after curve, up the side of a mountain, down the other side, and up the next, around and around and around, the ocean coming closer as we came down the mountainside and receding as we ascended, but showing its expansive body as we looked down from the top of the mountain. Suddenly, I began to wish that she would lose control of the car on one of those curves, that coming out of a curve she would keep the car on a straight path and we would take to the air, soaring through space to tumble down the side of the mountain into the sea. It was a beautiful day and I was with someone I loved and the ocean was below us, the mountains and the sky above and I wanted to die because maybe that would make a difference to people. I was so tired of words that could not exist in any other way.

But the car made itself one with each curve and we eventually came to Fort Ross where we stopped and got out to stretch our legs. The fort sat on the edge of a cliff, the ocean some thirty feet below. It was the first structure built by white settlers to California and I looked at the huge trees which comprised the walls of the fort and they were fear made manifest. These white men, Russians they were, had landed on the beach in one of the nearby coves and locked themselves behind the twenty-foot-high walls of a fort, locking themselves away from the sea, the mountains, and particularly, the Indians. But inside the fort they had built a church which protected them from any possibility of ever knowing the God from whom they had barricaded themselves.

We walked down into the cove and stood quietly for a few minutes watching the waves fall onto the shore. It was getting cool now and we went back to the car to begin the long drive back to the city. I was tired and didn't want to die anymore. Not then at least. Some other time. The intensity of the day, of being with Kris had exhausted me and I didn't want to die. But I was no longer afraid of dying. Indeed, I looked forward to it and would welcome it when it came. Maybe I would know the ecstasy of Joan and Craig and take my own life. More likely, I would die like Kerouac and John Coltrane who literally blew himself to death. When I reached forty, there would be no more words to write. It will have all been said in every way that I know and there will be nothing left then but the final, most profound statement of all.

There are those deaths which are the ultimate affirmation of God and every revolutionary begins to participate in the act once his life becomes a part of the revolution. When considered intellectually, it is frightening. When lived, it is exhilarating, it is good and right, as the sound and feel of dead leaves beneath one's feet on an autumn forest floor is good and right. I was no longer afraid to die; thus, I was no longer afraid to live.)

"They shall rest from their labors for they shall take their works with them," the priest read at Kerouac's funeral. And that is true for Joan Fox and Craig Badiali, also.

Eternal rest grant them, O Lord, and let perpetual light shine upon them.

Amen.

I continued commuting to New York each week to do the radio show and teach at the New School, as well as to be, all too briefly, with Margaret, the long-haired, soft-eyed, beautiful secretary of one of my editors. The remaining five days of each week were lived before the typewriter.

(ARTICLE: "My Life With Martin Luther King, Jr." *Evergreen Review*, January, 1970)

I only saw Martin Luther King, Jr. twice. The first time was in 1957 during my freshman year at Fisk University in Nashville, Tennessee. He had come to Fisk in the midst of the Montgomery bus boycott to deliver several speeches. The day he spoke to the student body I went only because attendance would be checked. I found a seat in the last row of the balcony and was asleep by the time King neared the end of his first melodious paragraph. I woke up some time later to hear him talking about three kinds of love, but went back to sleep when it appeared that he and I were on totally different wavelengths of love. Of course, in 1957 King was not the appointed and white-press-annointed leader. He was just beginning to be known nationally, and most blacks regarded him more with curiosity than anything else.

The other time I saw him was in Newark, New Jersey, in the mid-sixties. By this time he had the stature of the risen Christ and the nation was in the midst of We-Shall-Overcoming-Black-and-White-Together. The occasion was a rally sponsored by Local 1199 of the Drug and Hospital Workers' Union. I was a folksinger in those days, appearing at rallies and benefits to lead the audiences in singing freedom songs. When I sang in the South all I had to do was sing one note and the audience would be so much with me on the next one that I could've sung all night for the sheer joy of it. It wasn't like that in the North. Blacks had lost much of that ability to sing together and whites had never had it. So when it came time for me to lead the singing that day I dreaded it. It took about three songs to get the audience warmed up, and as I went into the fourth one they were just beginning to sing well together. Suddenly all heads turned toward the door, all singing stopped and there, walking into the auditorium, was the risen Christ. He was surrounded on both sides by members of his staff, one of whom I knew rather well. Although I was a little irked that Christ had decided to rise while I was singing, I had to admit that he and his staff looked impressive as they strode toward the podium.

The audience rose and applauded wildly. I stopped singing but refused to applaud. Instead I stared intently at Dr. King, trying to perceive what he might be feeling or thinking. But his face was closed to me. The thick lips curved neither up nor down. The eyes revealed absolutely nothing. His firm walk showed that he was aware that he was a public figure, but he didn't swagger as though he enjoyed it, nor did he attempt to shrink out of any sense of embarrassment.

The woman on King's staff whom I knew happened to sit directly in front of the rostrum where I was standing, and when she looked up and saw me we exchanged smiles. The people surrounding King had a certain style, particularly the women. It was a style that I called "old-line nigger," as opposed to "nouveau nigger." They were comfortable in their expensive clothes and wore their furs with that casual style it should take a family three generations to acquire. But they were as cool as you please, moving with an air of total confidence and assurance, which came, of course, from being a part of the King entourage. They were in, but they didn't flaunt it. Everybody knew they were in, and they knew that everybody knew, so they had no reason to be ostentatious or arrogant. My friend looked rather tired and bored, and when I spoke to her later, she said that they had been going from meeting to meeting for several days and she had had very little sleep. Dr. King, however, looked as fresh as a lily of the valley and as bright as the morning star.

Once the applause stopped I resumed singing, but I knew that it was useless. Everyone was waiting to hear King and wished that I would hurry up and finish, which I did. And I had to admit that I, too, was a little anxious to give myself up to the experience of being in h(H)is p(P)resence.

Some celebrities try to seem like "one of the boys" when they know they're being watched. They'll lean over and whisper to the person next to them in a too-familiar way. They'll step to the edge of the stage to shake the hand of someone they recognize and attract more attention to themselves. Dr. King didn't act like "folks." Bayard Rustin was on the podium that day and he leaned over (in too familiar a way), placed his arm around King's shoulder, and whispered in his ear. King merely inclined his head slightly toward Rustin and made no reply to whatever was said except to nod once.

When it came time for King to speak, he stood behind the rostrum without smiling or acknowledging the applause. I looked at him closely, particularly at his eyes (it is in the eyes that people tell us who they are), and they were empty. I was convinced of it. They were empty! But it wasn't as if they were devoid of all expression. They weren't, but

219

the expression which was there was that non-expression designed to be non-expressive. Looking into his eyes was like opening a door, and instead of seeing into a room, one saw a wall. King's eyes looked out over the audience, but no one could see whence he was seeing.

Finally the applause dribbled into the noise of people settling into their seats. He began. "Mis-ter Chaaaairman," he said slowly, and you could feel the tremors go through the crowd. A long pause. "My good friend, So-and-so," though he probably had never seen So-and-so or heard his name until five minutes before and was playing those politics that necessitate that the Great Leader recognize the existence of his local hosts. He continued down the podium, naming each person sitting there (skipping me, of course) until he had made sure no one was omitted. Then he began his speech.

His voice was deep and very slow. Each syllable had the timbre of a deep African drum. Then, imperceptibly, something happened. His voice began to lose its monotonous heavy timbre and to rise and fall in short strokes, and the crowd began to respond, to add their own tonal rhythms. Suddenly he and the crowd were locked in a passionate dance and King intensified the rhythms until the audience was shouting and getting happy as they had done under the spells of less sophisticated Baptist preachers a few hours earlier, and then King slapped his big drum once, twice, three times ("Free at last! Free at last! Thank God A'mighty, I'm free at last!" was how he gave the drum its final slaps at the March on Washington) and stopped, turned, and sat down. The audience went wild.

His speech was no more than seven minutes long, but within that brief time he had done what it takes other Baptist preachers an hour to do. He employed every technique so apparent in the March on Washington speech—the repetitive phrase, the quaver in the voice, the voice going high, then low, the elaborate metaphors. It was pure technique which extended back to slavery-time black preachers, but he had refined it and made it acceptable to whites without losing blacks. Even I was not immune to this black magic, but I was amazed to notice that as he spoke the eyes remained empty, an emptiness so profound that it was opaque. The voice was filled with emotion and expression, but the eyes did not flash or gleam or show any sign that he was aware of what he was saying. And I don't think he was. He had said it so many times that he knew how to pitch his voice for each response, how high to let freedom ring, and in what tone colors to paint the dream. He knew what they wanted to hear and he turned on his voice, but he wasn't there.

The applause was all that a Martin Luther King, Jr. had come to expect but, again, he did not acknowledge it. Nor did he deliberately ignore it. Rather, he gave the appearance of knowing that it would be unseemly for a man who was a spiritual leader to show any awareness of the unmistakable adulation the audience was demonstrating. He sat there while everyone stood and applauded with that fervor which is accorded dreams made manifest. I looked into that black audience and their faces shone with a celestial glow. They had looked upon His face and been within the sound of His voice and would talk about this day for years to come. ("Girl, he walked right by me. Closer to me than you are now." "I shook his hand! Yes, I did and I told him, 'Dr. King, you just keep on. We're with you all the way.'")

Eventually the hands which had filled the room with the noise of applause pulled out the handkerchiefs that had been stuffed in pockets and shoved into shiny black patent leather purses, to wipe the excited perspiration that Dr. King had brought from the glands of these hard-working, long-suffering and slow-dying beautiful people. They knew him, if I didn't. They didn't look into his eyes to see the person within. He was transformed in their eyes into the Deliverer and they were transformed in the sound of his voice to the Righteous.

He sat through the next speaker, as it was impolite to leave immediately. He then whispered something to the chairman and the chairman made the inevitable announcement that Dr. King had to be at such-and-such place in an hour and asked to be excused. As he got up to leave, the audience rose once again and the applause rent the heavens. I expected to hear a voice from above say, "This is my beloved Son in whom I am well pleased." Many people followed Dr. King into the hallway, I among them, as I wanted to say a quick hello to my friend. There I got my closest look at Dr. King and he did look tired, but I was impressed with the dignity (and there is no other word) with which he carried himself. He was a symbol and he was aware of it. He listened to the few words of those who clamored to shake his hand, listened intently, looking the person directly in the eye. But the eyes were still empty. Suddenly his aides hurried him into the elevator. The doors closed and he was taken away, as if by magic.

I knew as little about him after that encounter as I had known before. Who was he? I wanted to know what he was like when he wasn't behind a rostrum, when he wasn't leading the children to the Promised Land. I tried to imagine him in bed screwing, and couldn't. I tried to imagine him doing any of the things I did, like picking his nose, and I couldn't. After his death, I asked a close friend of his—someone who had known him for over ten years, who had been in meetings with him, gone to his house for dinner: "What was Martin like?" My friend shook his head. "He was the same way in private as he was in public. I never saw him any different. He was very aware that he was Martin Luther King and I guess nobody, except Coretta and Ralph [Abernathy] really knew him. And I wonder if they did."

I tried to tell myself that it didn't matter what he was *really* like. All that mattered was what he did. All that mattered was that he inspired black people to begin that long journey through the desert. But it did matter, does matter, because we've been cheated so many times by public figures with a certain image, only to learn that they are nothing like their image. That had been one of the painful lessons of my growing up—meeting famous people and finding that they were pyrite and not gold, as the public believed. I had seen famous folksingers backstage at concerts, getting ready to go on stage to sing protest songs, worry about whether they could outdo the previous performer. I had been standing in the wings as they came off stage after moving an audience to tears and the first words out of their mouths were, "How'd I do?" They sang about love and brotherhood and cared only about audience reaction, concert dates, and recording contracts. (And since Pete Seeger is the most famous folksinger, I feel I should stop all gossip and guessing games and say I'm not referring to him.)

I had heard the words of Martin King. I had looked upon him. He had moved me and yet he wasn't real. I couldn't feel a living person there. So it was with some curiosity that I picked up Coretta King's *My Life with Martin Luther King, Jr.,*[1] even though I knew she wouldn't let me feel him either. From what I knew of her through the grapevine, she was committed to the image, to the public person, to the myth, and though her book is filled with anecdotes and personal glimpses of Martin, it still leaves one with the sense that he was bigger than life. Throughout the book she draws analogies between his life and the life of Jesus, and she does it so well that when I finished the book I found myself wondering if I had indeed witnessed the Second Coming and failed to recognize it. I repeated to myself the gossip I knew about King, which was shocking but credible because it was not told maliciously. I recalled his duplicity during the Selma campaign, his cop-out in Albany, Georgia, his defeat in Chicago. I knew the inside stories of key meetings and the roles he had played in them. I knew that he wasn't a great leader, and that history may determine that Martin King was the worst thing that had happened to black people since Booker T. Washington. I told myself all these things in great detail and yet a doubt had been planted in my mind by his widow's book. But there was one passage in the book which struck me as significant, so significant that I wondered if Coretta King had been aware of what was actually being said.

During the Montgomery bus boycott, King decided that if he were found guilty on a particular charge he would go to jail rather than accept bail. Most of his associates felt that this would be a mistake. He said, "You don't understand. You see, if anybody had told me a

[1] Coretta Scott King, *My Life with Martin Luther King, Jr.* (New York: Holt, Rinehart and Winston, 1969).

couple of years ago when I accepted the presidency of the MIA (Montgomery Improvement Association) that I would be in this position, I would have avoided it with all my strength. This is not the life I expected to lead. But gradually you take some responsibility, then a little more, until finally you are not in control anymore. You have to give yourself entirely. Then once you make up your mind that you *are* giving yourself, then you are prepared to do anything that serves the Cause and the Movement. I have reached that point. I have no option anymore about what I will do. I have given myself fully." [2]

". . . finally you are not in control anymore," he had said. He was twenty-seven years old then, and suddenly, without warning or desire, he was projected into the role of national leader. He had lost control of events and, more important, the ability to control his own life had been taken from him. And I thought of Fidel Castro, whose original idea was to kick Batista out of Cuba and then let a more progressive government take over. He would not be a part of that government. He did not want any leadership position and said so. Yet he was forced to do the very thing he hadn't wanted. I remembered those three days in the heat of the Cuban summer of 1967 when Stokely Carmichael and I traveled through the mountains of Cuba with Fidel, getting up early in the morning to eat a huge breakfast of beef and plantain, visiting farms and villages until well after dark. We would stop someplace where Fidel's bodyguards would cook some more beef and plantain over an open fire and Fidel, who had not ceased talking volubly and excitedly from the minute he'd gotten up that morning, would talk late into the night. I came to know that Fidel wasn't an individual, that he had no personal life separate from that of being *el máximo líder* of the Cuban people. He was, in the most literal sense, the personification of Cuba and he exemplified the best in the Cuban people. A picture of Cuba would inevitably turn out to look and act and talk and think like Fidel Castro. He too had lost control and given himself entirely. But, with Fidel, I felt no distance between us. His eyes were not empty. There was very definitely a person in those big-pocketed Cuban military fatigues. I had no problem imagining him in bed with his girlfriend.

I turned back to Coretta King's book and opened it to the photographs, looking at them for the hundredth time, trying once again to get some feeling of who this man was. There he is, standing with two of his children in front of his birthplace. He has on a suit and tie. His legs are spread apart and the expression on his face is self-conscious. "I am Martin Luther King, Jr., standing in front of my birthplace with my children," this photo says. And there's the picture of him on his wedding day in a white coat, black pants, and black bow-tie, Coretta on his arm

[2] *Ibid.,* pp. 163–64.

and he grinning. The new groom and his beautiful bride, and he looks real, like so many pictures of black grooms I have seen encased beneath glass-topped coffee tables in the homes of bourgeois black America. Yeah, I know Martin in that picture. But he wasn't Martin Luther King, Jr. then. He was just a young black preacher working on his doctorate. There're pictures of him going to jail, pictures of him at the March on Washington, a picture of him in jail, and they all have that same stiffness, that same unreality. He is aware of the Nikons, Leicas, and Pentaxes pointed at him.

And then, then come the two human pictures. In the first he is seated on the sofa in the living room of his home with his wife and children, and the smile on his face is the kind of smile fathers have when they stop one day to look at their wives and children. They pat themselves on the back, feeling proud to have picked this particular woman to marry, who gave them these particular children. It's a man's smile that says, "I'm a man." The other photo is more revealing. Martin King, in formal dress, receiving congratulations from King Olav after being awarded the Nobel Peace Prize. The grin across his face, the dimple in his cheek, the eyes shining. This is one happy nigger! That's the only way I can put it, 'cause I know my people. It's one of those grins older black people turn on when they've gotten approval from white folks, and Martin's got it on. He's not Martin Luther King, Jr. in that photograph. Uh-uh. He's a happy colored boy. No dignity here, no manliness about him. He's gotten as high up in the white folks' world as any colored man can go in this life and he's so happy about it he doesn't know what to do with himself. So he grins.

The most revealing photo is the one of him lying in his coffin, the eyes closed, the mouth grim. In no other photograph have I ever seen the mouth of King set so firmly, so totally, so completely. (And the lips of the dead always mock life rather than affirm death.) I've never seen a man look so completely dead. I've seen bodies and photographs of bodies and none chilled me like this one. I remember the photographs of Malcolm lying dead, swathed in white cloth, and he looked like the "shining black prince" Ossie Davis eulogized him as. How noble Malcolm looked in death. The strength that was in that corpse. The dead Che looked like Christ. On a table in a bare room, half-naked, his scrawny legs, dirty feet, skinny chest and eyes half-opened, he looked like Christ. But King. I look at that photograph and it reminds me of the photographs of lynching victims. That's nothing but a po' black boy lying there. That's all. Martin Luther King, Jr. isn't there. The voice is gone and there is no applause. That's nothing but a colored boy lying there. Martin King looked like nothing but one stone cold dead colored boy.

And I understood then. Martin had lost "control," but unlike Fidel he had not replaced the individual soul he had lost with the soul of his people. He had lost control and no longer existed within himself or to himself. And Martin Luther King, Jr. was created in front of the crowds and the journalists and the television cameras. He was created in the sound of his voice, the movement of his gestures, the dignity with which he carried himself. Unlike Malcolm, he did not immerse his being in the soul of his people. Failing to do so, he was forever lost. He could no longer go back to the smile of the happy groom. And he didn't know how to go forward to totally lose his life and be made incarnate in black people. Thus he was lost, a thing in the eyes of the world, nothing to himself.

Two more stories from his widow's book. In 1960 King was sentenced to six months in jail for a traffic violation in Georgia. Coretta was deeply concerned because "my husband hated being alone. . . . He needed and depended upon the support of people he loved. It was always hard for Martin to be in prison, and this would be such a long stay." [3] I recalled the words of James Bevel, one of King's aides, who often taunted audiences with their fear of jail: "What're you scared of jail for?" he would ask. "When you say you're afraid to go to jail, what you're saying is that you're afraid to be by yourself. It seems to me that any man would welcome some time alone with himself. But most of us find that ourselves are the last people we can stand to be alone with." King didn't have to spend six months with himself, because a phone call from Senator John Kennedy resulted in Martin's release from jail, swung black votes to Kennedy, and put him in the White House.

The next incident occurred in 1963. Martin was arrested in Birmingham and put in solitary confinement. Coretta quotes him as saying: "Those hours were the longest and most frustrating and bewildering of my life." [4] But how can a man who had been to jail as many times as Martin King have felt that way? By Birmingham '63 he'd seen the inside of more southern jails than practically any man alive. But he never learned to deal with it. This time a phone call from Mrs. King to Kennedy did the trick.

That's why the eyes were empty. He knew that he did not exist except as an object—a "leader," a "public person," a "great man." Even to his wife it appears that he was the risen Christ and she was fortunate enough to be Mrs. Christ. Sometimes when Ralph Abernathy introduced King at mass meetings it would be with analogies to Jesus, and Martin Luther King, Jr. would not demur, would not feel any

[3] *Ibid.*, p. 195.
[4] *Ibid.*, p. 224.

embarrassment, because those were the times when he was alive. How does one endure the pain of knowing his own nonexistence?

On Martin Luther King's tombstone are inscribed the words: "Free At Last! Free At Last! Thank God Almighty! I'm Free At Last." Those are strange words for an epitaph. They're appropriate for King, though. He *is* free now. Myths can live more easily when there is no person who has to represent the myth. He is free now and I'm glad. He suffered long enough.

My friends that winter were the wind, which blew without ceasing, the fog, and a lone hawk, which flew out of the hills and into the wind almost every evening. I sat in the window seat, watching it stubbornly refuse to be blown backward. It would hang in the air, occasionally beating its wings and advancing forward only to be stopped by the full force of the wind. Occasionally, it would have to relent and allow itself to be pushed back, but always, with a few flaps of its wings, it would return to face the wind. After a while, it would leave, turning in a wide, arrogant arc, and fly in a line perpendicular to the wind. The next day it would return and I would sit and watch.

(ARTICLE: "Aquarian Notebook," *Liberation*, February, 1970)

Black people don't need any more deaths. Our history is filled with them. Sometimes it seems that dying is what we do best. We die on tenement roofs and in hallways, in bars, alleys, fields, in the street, and in bed. We die, we die, we die. Always we die.

Most of our dead are not even acknowledged. Fred Hampton and Mark Clark are shot and killed by the police. So what else is new? How many other blacks have died from policemen's bullets since? Where is the citizen's commission to investigate the circumstances of their deaths? Where are the statements of concern from the various organizations? They, too, were men, those blacks murdered before and since the Hampton-Clark deaths. No, they weren't prominent members of the Black Panther Party. They were just dudes who hung out, tried to make it from day to day. They'd never heard about Chairman Mao or Che and wouldn't know the working class from the fifth grade class. They were just down brothers doing their thing, whatever it might have been. And it just so happened that the cops didn't dig their thing, like they didn't dig Hampton and Clark's thing. So, they got wasted, like a white cop wastes a brother any time of day or night he feels like it.

To say that there is a national conspiracy to get the Panthers is to make the same mistake made by those Americans who honestly believe that the demonstrations at the Democratic Convention were a planned conspiracy. If the Chicago Seven *were* capable of a conspiracy, it would be abortive because they could never agree on a time and place to conspire. It is obvious that there was no need for anybody to conspire to "cause riots" in Chicago. It should be equally as obvious that the police of America don't need to conspire to get the Panthers. If you light a cigarette over an open can of kerosene, when it blows up in your face it wasn't a conspiracy.

The police have never needed more than the slightest whim to kill blacks, and when it comes to the Panthers, their already evident anti-black feelings are merely intensified. If there were a national conspiracy to get the Panthers, it would have happened like the Palmer Raids. One night when you went to bed, there would be Panthers. The next morning when you got up, there would be no Panthers. The government prefers to let nature take its course this time. A few cops in this town can't take the sight of the Panthers any longer and frame a few and shoot a few. A few cops in another city can't put up with it any longer, either, and likewise. The execution of a government conspiracy is swift and efficient. Three A.M. in 20 cities, 10,000 people are arrested. What has been happening to the Panthers is more a war of attrition, proof that the government does not feel them to be enough of a threat to conspire to destroy them. Let the cops who feel threatened do it.

We know very little about revolution when you come right down to it. We know a lot of theory, have read a snatch of this and a little of that and done a lot of talking to others who've read bits and pieces of something else, and we put it all together and come up with revolution. The Hampton-Clark murders make one wonder, however, just how many of us could psychologically survive the kind of revolutionary struggle which a student in Bolivia or Spain or Laos has to endure. In those countries, there are no Constitutional guarantees of freedom of speech and the press. Spanish students have been summarily given 20 year prison sentences for organizing campus demonstrations. And most of the revolutionary writers in these countries are either in jail or in exile. The Panthers have perpetrated the myth that because they have lost so many members by death, jail and exile, it proves that the government considers them a threat. Bullshit! It proves that some people in the power structure are pissed off. And who knows if they're pissed because of the Panthers' politics or just because they happen to be a bunch of arrogant niggers talking about offing "the pigs." SDS has been talking the same stuff in its way and has no martyrs to show for its effort. The Panthers seem to think that the progress of a revolution can be traced like earthquake tremors on a Richter Scale, only in this instance, the scale is the body-count. If the Government really felt that the Panthers or any of us were even getting close to bringing off a revolution, the number of hearses hauling our bodies to cemeteries would cause traffic jams all over the country. If the Government really felt itself in danger, there would be no *Liberation,* no *Guardian* and most definitely, no books being published by the likes of Abbie or myself. In fact, every book dealing with revolution would disappear from the bookstores and libraries in less than a week's time. If we knew history, even some American history, we would remember what happened to the IWW and what happened to a black man like W. E. B. Du Bois, who was unable to get a book or article published in any but a radical house or journal. And even when a radical house would publish one of his books, the distributors wouldn't carry it and neither would the bookstores. We forget what happened to white radicals in the fifties, musicians, actors, writers and workers. The government deported thousands, who were long-time residents, but not citizens, and fixed it so those it couldn't deport were unable to get jobs.

We use the term fascism so loosely that if and when fascism really comes to America, will we be able to survive it psychologically? We have been so pampered that we think we are what we are not. No government that feels threatened is going to feature the revolutionaries in *Life,* or interview them on the news, or invite them to Face The Nation and answer questions. America does believe, to a degree, in the dissemination of ideas, but we must not let that lull us into thinking that the government is going to uphold what we conceive to be our right to make revolution. No state, absolutely no state, will give its citizens the right to overthrow it.

We must use the Constitutional guarantees as long as we can, but we must not be psychologically dependent on them. The cops did not have the Constitutional right to off Hampton and Clark, but they sure as hell had the right—as cops. And, it should have surprised none of us that they exercised that right. If you tell a cop that you're going to off him and tell the government that you're going to overthrow it, then you are naive if you think that the cops and the government are not going to do everything within their power to prevent their own elimination. But we've had it easy. There has been such a liberal climate in the country that "movement personalities", like Abbie, Jerry, Tom, myself and many others are approached by lecture agencies to go around to college campuses and talk about revolution for anywhere from $500 to $1000 and more a night. We do it sometimes, but we are under no illusions that this comprises the essence of the revolutionary struggle. The Constitutional provisions of the right of dissent work to our advantage as long as we know in the very marrow of our bones that the revolution will be made without any Constitutional or humane provisions whatsoever. Instead, what seems to happen is that we actually believe that we have a legal right to make a revolution and then when the government begins to let us know that we don't, we start screaming and hollering and crying as if an injustice has been done to us. And instead of fighting to make a revolution, we end up fighting for the right to protest.

One of the easiest ways to destroy any organization is to get enough of its members on a merry-go-round to jail and the organization becomes a radical bail bonding agency. At some point we are going to have to realize that if we find ourselves in jail, we'll have to stay there. That's hard and cold. I know. But it's the only way to get out of the government's "moderate repression" trick bag. And, it's what revolutionaries in every other country in the world face. In South Africa, they have a special island where they put all the bad revolutionary niggers. The present Premier of North Vietnam, Pham Van Dong, pulled six years in the slams, most of it in solitary. Not only didn't the Viet Minh have time to raise bail, there wasn't bail anyway. We've had it easy so far and we must prepare ourselves and others for the experience which is to come, which is the *status quo* for every revolution which has ever been.

We are becoming victims of our own illusions and one sad result of it is that Fred Hampton and Mark Clark are dead. I see around me almost an entire generation of black youth being martyred needlessly and because I have been a part of the movement, because I have contributed my thinking to this revolution of ours, I must bear some of the responsibility for the needless deaths. It takes more than guts to make a revolution. It takes more than the courage to risk one's life for an ideal. It takes more than a willingness to die. It takes sense enough to know when to say "Advance" and when to say "Retreat." It takes sense enough to know when to fight and when not to fight. It takes sense enough to know what your organization can do and what it can't do. Because one has a gun and some bullets doesn't mean to go out and shoot a cop. Cops, guns and bullets are not in short supply. They'll be there whenever one is ready. Prior to that, however, one needs to build himself a base, so that when he proceeds to shoot that cop, he has minimized as much as possible the dangers of losing his own life. Example: The revolutionary struggle in Guinea-Bissau began with six men in the late 50's. They met and decided the time had come. Then, they proceeded to build their organization and spent four years among the peasants building their support and their base before the first shot against a Portuguese soldier was fired. Four years!

The deaths of Hampton and Clark were needless because they were totally without protection against what eventually happened. If they had had a base in the black community, the police would not have dared come in and shoot them in cold blood. The Black Panther Party has support within the black community, but it has no real base. Its base is among white radicals. Black America has related to the Panthers as involved spectators at a football game. They have not been involved as active participants. And because they have not, it is a simple matter for the police to come into the community and take off whomever it wants to.

The murder of Hampton and Clark is having an impact within black America. No event since the murder of Dr. King has been so unsettling. But the lessons which blacks are learning could have as easily been taught from history. Malcolm was killed, shot down in cold blood. That's the only martyr we need. All the teaching anybody wants to do can be done in Malcolm's blood. And, just in case anybody missed the point, King was martyred. So, if they would kill the man who brought the sword and kill the man who brought love, there is no further need for one drop of black blood to come spurting from a bullet wound. Just as it hurts the parent of a soldier killed in Vietnam that his child died for no reason, it hurts to say the same about Hampton and Clark. But it must be said in the hope that some lives will be saved. Black people cannot afford to be losing young warriors like Hampton and Clark. And undoubtedly, the Black Panther Party attracted to its ranks the young warriors of black America, the.young men and women who were willing to make the sacrifices, who were willing to risk their lives. And there is no commitment, no dedication like that of which a 19-year-old is capable. Now, they are in prison or dead or (and their number is not small) have left the Party in disillusionment for a myriad of reasons. The young are the revolution's most valuable resource. The Panthers have used that resource irresponsibly, endangering lives when it was not necessary, and, most of all, by adhering to a politics of romanticism, not revolution, a politics which enshrines the dead and does little for the living.

The murders of Hampton and Clark have touched off a whole new wave of support for the Panthers. And tactically, the Panthers should be supported, because it is in our own self-interest to do so. However, support of the Panthers while they are under severe attack means, in most minds, support for their politics. Indeed, all too many people see a vindication of their politics in the blood-stained mattress on which Hampton lay. This is no time for sentimentality (and there can be bleeding-heart radicals as well as liberals). That mattress is, if anything, a condemnation of Panther politics (and a confirmation of what we should've known all along about 'the man'). At some point, the movement will have to confront that and still continue to support the Panthers while they are under attack. The movement, however, has extreme difficulty in supporting anyone whose politics they might find objectionable, which is a reflection of our state of mind. Too often we judge people by their politics and, in fact, equate the two. This leads, of course, to factionalism, which is the present state of the movement. Though I find the politics of the Panthers to be, in great part, but not wholly, destructive, it is impossible to forget that the Black Panther Party is composed of individuals, is composed of young black warriors who are dedicated and committed and have much to offer. And if for no other reason than a desire to stop the next Fred Hampton from being murdered, I must oppose the organization and support the individuals in it whom 'the man' is trying to take off. This may seem contradictory, but it is an attitude which is essential in a revolutionary movement. Gandhi put it in a religious framework: "Hate the sin and love the sinner."

In a revolution there are martyrs. Nonetheless, because we accept death as inevitable it means that we must be all the more careful to be as sure as we can that those deaths which do occur are inevitable and do not become inevitable after the fact.

The deaths of Hampton and Clark were needless, but not meaningless. We must see to that. But we can only invest their dying with meaning if we recognize and destroy the weaknesses and shortcomings within ourselves. At present, these are many. If we fail, it will be more because of our own shortcomings than the objective circumstances. If we continue to gauge our progress by the intensity of government repression and the number of martyrs, then we have already failed. Even though I recognize the inevitability of death in a revolution, I cannot wholly accept it. Any death is one too many. And for every death we suffer, we must ask ourselves: did he have to die? Could it have been avoided? Did we do something wrong that made his death more of a probability than a possibility?

We must share the responsibility for the deaths of Hampton and Clark, all of us, like myself, whose words and actions have helped to create the unnatural climate of violence which now surrounds the movement, all of us who have used the rhetoric of violence helped to convince others to commit their lives. We, however, could not protect those lives once they were committed, and, we should have been able to. Sometimes martyrs are created from the guilt of the living.

Che said, "In revolution one wins or dies." If I may be so presumptuous, I would like to amend that. In revolution, one wins and dies. Black people have done enough dying.

(ARTICLE: "Aquarian Notebook," *Liberation*, March, 1970)

When the black radical movement began in 1960, it adhered to the philosophy and tactics of non-violence. There were few within the early black movement who believed in non-violence, but it was accepted out of respect to Martin Luther King's position within the movement, and, also, because it seemed to work.

The first decisive challenge to the concept of non-violence and King's leadership came from Malcolm X, who ridiculed non-violence and extolled the right of self-defense. This was one of Malcolm's primary ideological contributions during his brief career. He was the first to present an alternative to the thinking of King. Though there is, of course, no direct relationship between Malcolm's words and the rebellions of Birmingham, Harlem, Bedford-Stuyvesant and Rochester in 1963 and 1964, Malcolm provided the beginnings of an ideology of violence. For him, violence was essentially an act asserting one's manhood. Although he occasionally spoke of guerrilla warfare in the last months of his life, primarily, he saw violence as an act of self-defense. It was also a matter of simple common sense. One had the right and duty to defend himself, his family and his community.

The ideology of violence received its greatest and fullest expression in Frantz Fanon's *The Wretched of the Earth*. Fanon was the psychologist of the colonized and he saw violence as a spiritual act in which the colonized were cleansed of their slavery and simultaneously born as free men. In its initial phase, violence was less a tactic of the revolution than an inevitable result of the colonized state, which, in itself, was one of violence. Thus, the counter-violence of the colonized, when he turned on the colonizer, was a psychic necessity and inevitability.

H. Rap Brown was the first national black leader after Malcolm who articulated an ideology of violence. (While Stokely Carmichael was by no means non-violent, a philosophy of violence was never an important part of his rhetoric.) Brown articulated in 1967 what many accept now as fact—that blacks are facing imminent annihilation. The only response to this, according to Brown, was to take up arms.

By 1967, the blacks of the North had shown themselves to be more than ready to use violence. The summer of 1966 was the first big summer of urban rebellions, rebellions which were to reach their peak in the days following the assassination of King in April of 1968. The violence of the rebellions was marked by the destruction of property and, though projected by the press as being anti-white, no rebellion moved outside the black community. In fact, more blacks died in the rebellions than whites. It was a violence directed against economic oppression and the police.

By 1967, however, the dominant tone of the black movement had shifted to that used by Malcolm. It was a violent rhetoric, which does not mean that violence was always articulated. But it was a rhetoric which was designed to frighten whites and anger blacks. It was a violent rhetoric because it was an anti-white rhetoric. Although the physical acts of violence were not directed against whites, psychic violence was. Thus because of its rhetoric, the black movement became a violent movement.

While the physical violence of the rebellions was spontaneous and unorganized, there were three attempts to organize around the concept of physical self-defense in the sixties. The first came from Robert Williams in Monroe, North Carolina. Williams, an ex-Marine, organized black youth to defend the community against the attacks of the Klan. The eventual result was Williams' going into exile to save his life. The second attempt came in the mid-sixties with an organization called the Deacons for Justice and Self-Defense. They were a group of young black men who respected the CORE workers who came into Louisiana to organize but could not accept CORE's non-violent philosophy. They organized to protect these workers and soon became an organization that could be depended upon to go anywhere they were needed. Quietly, almost anonymously, they policed demonstrations and marches. Their presence deterred white violence in many instances. The largest and most successful organization which organized around the concept of self-defense was, of course, the Black Panther Party. It was originally called the Black Panther Party for Self-Defense and viewed its primary responsibility as defending the community against the police. The Panthers made the gun visible and the rhetoric and instruments of violence had a great impact on the minds of blacks.

Of those who have articulated an ideology of violence, Malcolm X seems to have been the only one whose purpose was not to bring about violence. In an interview with Marlene Nadle of the *Village Voice* a few weeks before his murder (and published in the *Village Voice* of February 25, 1965) he spoke candidly about his rhetoric of violence. He used it as a tactic, he said, because America responded only to violence. Thus, he hoped that the threat of violence would be enough to make America reform itself and eliminate the actual necessity of violence. Coretta King in her book on her husband reports a conversation she had with Malcolm X when he came to Selma during the demonstrations in 1965. She says that Malcolm told her that he wanted "Dr. King to know that I really didn't come to Selma to make his job more difficult. I really did come thinking that I could make it easier. If the white people realize what the alternative is, perhaps they will be more willing to hear Dr. King." Of course, it is very possible that Malcolm was trying to "hustle" both Marlene Nadle and Coretta King. However, it is equally as possible that he was consciously using the rhetoric of violence in the hopes of avoiding the actual violence which he knew was going to erupt from the ghetto if nothing was done.

If this is so, Malcolm seriously miscalculated the effect of the word. The word actualizes and makes real that which before was vague and unformed. Indeed, the word is the act and once Malcolm began to articulate an ideology of violence, he had unleashed the actual violence he hoped to avoid.

Within the black movement of the sixties, the concept and use of violence underwent some very rapid progressions. No matter what he thought privately, Malcolm articulated a concept of violence as an act of self-defense. In the thinking of Fanon, violence was simultaneously an act of self-defense and assertion. In the thinking of H. Rap Brown, it was the necessary act of survival. In the thinking of the Black Panther Party, it was a principal part of their program. In their military-like uniforms, use of military nomenclature, and rhetoric of violence (and violent rhetoric), the Panthers became the first national exponents and representatives of violence within the movement. They defined their revolutionary intent in the words of Chairman Mao: "Power comes from the barrel of a gun." They were a military organization which became a military-political organization. (During the days when SNCC and the Panthers were discussing a coalition, SNCC wanted the Panthers to view themselves as the military wing of the movement, with SNCC being the political. This is the way other revolutions have been organized, with the military under the control of the political. For example, Chu Teh was head of the Chinese Red Army, but he and it came under the control of Mao and the Central Committee of the Party. The Panthers, on the other hand, wanted to absorb SNCC into its structure, with no separation between the military and political wings. This is the way the Cuban revolution was organized. Fidel was the military commander and political leader. The guerrillas were warriors and political workers. When SNCC refused to be absorbed into the BPP, the Party at that point began to expand from a self-defense organization into a political party.) The Panthers did not extend the ideology of violence beyond what Malcolm had articulated, but merely emphasized it more than anyone had done previously.

The violence within the black movement comes from two very disparate sources. One is the obvious violence which has been done unto blacks—psychic, cultural, and physical. The violence of the urban rebellions has been in direct response to the violence which has been the climate in which blacks have been forced to live. It is this violence which Fanon describes and analyzes in *The Wretched of the Earth*.

Philosophically, however, the rhetoric of violence has been a reaction to the non-violence articulated by Martin Luther King, as well as a response to the violence of the system. Non-violence was a turn-the-other-cheek philosophy. King admonished blacks to love those who hated them. King believed that the key lay in the ability of blacks to endure longer than whites were able to hate. It was a concept of non-violence which was doomed to failure, because it went against the history of a people who *had* endured as long as they had been hated. It was a concept of non-violence which denied manhood to a people who had always been denied manhood. And, as a concept, it did not gain many adherents. While King was sincere in his use of it, to most it was a tactic to be used as long as it got results. It might be argued that King was a poor practitioner of non-violence (though there is no one with whom he can be compared except Gandhi and the particulars of their situations are too different to make for fruitful comparisons). While King and his organization had the ability to train thousands in the tactics of non-violence (as in Birmingham in 1963), he was not able to transform those who used those tactics. And King himself never became the moral leader that Gandhi was. King used massive civil disobedience within a very limited framework, but he never focused the struggle in its moral roots. Unlike Gandhi, Cesar Chavez or Dick Gregory, King never fasted, in jail or out. It is in the act of fasting, however, that non-violence achieves a moral intensity and purity which it cannot achieve otherwise.

King's greatest failure was an inability to communicate the concept of non-violence in historical language which would have communicated to blacks. Why should we be non-violent, blacks wanted to know? That's what we've been for four hundred years, except to each other every Saturday night. Perhaps, the failure to communicate the concept is a failure of language. The opposite of violence is not its absence—non-violence. The very word commands one *not* to do something. But it does not say what one should do. In King's mind, non-violence was active and dynamic. It was an act of love. However, he could only communicate passivity to a people who viewed themselves as having been sheep, dumb before the slaughter. While King did exhort blacks to love the enemy, he did not say how one loves that enemy. He did not say how one communicates love to someone who has had his humanity destroyed. How do you grasp the core of a man and transform him? This was the aim of the non-violent movement, an aim which King did not articulate often enough or well enough, for he became a political leader with a spiritual rhetoric. Gandhi always remained a spiritual leader who was also political leader.

The word which has been erroneously translated as non-violence is *satyagraha,* the word which Gandhi himself used. And when translated accurately, it means something totally different than "non-violence." *Satyagraha*—with the force of one's soul. This is more than not being violent. It is an act of creative love. With the force of my soul, I will change yours. It is what Henry Miller meant when he wrote, "One who

235

is really a force, a mouthpiece of God, will make himself heard without opening his lips."

Unfortunately, non-violence in America has been too often propagated by people who knew nothing of *satyagraha*. Too many of them think non-violence means not striking back. In actuality, non-violence has nothing to do with refusing to hit somebody. Non-violence (*satyagraha*) is an attitude of the soul, making it possible to admit the necessity of violence without being destroyed in the use of violence. *Satyagraha* seeks to avoid the use of physical violence; however, sometimes, it is one's only defense. It is the only way in which one can insure his physical survival and that of others. In that instance, and, only in that instance, is physical violence permissible. Underlying the use of physical violence is this attitude of the soul, *satyagraha*, and it is this, and only this, which will make the revolution a reality. Violence is incapable of doing this, for revolution is the moral transformation of Man.

Within the movement, violence has come to have a value in and of itself. Most of us have come to violence, not from necessity, but from playing the roles of revolutionaries. We still lack a basic understanding of what it is to be revolutionary. Could we, after a small skirmish, tend to the wounds of those we had just shot? Could we shoot a cop and then fix up his wounds, if he were left in the streets to die? Not as long as we think of and call cops "pigs." It may be a great purgative to scream "Off the Pig," but it will never never be revolutionary. Indeed, what have we become when we call someone a "pig"? And while I understand the psychological necessity that impels blacks (including myself) to refer to whites as "honkies," do we become more human when we do so? (Perhaps we do, in the long run, if we recognize that it was historically necessary to call people "pigs" and "honkies," that we were not talking to them, but to ourselves. That we were cleansing ourselves by screaming these epithets. However, there is no guarantee that we will progress beyond that and if we don't, then what was historical necessity becomes an historical end and we have become no different than those we dehumanized in the words "pig" and "honky.") If we lose our humanity, then it is utterly impossible for us to create a humanistic society. Power does not come from the barrel of a gun. Only bullets. When one pulls the trigger of a gun, he is making an irrevocable decision about another's right to existence. It is a decision which must always weigh upon one with excruciating pain. It is a decision which one must feel he is forced into making and once forced, it is a decision to be avoided except when necessary for the sake of one's own survival.

Not only does power not come from the barrel of a gun, does power have anything to do with revolution? We have defined our struggle as one in which power must be wrested from those who now hold power.

This is not necessarily revolution. Indeed, it is altogether possible that within that kind of framework revolution is impossible. The humanistic society will not be created by government edict, revolutionary or otherwise. That society will only come about through the living of it. It is the quality of lives which must be changed. We think now that it is necessary to destroy the state and create another one before that can be done. That may be an illusion.

Dave Dellinger has often said that non-violence as a creative force has scarcely begun to be even understood. Before that can happen, we must realize the necessity for it. We must realize that it is in becoming agents of *satyagraha* that the revolution will be made flesh. We must get rid of the old images of non-violence and recognize how *satyagraha* has already functioned within the movement and consciously begin to explore it and use it. The biggest example of *satyagraha* in the sixties was not the non-violent movement but the Yippies. And I don't think I am stretching a definition. I am talking about how a generation of youth were spiritually transformed without the use of violence, but through the soul-force of others. (And soul-force is different from charisma. King had the latter, but not the former.) SDS may have politicized thousands; Abbie and Jerry spiritualized hundreds of thousands. An entire nation may become politicized (in the way that we want them to of course), but unless that nation undergoes a spiritual transformation, there has been no meaningful change.

Violence is necessary, but it must not be the core of our struggle. In too many minds, it has become that. As long as it remains that, then those who call themselves revolutionaries are nothing more than glorified bandits.

On July 12, 1967, my wife gave birth to our second child, a son. July 12 also happened to be the first night of the Newark Rebellion and on that night, as I sat at home filled with the intense emotions of the two events, I wrote a poem. A year later I incorporated part of the poem into my *Guardian* column of July 13, 1968 and would here like to repeat it:

"As we destroy, let us not forget that it is only so we may be more human.

"As we destroy, let our exaltations not be for the blood that flows in the gutters, but for the blood that may more freely flow through our bodies.

"We must destroy in order to live, but let us never enjoy the destroying more than the New Life, the only reason for the destroying.

"If we forget, then those who come afterward will have to destroy us for the Life that we, in our destroying, failed to give.

"Revolution does not mean us against them. The revolutionary is a midwife seeking to give birth to the full potential of man. Involved in that most difficult of all births is our fighting against them, but let us not confuse that fight with Revolution."

We are all agreed that the end we are struggling toward—a humanistic society—is good. However, the means we use to achieve that end can make achieving it impossible. Indeed, it is altogether possible that the means is the end and there is nothing more. The end is the creation of a humanistic society. The means is to invest every act with humanity.

I wonder now how I could have written so much that winter. In addition to the material reprinted here, there was a long essay analyzing the politics of Stokely Carmichael and Eldridge Cleaver for Dotson Rader's short-lived, soft-cover magazine, *Defiance*; an introduction to Rosa Guy's book, *The Children of Longing*; the introductory notes for an anthology compiled by Rae Pace Alexander called *Young and Black in America*; three reviews and a long article for the *Sunday Times Book Review*; an article on children's literature for *Publishers Weekly*; essays for *Evergreen Review* on black writers and white publishers, and on Ousmane Sembene's film, *Mandabi*, and I began a new column called "To the Tribe" for Walt Shepperd's unsung but influential paper, *Nickel Review*.

When Robert Nemiroff, the husband of the late Lorraine Hansberry, asked me if I would be interested in writing an article about her for the *Village Voice*, I didn't know how important it would be for me. Except for *The Sign in Sidney Brustein's Window*, I was unfamiliar with her oeuvre. I read all her plays, as well as letters and articles Bob made available to me, and with her, I touched once more those qualities I had found in W. E. B. Du Bois—an uncompromising honesty and a clarity of vision. She became my model that spring for who I wanted to be as a writer and as a person. Indeed, at long last, I knew of someone who had been a good person and a good writer. (The essay about Lorraine Hansberry was later expanded to become the introduction to *Les Blancs: The Collected Last Plays of Lorraine Hansberry*.)

(ARTICLE: "Young, Gifted and Black: The Politics of Caring," *Village Voice*, May 28, 1970)

The rise and fall of a writer's reputation is not much different from that of a stock. One year everybody wants a "piece of the action."

The next, it's almost as if that particular stock hadn't been on the market the year before. That writers are subjected to such is no reflection on them. It is a reflection of that strange, unreal world in which the writer must function—the world of publishers and agents, reviewers and reviews, and that small minority of the population which buys books, or attends the theatre. Indeed, a writer's reputation may have very little to do with what he or she writes, but more with the personality which is publicly projected. One writes, but that does not mean one is a "writer." The former does not necessarily lead to the latter, but for all too many who write, it does. And, conversely, a writer is not necessarily one who writes, for a writer is a social role, a character in a bad play, a mask worn at after-five cocktail parties at the Chelsea. And those who write and begin to play the role of being "writers" cease to be human beings at some point. Instead, they become "literary figures," major or minor, and once they become such, they cease to write or merely write about being "literary figures."

Lorraine Hansberry was a rarity and just how rare she was we are only beginning to realize, five years after her death at the age of 34. Her reputation rests wholly upon one play, "A Raisin in the Sun," a play which has been consistently misunderstood and misinterpreted. Her second play, "The Sign in Sidney Brustein's Window," was even more misunderstood, and because it was not a Broadway hit, it did not serve to enhance the acclaim she received from "Raisin in the Sun." And three months after "Sign" opened, Lorraine Hansberry died and the play closed.

Until the Off-Broadway presentation of "To Be Young, Gifted, and Black," Miss Hansberry had become a part of theatrical history, which is to say, forgotten. After all, she wrote before the days of black power, black consciousness, and revolution. It was assumed that there was nothing in her works relevant to the ethos of the late '60s. After all, this is the era of the "new black playwright" and the toughness of LeRoi Jones and it seems that the literary and theatrical establishment can only accommodate one kind of black writing at a time. Generally, that brand of black writing seems to be one which will serve more as therapy for the guilty and the anguished rather than sustenance for pilgrims. Thus, when one thinks of black writers today, the name of Lorraine Hansberry does not come quickly to mind, and, if any name should, it is this one. She not only foreshadowed much of what is thought to be "new" in black theatre, she exemplified a model which has been ignored, to the detriment of us all.

"To Be Young, Gifted, and Black," both the Off-Broadway presentation and a new book (Prentice-Hall, $8.95), are attempts to show us the errors of our ways. Those who saw the dramatic production will not be duplicating an experience by reading the book. The book includes more material, as well as photographs and some of Miss Hansberry's own witty drawings. It is composed of excerpts from her writings, public and private, published and unpublished. The result is, on one level, a sensitive autobiography (thanks to the skill of Robert Nemiroff in weaving the disparate parts into an eloquent whole). On another level, it is the expression of a vision of the realities and possibilities of humanity. It is not surprising that most young black writers do not find their inspiration in her, and it is a pity. "Raisin in the Sun" is looked upon as an "Uncle Tom" play, because the Younger family moves out of the ghetto and into a white neighborhood. This is true, but it is not what the play is about. Miss Hansberry was concerned with blacks not as representatives of a particular political attitude, but as people, as black people, and she set herself the task of describing the contours, subtleties, and dynamics of black life. "Raisin in the Sun" is a good example of Mama Younger's advice to her daughter in the play: "When you starts measuring somebody, measure him *right*, child, measure him right. Make sure you done taken into account what hills and valleys he come through before he got to wherever he is . . ." Lorraine Hansberry "measures" all of her characters "right." And in "Raisin" there is a surprising range of characters—Mama Younger, who has survived and won; her son, Walter, the castrated black male; his wife, Ruth, who sees the castration and is unable to stop the knife; Beneatha, Walter's sister, who would be described today as a young black militant; and Joseph Asagi, an African student, with a vision of the new, of what is to come. Within one apartment, Lorraine Hansberry capsulized so much of black life on a myriad of levels—the contrast between Walter and Joseph, the former seeking to find his self-respect through success in the terms laid down by the system, and the latter, who has found his through revolutionary involvement and commitment. And the women. It is like a history of black women at a crucial moment in history, all of them beautiful in totally different ways, all of them strong in totally different ways. If one thinks the play is preaching integration, then one had better check himself, because his own sensibilities have become warped.

It must have taken a lot of guts to follow "A Raisin in the Sun" with "The Sign in Sidney Brustein's Window," to follow a play about blacks in the ghetto with a play about white intellectuals in Greenwich Village. That's why the play confused so many. They expected Lorraine Hansberry to repeat herself, to write "Return to Raisin in the Sun." She didn't. She followed her vision and produced a very significant play.

Sidney Brustein is an intellectual who no longer cares. At one time, he was politically active and involved, an idealist, and although it is never made explicit, it is clear that he went through the McCarthy period and was broken by it. Since that time he has been trying to reconstruct his life, to give it a meaning as significant as that which it once had, and he has merely drifted from one failing endeavor to another. He has adopted a mask of cynicism, and his wife, a young aspiring actress who works as a waitress, is the constant target for his bitterness and self-hatred. The play delineates the reconstruction of Sidney.

The play was produced a year and a half before white liberal intellectuals were to be confronted by the spectre of black power. "Sign" was a conscious warning. Lorraine Hansberry was speaking to those white intellectuals of her own generation and telling them to prepare themselves for what was to come. And, in fact, had already come, for LeRoi Jones, a Villager in good standing, had already stunned his former associates by his new black plays, by his aggressive anti-whiteness. Unfortunately, they didn't have the slightest idea what she was talking about, and by this time, Lorraine lay dying.

On another level, however, the play is a warning to those of us who are now young as Sidney once was and who will be growing older, as Sidney was doing. Where will we be 10, 15 years from now, with our books, our record collections, and our dreams? Where will we be if (or when) the bubble bursts? We are young now, but one day we will have been to one demonstration too many and heard the same speeches once too often. All of us will, in one way or the other, have to walk the painful road walked by Sidney Brustein and I hope that at the end of it, we can say, as Sidney does, that he is "a fool," "A fool who believes that death is waste and love is sweet and that the earth turns and men change every day and that rivers run and that people wanna be better than they are and that flowers smell good and that I hurt terribly today, and that hurt is desperation and desperation is—energy and energy can *move* things . . ."

But maybe that's why Lorraine Hansberry is not a blue-chip stock in today's literary marketplace. Her idealism is of a kind that we don't have any more. She believed in the ultimate goodness of people, believed "that one cannot live with sighted eyes and feeling heart and not know and react to the miseries which afflict this world. . . . What I write is not based on the assumption of idyllic possibilities or innocent assessments of the true nature of life. But rather . . . that, posing one against the other, I think the human race does command its own destiny and that destiny can eventually embrace the stars." But romanticism is not fashionable in our time. Indeed, maybe Lorraine Hansberry was the last of her kind and if that is true, then chaos and barbarism stretch before us into infinity.

Lorraine Hansberry was, however, political in the sense that we in the '60s were. She was involved in the civil rights movement and in radical politics. But she did not subordinate herself as a person to her politics. Throughout "To Be Young, Gifted, and Black," she shows her awareness of the impending black revolution, of what we now call the Third World, of imperialism, capitalism, and the rest. She was a political radical, but her politics were not dogma learned by the mind, but a feeling of one-ness with her people and all people. My God, how we need her today. She knew that politics was not ideology, but caring. Politics is that quality of becoming more and more human, of persuading, cajoling, begging others to go with you on that journey to be human. And everything else—ideologies, strategies, tactics, slogans—are only means to that end (and it is questionable just how good they are as means). But, today, it seems to be the rule that the more political one is, the less human he is.

Perhaps the greatest irony in Lorraine Hansberry is that so much humanity should have come from the life and work of a black woman. Then again, it is quite logical. She had been tempered by the fire and emerged briefly to let her own light shine. She knew that blackness was the basis of her existence, not the totality, and that if it becomes the totality, one can only be consumed by the fires of one's own rage and frustration. Lorraine Hansberry is the black artist who lived beyond anger, which is not to say that she wasn't angry. She was, but anger did not define her art. If one quality did, it was compassion, the kind compassion which can slap a face as easily as it can kiss a cheek, which can curse as easily as it can tease.

She stands as the quintessential model, not only for her vision, but for her integrity in the expression of that vision. Indeed, Sidney Brustein and Walter Lee Younger are brothers and it took a certain kind of courage to be able to see it and express it. A young, gifted, and black writer could not do better than to set himself the goal of being worthy of this woman.

Writing this essay reminded me that identity is being known to one's self, without caring or expecting that identity to be shared or affirmed. It was to be like the ocean. I had known since that spring day in 1959 sitting on the rocks above the ocean at La Jolla. But to know was not to live the knowing. Forcing myself to expose the interior reality in print was one aspect of learning to live my life as I knew it. Not being ashamed of my relationships with white women was another. But I learned to accept the totality of my being with its disparate selves by watching Margaret dance with her life, and mine, for a beautiful year. She lived her selves, regardless of how they appeared to contradict each other. She could love and sleep with me and be enraged when her boyfriend slept with other women. She could prepare leaflets for a feminist demonstration while swooning to the most sexist Mick Jagger song, extol the virtues of natural food while sitting across from me in an Italian restaurant. It was she I talked to during the week I agonized over whether to stop writing for *The Guardian*. "Fuck 'em!" she advised with a shriek as we walked along Second Avenue. "Goddam Stalinists! What th' fuck do they know?" It was, perhaps, the most cogent political commentary I'd heard throughout the sixties. She was the first woman I loved who was not intellectual, and, at first, I was afraid to be with her, not knowing what we would talk about. But being with her was easy, because she cared about all of me, not only my mind. She helped me learn that love does not reside in what you say, but in who you are.

Because of Margaret I fulfilled a childhood dream and moved closer to the burial of my marriage, for one April night in 1970 I made Michele visible. Margaret and I went to see the film, *Woodstock*, and in the final frames, Jimi Hendrix greets the dawn with an extraordinary, lyric guitar solo. However, I was transfixed by the small gold earrings he wore, and entranced by how beautiful they made him look. The next evening, Margaret pierced my right earlobe and I became beautiful, too.

I wondered how Arlene would react when she saw me, because since the beginning of our marriage, I had periodically asked her how she would feel if I pierced one of my ears. She'd always responded by looking at me as if I'd announced that I was having a homosexual affair.

Two days later she met me at the Martha's Vineyard airport as she always did, and was about to greet me when she noticed the gold stud gleaming against my brown skin. The greeting caught in her throat. Her mouth closed and she didn't address a word to me for the remainder of the day.

That evening I was standing before the bathroom mirror admiring my feminine self when I noticed her standing in the doorway. "I'm sorry about the way I reacted. It just took me a little time to adjust to it. But I think you look kinna cute." There was a tremor in her voice, and I looked at her and saw her eyes doubting that she knew the person before her. I wondered, too, because, suddenly, I didn't care if she approved. I turned back to the mirror, and instead of seeing myself, I saw who I had been in relation to her for the past eight years. There was the young boy, unsure of himself and in fear of loneliness, handing his life to his sun-lit bride. In return for protection from loneliness, he accepted her thrashings, her demands, and punished himself with guilt when he failed to be who she wanted him to be—a man who lived only for her. For eight years, I had wanted her approval of my life, wanted her to say that it was all right for me to go south, to go to Hanoi, to rent a studio, to buy a bicycle and roam the midnight streets, which I had done the previous year so I could be alone. All the letters I had written explaining myself to her had been appeals for approval, petitions wanting her to sanction my being. Even though I had acted, sometimes brutally, without her imprimatur, I had never ceased longing for it, and though she had always given it after the fact, I had paid for it by her consequent resentment. But that night when Margaret and I pushed our way through the slow-moving crowd outside a Third Avenue movie house, I turned to her and said, timidly, "How do you think I'd look if I got my ear pierced?" "I think you'd look adorable," she replied, smiling, and I was free. (I could not understand why I doubted Arlene's ardent declarations of love until the night Margaret said, "I like you." Arlene never said that, and I don't think she could have, because she experienced me only in relation to her needs. When I satisfied them, I was loved. When I did not, I was hated. After I left, I knew that if I ever married again, I would be content to be liked. If love did not follow, I could go to the movies and see it.)

Standing before the bathroom mirror, I realized, finally, that my life was not a subject for discussion and I would never get into an argument about it again. It was a gift presented to me, which I could give or withdraw from others, and a pierced ear, with a golden stud, was a plainsong of praise.

3

Summer. We moved to a house on State Road in the center of Gay Head, and from the small room with the sloping ceiling on the top floor, I looked up from the typewriter on to the Atlantic Ocean, and Portugal somewhere beyond the horizon line.

The silence between Arlene and me was so familiar now that it had acquired the illusion of intimacy. The first six months of 1970 were the best of our marriage, at least for me, because I had been able to write without the annoying intrusion of mundane marital tensions. Arlene had begun, finally, creating a separate life by organizing a free nursery school. It was the ultimate irony of our marriage, because she had wanted to be a preschool teacher when we'd met. "You're too brilliant to waste your mind on children," I'd told her, an indication of the contempt in which I held children then, and I apologized that summer for influencing her life so wrongly. She had the gift of being able to enter a child's world wholly and she loved being there. I wished, sometimes, she had been able to so enter mine.

I could not live in a child's world then, and Arlene frequently criticized me for not assuming the role of father, except as disciplinarian. But I had never been a child, had very few, if any, pleasant childhood memories, did not know what a father was, and wasn't particularly interested in learning. I couldn't understand why my children addressed me as "Dad," for no such person existed. Yet, once I learned to share silence with them, which I could only do when Arlene was absent, a relationship was created between us. My only pleasant childhood memories were the times of silence shared with my mother while she cooked, or with my father while riding in the car alone with him. I did not know how to explain this to Arlene, and felt guilty when she came home from a meeting or a trip to learn that I hadn't played with the children. "What did you do?" she'd want to know. I could only say, "Nothing." The children understood, I think, that I had brought them into the nave of myself where words had no existence. Only in the silence could I say to them, I am here, and only in the silence could I hear them say, so are we. Ultimately, there is nothing else to be said.

4

The end came at the crepe paper remains of the children's birthday party that July. It assumed the only form it could have: Arlene told me that she had had an affair.

I had known, because after seven of them myself, I had recognized the signs—the flustered joy on seeing a certain person unexpectedly in the store or at the laundromat, the glance toward a particular house as she drove me from the airport, the brief, *sotto voce* phone conversations. The conclusive proof came when, two weeks before her confession, she told me that she no longer knew what was real and what wasn't.

I knew the feeling well, because to have an affair was to admit a new reality into one's self, one so important that it threatened to drown you in the depths of its beauty. However, the new reality could not be given to the one with whom you'd always shared joy. You couldn't run through the door on a sun-washed afternoon, your body still radiating the heat of another's nakedness, and announce, "I just slept with the most fantastic person I've ever met!" The joy had to be buried in some cobwebbed corner of your soul where your spouse couldn't see it. But this was the most wonderful occurrence of your life and a hundred times a day you stopped just before you blurted, "Come see! Come see!" while grabbing your spouse's hand and leading him/her with high-arched skips to the place in the woods where you found the dawn-blue robin's egg. But it could not be. Not only must you keep silent, but you had to pretend that you were who you had always been, that the best thing to happen to you recently was finding a gas station with gas a penny cheaper than you had been paying. But you were not the same person and never would be again. Your past, and the spouse who belonged to it, were like the dream ghosts which hover on the outskirts of waking. But those dream remnants were what your spouse, friends and neighbors considered real. How could they? Didn't they see that you had just been crowned with the galaxy? They didn't, and after a week of trying to live in a reality which no longer existed for you, and always suppressing the one which did, you could not distinguish subjective and objective reality, because, for the first time in your life, the two did not correspond.

By my third affair, I had learned to keep my marriage separate from my affairs by allowing the marriage existence only in the presence of Arlene, and the affair only with my beloved. That was the psychology for successful extramarital relationships. The moment of sadness at leaving your beloved could not be allowed to connect itself to the moment you saw your spouse. (But the joy you knew on leaving your spouse could be the wings speeding you to your lover.) During those first days of July when Arlene cried out to me repeatedly, "Julie, please help me! I'm losing my mind!" I said silently, "The first one is the hardest. Don't tell me about it." But she had to. It was the most forceful way of telling me and herself that the marriage was finished.

We sat on the screened-in side porch, and as I listened, my mind did not dispute her right to do what I had done more times than she knew. My emotions, however, were rotted with jealousy and possessiveness, and they implored me to scream, cry and curse her. My mind lashed me scornfully for being unable to accept from her what I extolled in myself. I knew my emotions were wrong, but they existed. Unwilling to accept their existence and unable to allow them expression, I could only hold them inside and loathe myself for having them.

However, when Arlene ended her confession by telling me that all she wanted was for me to help her feel sane again, I looked at her, paused, and said, evenly, "Describe to me in what way you feel crazy." It was the single most strange instant of my life, because in the pause between her request and my response, I disassociated myself from my emotions, and for the next two hours, I listened as she detailed her feelings of the past month, and analyzed for her what she had experienced as if I were an anthropologist classifying bone chips. She needed me, and I needed to be needed. Ours was the perfect marriage of defects, and it was alive and well.

"I feel sane for the first time in a month," she finally said. I was glad. "Are you going to be O.K.?" she continued. I nodded. I was sure I would. My emotions just needed a few days to memorize the lecture notes on open relationships. I went upstairs to my study, lay on the narrow bed and cried.

I cried for four months. It was an uncontrollable sobbing, a force which possessed me without warning as I sat at the breakfast table, in airport waiting lounges, or in a casual conversation with a friend. I did not know what was wrong. Was I so typically male that I lived by the double standard? I didn't think so, for I had easily forgotten the affair she'd had while I was in the South. One day as we drove down-island to look at a house we were buying, and which I knew I would not live in, I said, suddenly, "I feel like I've been killed." She responded angrily. "All I did was sleep with one guy. What's the big deal?" But that was not what

247

I was talking about. I knew only that my body said that she had murdered me.

Suicide became my lover. There had been times when I had not wanted to live, but this time I wanted to die. I went into the bathroom several times a day and held the bottle of Excedrin tablets in my hand lovingly. I imagined opening it, swallowing the contents, and then lying on the bed to wait for death. I particularly enjoyed fantasizing Arlene's discovery of my body. Always, though, some force gripped my hand and would not allow it to pour out the bottle's contents.

Each afternoon we went to the beach and while Arlene and the children played in the waves, I lay fully clothed on the sand, staring at the other successful men with their wives and children. How many of them were living in a soap opera, too? Was this success? An attractive and articulate wife, two beautiful and intelligent children, a VW microbus, a cat, a home on Martha's Vineyard, and a biographical sketch in *Who's Who in America* which had no resemblance to my life? How banal I had become. So much so that Arlene and I were both infected with gonorrhea that summer and didn't know, at first, who had given it to whom. (The three women with whom I'd been sleeping passed their VD tests, I later learned.) All that remained were wife-swapping parties, and Arlene had already suggested that I have an affair with one of her best friends. (If only the friend had asked.) I had become a member in good standing of the liberal-intellectual-bourgeoisie. I could see myself living in that house in the woods, which I'd dubbed, "The House That Revolution Built," and once or twice a week inviting another couple over with their two children, to eat thin slices of imported ham and cheeses with expensive crackers, to sit down to dinner before the round oak table (and you can't be an intellectual without a round oak table, preferably one bought very cheaply at "a tag sale in the Berkshires," or "at this junk shop we found on a backroad in Connecticut"), to talk knowingly about what was happening in the country (and we would really know, because we knew people who knew other people who said . . .). I could see myself achieving a minor reputation as a writer, ensuring modest sales of my books, and with success certain, I would watch my children grow into successful adulthoods and marry about the same time I burned the mortgage. If I were lucky, I would be drinking so much by then that I wouldn't recognize how much I had betrayed that boy who had wanted to be the black James Joyce. Sitting on the beach on those summer afternoons, I realized that my life was no different from that of any middle-echelon business executive, except that on my descent into banality, I could quote from two thousand years of literature and hum portions of Bach cantatas.

I had to begin again, to once more awaken in terror on the morning of my Commencement. But how? I did not know if such was even possible. I could not leave in anger at Arlene, rejecting what I had become with her. When one's living leads to a present he cannot accept, that living, which is one's past, cannot be repudiated. It must be invited to a powwow, and the peace pipe passed back and forth beneath the bejewelled night sky. If one does not make peace with the past, it will simply return at some unexpected time in the future, painted with the colors of war and shooting swift, silent arrows.

I knew I would leave, but I counseled myself to wait patiently for the right time.

By the middle of August, I was surprised to find myself at the typewriter. It was an unconscious act, wholly unrelated to the crisis of my life. But I prided myself on being a professional, and the show always goes on. During the next two months I wrote a book of tales for children, published in 1972 as *The Knee-High Man;* a short story, "The Valley of the Shadow of Death," published in *Black Review No. 2;* reviews for *The New York Times Book Review* and *Life;* an article on black separatism for *Ebony,* and an obituary of Jimi Hendrix for *Evergreen Review.*

(ARTICLE: "Jimi Hendrix: Goin' Toward Heaven," *Evergreen Review,* December, 1970)

When Brian Jones of the Rolling Stones died earlier this year, you knew it was only the beginning. That fantastic period of euphoria, of the ecstasy of the virginal newness of the sound of rock could not last forever. Rock is a highly intense music; it is pure energy turned into sound. It is also a dangerous music because of its ability to so totally and completely capture the listener, filling him with the joy the touch the feel of the combination of sound and words and rhythm known as music. When one listens to rock, he knows why Plato wanted to control the musicians and poets in the Republic. No state can hold itself together if, in some way, it does not maintain control over the arts, particularly music, the most immediate and sensual of experiences.

If it is a dangerous music to listen to, how much more dangerous it must be to and for the musicians who make it. When playing well, the musician gives of himself until there is nothing left inside. He leaves the stage drained, empty, and yet, the conditions of the business demand that he must pack his equipment, get on an airplane, and go somewhere else to do it again the next night and the next and the one after that.

There is a price one pays for being an artist, and that price is paid in the emotional energy expended in the creative process. The writer, alone in his room with his typewriter, has his own peculiar problems of creating, and, at the same time, remaining one step removed from what he is creating, analyzing it, criticizing it. His problems revolve around a kind of schizophrenia; a constant battle to maintain a balance. The musician, however, is an intimate part of the act of creation. He is both creator and audience. He strikes a chord on his guitar and that chord creates responses in him. He is not outside, as is the writer. (A degree of detachment from what he is writing about is necessary for the writer at the instant he writes. He must not feel as he writes, particularly if he wants to successfully make his readers feel. The musician must feel what he is singing and playing or he will not make the listener feel.) He plays, and not only does the music he plays set off responses within him, it sets off responses in his listeners, and their responses in turn affect him, pushing him to do more and more. "You really want to turn those people on," Hendrix told an interviewer. "It's just like a feeling of really deep concern. You get very intense. That's the way I look at it. That's natural for me. Once you hit that first note, or once the first thing goes down, then it's all right."

The great musician, like any great artist, becomes the servant of his art and his life becomes a sacrifice to it. ". . . the deeper you get into it the more sacrifices you have to do, maybe even on your personality or your outward this and that. I just dedicate my whole life to this whole art. You have to forget about what other people say. If it's art or anything else . . . you have to forget what people say about you sometimes. . . . You have to go and be crazy. Craziness is like heaven. . . . Once you reach that point of where you don't give a damn about what everybody else is saying, you're goin' toward heaven. The more you get into it, they're goin' to say, 'Damn, that cat's really flipped out. Oh, he's gone now.' But if you producin' and creating, you know, you're getting closer to your own heaven. That's what man's trying to get to anyway." (Jimi Hendrix) Yet, while he is being sacrificed, he must survive so that the sacrifice may be renewed with each dawn. There has to be some way for the musician to replenish himself after he leaves the stage and slumps in a chair backstage. Alcohol, dope, and sex are the most common means. Writers and artists have availed themselves of the first and third more than the second. (See Mailer's *Advertisements for Myself* for an account of what drugs can do to a writer.) For the musician, however, drugs provide something. Maybe it's nothing more than a way to continue to feel (once the music has stopped), and yet simultaneously escape. Escape from the demands of the music, the demands of the audiences, and the demands of the way of life.

Perhaps, too, drugs provide an escape from the loneliness. How, you ask, can a Jimi Hendrix or a Mick Jagger, idols of millions, be lonely? The great musician, like the great artist, cannot help but experience the loneliness of the long distance runner, for that is what he is. The musician knows, as he stands there, the lights dancing over him, the faces looking up at him, that who he is is of no concern to those listening. He must do his duty—make music. Afterwards, there are the young girls offering their bodies, not to a person, but to an image, a thing as it were, a musician. And after a while, you, as a person, cease to exist. You are a name, a face, a fuck, the producer of certain sounds, a demigod who can make people feel themselves and others in ways they never imagined. But you, the person, no longer exist. "Jimi was always gettin' pretty upset about the fact that people would put pressures on him to play the hits. 'All of you people . . . have you really come to see me, or have you just come to see Jimi Hendrix, "star," and you want to hear "Foxy Lady," and you want to hear this, or do you really want to see me try and give you some music that I want to play?' And nine out of ten, Jimi comes onstage with that feeling that he wants to play for those people because they've presumably come to hear him and his musical mind. And they don't want to know about it. So he would end up, he would play a couple of things that they knew, and he would play a slow blues for himself, and it would be to any musician's ears a completely mind-blowing and really creative thing that would be so complete and good. And the audience would still shout for those other things. So when he hears that, he's really felt that he's poured something out and that's the real him as a musician, and they haven't even known about it. So he just gets bitter about it—'Okay, you want this, you got it, blam, blam, blam. I'm through and that's it.'" (John Mayall) After a while, the dichotomy between who you know you are and can be and who they want you to be becomes too much. Bob Dylan split to the country. The Beatles stopped performing live. Joan Baez ceased to be a serious performer, preferring political involvement.

Jimi Hendrix, like Brian Jones, accepted the way of life of the musician. He was flamboyant in dress, flamboyant onstage, and, for a while, his private life seemed to be little different. Of all the rock groups, the name he gave his was the most revealing—the Jimi Hendrix Experience. That was it—an experience of the highest order, and music was merely the means toward that experience. Listen to Hendrix on a stereo headset and feel the notes pierce through the center of your head, the sound jumping from one ear to the other. His music, like all great music, was a total experience. So was he.

Then, about two years ago, something happened. He had become a star and was becoming less of a musician. He went onstage and gave them what they wanted, and, afterwards, hated himself. The joy of just making music could not coexist with the demands of stardom. "I hate for little kids to come flashin' on me sayin', 'Oh, wow! You played tonight!' knowing all the time you played bad. That's because they're flashin' on me. That's too much burden on me. I'm just like them. Forget about names as long as the whole stuff is constantly moving toward gettin' things together. I don't disrespect them. I appreciate it, but it hurts me almost inside sometimes. That's just my own little hang-up though." (Jimi Hendrix) It was more than a "little hang-up," as he well knew.

His group broke up and he went to the country to get himself together. He returned with a new group whose name was just as revealing as that of the first—the Band of Gypsys. He had gone from being an experience—the quintessence of Being—to being a gypsy, a wanderer. And one knows that gypsies do not wander voluntarily, but that they are forced to move from place to place. It has now become their way of life, but it is a way of life that is imposed upon them. Their traveling is merely a way of adapting to circumstances. Jimi had become a wanderer, fleeing from the demands of what it is to be Jimi Hendrix, a musician of the highest order. (And the music of the new group differed in tone and mood from that of the Experience. It was a moody, minor-keyed music, simpler and less frenetic than that of the Experience, but lacking in the incredible exuberance and joy of that earlier group.)

The Band of Gypsys did not last long, and the Experience reorganized and broke up again, and Jimi eventually returned to England, where he had first become famous and where, it seems, he felt most at home. And it was there that the drugs he was reported to have used did to him what they had done to Brian Jones. At age twenty-seven, the greatest musician in rock was dead.

I felt particularly close to Hendrix. I never met him and never even saw him perform live. But he was black, and I felt a personal bond between us. I could look at him and know where he had come from, what his childhood and adolescence had been like in Seattle, the quitting school at sixteen to join the paratroops, and then the years of apprenticeship with black musicians like Little Richard and the Isley Brothers.

Where I felt we were closest, though, was when he decided to walk across that line his race had circumscribed about him, when he went to England and became the Jimi Hendrix we know. At a time when black nationalism was on the rise, when Black Power was the order of the day, this black man chose something else—to free himself from other people's conceptions of who he was by merely being himself. He entered another world, a world where he didn't have to deny his race or make a profession of it either. He merely used it as the foundation on which he built his incredible temples of sound. ("I'm representing everything as far as I'm concerned," he said.) And I know the tensions and conflicts he must have felt being an idol to millions of whites. My God, how lonely he must have been, knowing as he stood before an audience that the one part of his being that audience couldn't (or wouldn't) take into themselves was the fact of his race. ("I don't even think of Hendrix as black," said Alvin Lee of Ten Years After. "Hendrix is Hendrix.") But he built his erotic performances out of his black experience (witness his performance in *Monterey Pop*) as does James Brown. The difference between the two, however, is the difference in the audiences for whom they performed. Jimi's audience could not respond in kind. They were turned on, but for all the wrong reasons. They thought he was a good showman and never knew that to dance, to be erotic, is to propel one's self into the vortex of the rhythms of the universe, to the source of life itself.

Explicit eroticism began to play less of a role in his performances. Perhaps he realized that what he knew as fundamental to life and his black experience had merely become a gimmick, something he was expected to do, something audiences came to see but not to be a part of. They mistook the movements of his body for the Jimi Hendrix Experience.

In the last year he performed before black audiences in Harlem, and his music was beginning to expose more of his black roots. Something was on his mind. It seems as if he was beginning to feel a need to come back home. Everybody thought it didn't matter that he was black. To them, that was not important. To Jimi, I think it was, but no one ever knew it except other blacks who felt from him what no white could.

The way I will always remember him is as he was shown at the close of the Woodstock film. It is the last morning of the festival. The sun is coming up and Hendrix is the last performer. And, as shown by the cameras, there he is . . . alone, quiet, and looking peaceful in a way I had never seen a person look. He seemed at one with himself. He has been playing for almost two hours when he appears in the film and, at this point, he is, in his words, "just jamming," and he tells people they can split if they want to. Then, after an instrumental with the group, he plays that incredible solo rendition of the "Star-Spangled Banner," which is like a history of America in sound, and then he breaks immediately into "purple Haze." Without a pause, he progresses into a very quiet, lyrical instrumental that seems to grow from the dawn and the littered, now almost deserted fields of Max Yasgur's farm. While he played, there was scarcely an expression on his face. The camera shot mostly from the side, and you could see that magnificent profile, the mass of hair on his head tied with a flowing scarf folded in half, and the (what looked like) mother-of-pearl studs in his ears. And then it was over. He said, "Thank you," and walked away.

I'll miss him. He was important in my life and I often referred to him jokingly to my friends as "my leader." But it wasn't a joke. He was black, and because he was, and because he chose to be what he was, he helped me to keep from getting trapped in a politic of blackness wherein I would have denied the humanity of others, and, thereby, my own. He helped me to keep struggling to be me because he chose to be himself.

Now he's paid the price of being who he was. The drugs were the immediate cause. But it was the music that killed him. God extracts a price from those He chooses to be His messengers.

For a while I'll feel rather lost without him, as I did when Malcolm X and John Coltrane died (the only other deaths that I have ever felt in the fiber of my being). I depended on Jimi Hendrix in a very fundamental way. Now I've got to continue on my own. And I've got to do it not only for me, but for him, too.

But someone named Jimi Hendrix was there when I needed him. Because he lived, I am a little more who I am. (Now, excuse me, while I kiss the sky.)

All quoted passages are from a remarkable book, A World Bold As Love: Rock, *by Douglas Kent Hall and Sue C. Clark. Cowles Book Co., Inc. New York, 1970—J.L.*

I wrote, and afterward, rereading what I had written, wondered where the words and ideas had come from. My consciousness was unrelieved pain, and yet, my words had their typically even, quiet tone. I could only conclude that the writing came from somewhere within me that had nothing to do with the circumstances of my life, and perhaps, it was that which was the counterweight to the death I still wanted.

One particular essay nagged at me throughout the summer, demanding to be written. I tried to ignore the necessity of doing so, hoping that someone else would write it. The occasion was the trial of seven members of the Black Panther Party in New Haven, who were accused of torturing and murdering Alex Rackley, another BPP member. The three Party members who had actively participated in the murder had admitted their guilt. Yet, black and white radicals had been demonstrating on the New Haven Green, and many articles were published in the radical press demanding that the New Haven Seven be freed, because it was impossible, so the radicals claimed, for blacks to receive justice in America. I waited for weeks, hoping someone else would say, murder is murder. No one did, and I watched while friends I loved, like Abbie Hoffman, Jerry Rubin and Dave Dellinger demanded the release of the New Haven Seven. I didn't want to risk losing their friendship, particularly Abbie's, but to remain silent would be to risk losing myself.

(ARTICLE: "Aquarian Notebook," *Liberation*, Autumn, 1970)

Every whole consists of two halves. Each half can be composed of myriad parts, each contributing to the composition and character of that half. After the Woodstock Festival last summer, we mistakenly viewed it as being the whole, not realizing until the bad karma and murder at Altamont that Woodstock had merely represented one-half. Together with Altamont, however, we got a picture of the whole of the new culture.

The trial of the Chicago Eight was also thought to represent a whole. Within its myriad parts, the Movement was synthesized and represented in the persons of the defendants. What the Movement opposed was represented in the judge, prosecutors, prosecution witnesses, and the jury. The Chicago trial was almost like a morality play, so clear were the lines between "good" and "evil." And, we mistook that trial as being truly representative of the Movement.

The trial of the New Haven Seven, however, indicates that the Chicago trial was merely one-half of the whole, the Woodstock half. The trial of the Black Panthers in New Haven is the other half, the Altamont. And, unfortunately, we have been loath to recognize what that trial really means for us.

The facts in the case are simple. Alex Rackley, a member of the BPP, was tortured and murdered. Many members of the New Haven chapter were arrested and charged with various degrees of responsibility for the acts. Warren Kimbro and Lonnie McLucas were charged with the actual murder. George Sams was an active accomplice, giving the orders. And, according to Sams, he was merely carrying out orders he had received from Bobby Seale, thus making Seale a co-conspirator. Except for Seale's alleged complicity, the facts are indisputable. McLucas and Kimbro have each admitted participating in the torture and of firing one shot each into Rackley. Sams has admitted his role. Thus, from the legal point of view, it is an open and shut case. George Sams, Warren Kimbro, and Lonnie McLucas were principally responsible for the death of Alex Rackley.

However, the legal approach always omits the human factor and it is with the introduction of the human factor that the picture becomes much more complicated. McLucas says that he participated in Rackley's murder under the threat of death, that he was coerced. Kimbro says much the same. George Sams is pictured by the Panthers and the underground press (which always falls obediently in line behind the Panthers, never questioning where the parade might be leading) as a psychotic and an agent provocateur. Indeed, Sams becomes the scapegoat, the one on whom all responsibility and blame is placed. From the evidence at hand, it seems clear that Sams is a psychotic, that he probably was an agent, and that he is a very sick person. The evidence also makes clear that he did use coercion and threats against McLucas and Kimbro, that they were fearful of their lives. It is on these aspects of the case that people in the Movement have seized and emphasized. [The underground press tells us that the BPP is being persecuted in New Haven and that the defendants are being railroaded.] Movement journalists want us to believe, in fact, that the Panthers are not guilty of murder, though they admit that they did murder Rackley.

This is sad. On the one hand, we can self-righteously cite the verdict of the Nuremberg Trials when we want to condemn the military establishment and the politicians. We can say to them that you are personally responsible for what you do, that you do not have to follow orders and there are no extenuating circumstances. Yet, we can turn right around and become Adolf Eichmanns, eloquent apologists for the Movement's My Lai. In other words, our morality is used to condemn others, but it is not to be applied to ourselves. We can react with outrage when four are murdered at Kent State, but when a professor is killed in the dynamiting of the Mathematics Building at the University of Wisconsin, we don't give it a second thought. When they kill, it is murder. When we kill, there are extenuating circumstances. It was an accident, we say. The blast went off too soon.

What kind of revolutionaries are we? Or, do we even deserve that name anymore? The murder of Alex Rackley was an important occurrence in the history of the Movement. It was the logical culmination of the politics we have been espousing, a politics of violence-for-the-sake-of-violence, a politics which too quickly and too neatly divides people into categories of "revolutionary" and "counter-revolutionary." The murder of Alex Rackley is the result of a politics which more and more begins to resemble the politics we are supposedly seeking to displace. Mary Breasted in the *Village Voice* of September 17, 1970, describes a scene from the Philadelphia Constitutional Convention. It is more revelatory than she obviously intended. Michael Tabor, one of the New York Panther 21, is the speaker.

> "He . . . gave a loving description of the Panther version of self-defense.
> " 'It means if the pig moves on you today and he's got a gun, and, you ain't got a gun, Christ, hippie, you ain't in a position to deal with him,' he said, adding after a pause, 'but come sundown . . .'
> "The crowd in the gym caught his meaning. They broke into happy laughter, cheering and applause. He couldn't resist continuing his violent fantasy.
> " 'You go up on the roof . . .' (Another pause and more cheers.)
> " 'You put your finger on that index . . .' (Cheers again.)
> " 'You get him in your sights . . .' (Cheers)
> " 'And you pull that trigger . . .' (Wild cheers)
> " 'That's self-defense. Cause if you don't get him today, he's gonna get you tomorrow.' (A great ecstatic roar.)"

This is not the politics of revolution, but the politics of psychotic fantasy. Under no circumstances can murder *qua* murder be advocated and glorified. And, for it to be cheered and applauded is even more sick. It is one thing to advocate the necessity to defend one's self. Malcolm X did it simply and eloquently. It is another thing, however, to lovingly describe an ambush with an almost sensual delight. In Miss Breasted's parenthetical descriptions of the audience's responses to Tabor's remarks, one does not see a gathering of revolutionaries, but only the Romans in the Coliseum, cheering and applauding the deaths of the slaves.

The trial in New Haven represents that other half of the Movement, that half we do not care to see or acknowledge as even having an existence. Because we have invested ourselves with Absolute Virtue, we cannot see when we are wrong, when we are moving away from where we say we are going. We perform incredible mind-calisthenics to remove all responsibility from the shoulders of McLucas. George Sams becomes our scapegoat, just as students and blacks become the scapegoat for America's sins. Yet, McLucas is responsible for what he did. But, he belonged to an organization in which the individual is required to give up his own mind to that of the organization and any deviation from the official "line" results in that individual's expulsion. The Movement has spawned organizations which turn out robots, who, at the sight of another person, start talking revolutionary ideology, who view the world and other people through the narrow, inverted eyes of doctrinal politics.

The trial in New Haven raises serious questions about the functioning of the Black Panther Party. How was it possible for one individual, George Sams, to terrorize the New Haven chapter, as it seems clear he did? Why was not even one individual able to pick up a telephone and call the national Panther office in Oakland and inform them as to what was going on? Seale, a national officer, was in New Haven while the torture was proceeding. Yet, not one member of the chapter was able to talk to him privately for a minute, or to slip him a note. This is unthinkable until we remember that no one, except a child, had the courage to call the naked Emperor naked. All revolutionary organizations find discipline necessary; however, when discipline is so strict that basic human morality is suppressed (and always in the name of the "people"), then, that is not discipline. It is totalitarianism. The Panthers have taken great pains to continually inform us that they are the "vanguard." If they are, then it is their responsibility to be shining exemplifications of humanity revolutionized, the New Man. So far, and particularly in the New Haven case, there is nothing more evident than humanity inverted.

The BPP has gone through some confusion trying to make it appear that they are, once again, the victims of persecution in the New Haven trials. Immediately after Rackley's murder was discovered by the police and a finger pointed toward the Panthers, they maintained that Rackley had been an agent and had been tortured and murdered by the police. It was very much later that they began saying Rackley was a member in "good standing" and had been murdered by Sams, who was framing others. And, when McLucas and Kimbro confessed their parts in it, the responsibility was shifted even more to Sams. Cleaver maintained in several articles that he had always been suspicious of Sams, that Sams had been expelled from the Party and had only been reinstated at Stokely Carmichael's urgings. (Carmichael was, at the time, an officer of the BPP.) That, in fact, Sams had been brought into the party by Carmichael. In other words, everyone is to blame, except those responsible for the deed. Even if Carmichael did bring Sams into the

Party, what kind of organization would expel and then reinstate a person at the urgings of one individual? An organization has criteria for membership that are supposed to be independent of the existence of any one individual. This is particularly true of a revolutionary organization. The logical conclusion one reaches from Cleaver's comments is that, in reality, Stokely Carmichael killed Alex Rackley.

Although massive demonstrations had been promised for New Haven, they have not materialized. Perhaps that is because the trial is not a clear-cut example of Movement virtue vs. American iniquity. Perhaps people are uneasy about the entire case, but afraid to voice their uneasiness and doubt. Yet, Movement leaders and personalities continue to see the New Haven trial as another example of the Government's attempt to wipe out the Panthers.

In actuality, what is happening in New Haven is a tragedy for the Movement. George Sams is not responsible for the death of Alex Rackley. Neither can total responsibility be placed on the shoulders of Kimbro and McLucas, though they pulled the triggers. The responsibility lies with the kind of politics they have been articulating. Kimbro and McLucas are tragic victims of that. It is not the Government which is responsible in this instance; it is us. We have become the good Germans. We see the troops go by, the blood dripping from their hands, and we cheer, "Power to the People" and "Right On." Our involvement in the rhetoric and emotions of violence have so distorted our vision and warped our minds that we are now capable of perpetrating the same acts of inhumanity as the Government.

It should be impossible for a revolutionary to conceive of himself doing certain things. Torture is one of them. To torture another person means one must suspend all human feelings not to feel the pain of the other. McLucas testified to his own sickness and revulsion at the torture. Yet, his humanity was not strong enough to force him to risk his own life to stop it, or (and this is more likely) his humanity had been sifted through the sieve of dogma and doctrine and his head tried to justify what his heart was sickened by. And that is the politics too many of us exalt—a politics of the head. But the revolutionary's politics, while guided by his head, are never disconnected from his heart. It is the feeling of love for humanity in his heart which his head seeks to make concretely manifest. That is the soil, the only soil, from which the revolution can grow.

If the murder of Alex Rackley is seen as nothing more than what can happen when an agent gets loose in your organization, then, we are finished. If George Sams is held wholly responsible for Rackley's murder, and not our politics, then there can be no revolution coming from us. McLucas and Kimbro are not revolutionary martyrs. There is no glory surrounding them. They are deserving of all our compassion, pity and tears, because as we cry for them, we cry for ourselves and what we have allowed ourselves to become.

We must stop trying to excuse the murder of Rackley. There is no excuse. We must face that very painful fact and learn from it. If we don't, it will happen again and again.

We are never so much the victims of another, as we are the victims of ourselves.

The editors of *Liberation* held the essay for three months after it was submitted. Finally, I had a tense meeting with them early that fall, in which they argued that the prosecution could use my words against the Panthers. I'd been aware of that as I wrote it, but if the use to which my words could be put was to be the sole criteria for writing, I would have to stop. But as the old ones were fond of saying, "The Devil can quote Scripture as good as God." The meeting ended without agreement, but to the magazine's credit, they published the essay. My relationships with Abbie, Jerry and Dave emerged unharmed.

5

Summer dwindled into cooler, pre-autumn days and I waited for a sign of deliverance. It came in Santa Fe, New Mexico, at the beginning of September, where I went to speak at a conference. Carol was sitting cross-legged on the floor the evening I spoke, and I felt myself directing my words to her. Before I heard her voice, I felt known by her, and when we finally spoke, my life was handed back to me.

The conference ended, however, without either of us talking of what was so evident: We loved each other. But we couldn't talk of that because there was no chance to live that love. She was in the process of moving from her apartment in Cambridge to California. I wrote her after I returned to Martha's Vineyard and she called from California, and said, "I'll come if you want me." I did, but did not tell her so. To leave Arlene for another woman would abuse her, Carol and myself. I did not want to leave Arlene unless she agreed that I should. I was not seeking her approval this time, but it was important to the eight years we had together, however painfully, that my leaving be devoid of the slightest suggestion that I was rejecting those years, or her. She had to know that my leaving was merely a prerequisite for finding my life. If she understood and accepted that, my leaving would be the same for her.

A few weeks later, I had a dream. Arlene and I were asleep. I was awakened by our daughter's crying outside the bedroom door. I did not want to get up to see what was bothering her, and as she continued crying, became angry, because Arlene continued sleeping, undisturbed. The crying increased, and I heard a noise and realized that someone was attacking her. The noise and the crying became louder, and I was frantic. I tried to wake Arlene, but she seemed to sleep all the more soundly. As I started to get out of bed to see what was happening to our daughter, Arlene rolled on top of me. I told her to get up. I could hear our daughter screaming louder, and I yelled at Arlene, "Get off! Get off!" She did not move. I pushed at her and she became heavier, pinning me to the bed. Hysterically, I began pushing at Arlene, and her body seemed to acquire weight with each push and I started to suffocate. Finally, in a final desperate effort and in sheer terror, I pushed at her, and awoke to find myself sitting upright in bed, trembling.

I sat there, and the dream's meaning was evident. My life was, indeed, being suffocated by her. The child outside the door was not our daughter, but me, and I was in mortal danger. I did not understand how I could be myself and my daughter simultaneously in the dream, but I knew it was true. (Only while working on this book did I happen to read an essay of Carl Jung's on synchronicity, where I found the following: "Any essential change of attitude signifies a psychic renewal which is usually accompanied by symbols of rebirth in the patient's dreams and fantasies." That girl-child being attacked was the new me, the infant, unknown self.)

The dream was the final sign. I left, and it did not matter if Arlene understood. I explained why I had to leave, but regardless of how much I told her that I cared about her, that I wasn't rejecting her but choosing myself, understanding would not relieve her pain, or even be a consolation. Understanding could not obscure the central fact of my leaving: Once I had needed her; now I didn't. Her presence in my life represented death.

But what is flawed at its birth can never be made whole. The flaws can be disguised, but one day the finish wears off. We had used each other like putty to fill the cracks in our young souls. Any marriage I entered would have been the same, given who I was then. Our fate is not visited on us; we attract it. We rise to the surface and grab the fly, only to feel the hook tear through our mouths, until we learn to see a lure and know it for what it is.

Thus, there was no blame. Our time had ended. It was time now to cross the great water.

VIII

1

October 18, 1970
(Journal)

It has been five days since I left Arlene. A lot of me is here [Cambridge] with Carol and a lot of me is still there with Arlene. And I guess it'll be that way for a while. It is difficult to end a life with one person and begin a new life with another person in the same motion. Maybe it's even foolish to try.

The last day or so I've had all kinds of doubts and anxieties. Part of it is guilt, of course, over leaving. . . . Most of it is just a matter of time, of letting time kill the responses and reactions I've carried for eight years and letting new ones be born. It's going to be hard, though. Harder, perhaps, than I realized. One can carry his past with him to such a degree that it literally becomes his present. It literally transforms all he feels. And that's one of my problems. To live more and more in the present.

The older one gets, the more complex life seems. Maybe one gets more and more conscious of the many levels and dynamics with age. It's always been this complex. I'm just learning that.

Well, I've enlisted for the duration. Will ride each current to see where it goes. If I drown, at least I wasn't afraid to ride. To live a spiritual existence is much more precarious. Whatever happens depends on me. Sometimes the thought is exhilarating. Sometimes not. I have exchanged the known—life with Arlene—for the unknown. It is like beginning again, except into the new life I carry an old one, which can destroy the possibilities of the new. And I have to have the strength and courage to make sure it doesn't.

263

I know that probably one of the things that has gone through your mind is the "unfairness" of my leaving, that I leave to lead the life I want to, unencumbered with children. . . . From the inside, though, it looks different.

Yes, it is undeniably true that I will not have to live twenty-four hours a day with two children as you will. And if that's taken as the sole criteria of fairness, then I am unfair. I guess something I've always thought of as "unfair" is how people always give their sympathy to the women when a couple breaks up. They never consider that the man may have deep feelings about his children, may find some emptiness in himself because they will not be as intimate a part of his life anymore.

In a way, I think we, as individuals, face the same basic problem: Building lives without the other. And if the prospect is alternately exciting and depressing for you, it is the same for me. There was a certain security in our being together, a security because we were dealing with what was known, what was familiar. Now, perhaps more even for me than you, there is nothing but the unknown. And, sometimes, it scares me. I want to come back, because no matter how bad it got, at least being with you was familiar. Being married was familiar. There were few dangers. Now there are many. I am haunted, of course, by the thought that I should not have done what I have done, that I am making a mistake. Yet, I know that it is not a mistake. Still, there is the fear.

2

The mistake was living with Carol. I was unfit for human consumption, and especially incapable of responding to the kind of love Carol offered. "I sing your praises," she wrote me in her first letter, and though I couldn't imagine what she had found to sing about, I wanted to believe that there was something. The first week we lived together, she took me to clothing shops, because, "You should dress in the colors of the sun," and I, whose wardrobe had always consisted of monochromes, became a rainbow. "Celebrate yourself," she told me. I didn't know how, but I wanted her to teach me.

Carol is the only genius I've ever known, and the intensity of living with her was, at times, unbearable. A graduate student in psychology and religion at Harvard, she was also an artist and a poet, and our life together was one of conversation more incredible than those I'd shared with Arlene. Carol and I lived on her king-size bed studying astrology, the *I Ching*, and the Tarot, talking about Tillich, Jung, Buber, dreams, the structure of language, and the gifts bestowed on her by her Sioux mother. We buzzed through the streets of Cambridge in her yellow MG, the top down, regardless of how chilly the autumn weather was, and each week she flew with me to New York for the radio show, and the television show I had begun hosting on WNET.

Every other weekend, however, I went to Martha's Vineyard to see the children, for I wanted them to know that I was only absent from their home, not their lives. Being with them, however, meant being with Arlene, making it almost impossible for us to internally separate from each other.

It was no way to begin a life with another person, and after the ecstasy of the first weeks, life with Carol seemed no different than it had been with Arlene. (Months after I left Carol, I cast her horoscope chart and, to my dismay, it was almost identical with Arlene's.) Carol could not live with a writer, either, but that was what I was, and I vanished into the typewriter to do record and book reviews for *Rolling Stone*, columns for *Liberation*, an article for *The New York Times* Op-Ed page, and to begin a book of historical fiction, *Long Journey Home*. Carol could not accept my self-absorption, and retaliated with sharpened silence, and I began wandering around Harvard Square, looking for a home in the bodies of Radcliffe girls. But, having always had relationships happen to me, I did not know how to make one happen. Death returned.

November 2, 1970
(Letter to Arlene)

I'm beginning to feel as if there's a fatal flaw within me which makes it impossible for anyone to really live with me. And, if that's true, I know what it is. It's that my life is pledged to something else. God, shall we say, though that won't communicate anything to you. I've been on the verge of tears for the last day, and am sorta blinking back the tears now. . . .

I spent a good part of yesterday with the *I Ching*. Thank God for it, because it helps to bring to consciousness a lot of things within me which are unconscious, which I can't get at any other way. One of the things I asked was, "What do you think of my having left Arlene?" I asked because everything within me was saying that I should ask you if I could come back. . . .

Well, I got Hexagram 47 "Oppression, Exhaustion"

THE IMAGE

> There is no water in the lake:
> The image of EXHAUSTION.
> Thus the superior man stakes his life
> On following his will.

> When the water has flowed out below, the lake must dry up and become exhausted. That is fate. This symbolizes an adverse fate in human life. In such times there is nothing a man can do but acquiesce to his fate and remain true to himself. This concerns the deepest stratum of his being for this alone is superior to all external fate.

. . . the above seems to describe my situation so accurately. Our relationship as it was constituted had exhausted itself and there was little I could do "but acquiesce in my fate and remain true to myself." But it is so hard and I can't help but wonder if it's worth it. . . . My internal reality is so strong and so much more real to me than anything else that, I guess, there is always a veil between me and others. . . . I live most fully and completely inside myself, not with others. . . .

. . . I guess I had to go through this experience to really . . . recognize that God demands that I give all of myself to Him, to the work He says I must do, that maybe if I do that, then I'll find some kind of inner peace and as long as I resist and fight Him, as long as I keep thinking that I have a right to try and be happy in the ways that others are, I'll be in pain. . . .

Articulating the pain did not, however, alleviate it. I still bled from the summer's wounds, and they reopened whenever I remembered my shame and self-hatred at my reaction to Arlene's affair. Why had I been unable to accept it? Why had I felt destroyed?

> November 13, 1970
> 2:30 A.M.
> (Letter to Arlene)

I know that it will be quite a long time before the pain of this summer recedes for me. . . . In trying to figure out why I took it so hard, you suggested that it might have something to do with

266

feeling possessive. I partially accepted that, but it didn't feel right to me. And then this week it hit me just what it was all about. When you told me, it meant that I no longer belonged to you. Does that make sense? When I say that I'm not rationalizing and really saying that you no longer belonged to me. I've never felt that, but I've always felt that I belonged to you. . . . Too, I belonged to the island and because I no longer had you, I no longer had the island. Thus I was utterly alone—without person or place.

. . . I go back to that feeling I had when we met that I had to marry you. It was a very necessary thing to me, because I needed that to do anything else. And, as long as I knew I belonged to someone—you—then, everything else wouldn't be as difficult. . . . What do I mean by belonging? I guess I mean something which makes me feel like someone in this world provides some kind of refuge. You know that feeling of belonging. You like groups. I don't think I've ever had that feeling of belonging except with you and the island. . . .

. . . I guess another reason I felt that I no longer belonged to you was because I felt that your affair was a settling of the score with me. It was something you had to do to maintain your own sense of self-respect in the face of my affairs. I felt that Ronald didn't exist as a person for you that much, but he was someone who was available, who was sweet and gentle and thereby met certain standards for you. But he sorta got caught in the middle of something which had been going on for eight years. And this is not to say that you didn't like him for himself, also. But also involved was just the whole idea of having an affair, because you wanted to have one; you wanted to feel young and romantic; you wanted to even things up with me a little. You were trying to work something out in our relationship as much, if not more, than you were trying to have another relationship. . . . Perhaps all of those mixed emotions contributed as much to your feeling of insanity as much as your not being able to tell me.

In a letter, she agreed that the act had been directed at me: I was supposed to feel murdered. She'd told me about it, not only to relieve her guilt, but to force me to do what she could not—leave. (If she had met a man with whom she shared love, I would not have been destroyed. Love happens; it is good, and will not make one insane. She had played a game, and I was the ball slammed across the net.)

But I could not blame her. The death was rooted within me, because I had fled from loneliness into marriage, fled from it into the revolution and blackness. (The knowledge of our essential loneliness is always there, pressing at the backs of our eyes, echoing in the caverns of our souls, and we try not to hear the hollow sounds and think we have triumphed when we hold another and say, "I love you," think we are safe in the vise of another's thighs, think that we have overcome when we raise clenched fists high into the air, as if they were tiny flags to be waved at a parade. We think we have conquered what can only be embraced when we proclaim, "We are an African people," or walk a picket line to show our solidarity with the "oppressed of the Third World." I had tried to believe that the road to salvation could be picked out of the granite mountainside with red, black and green pickaxes and subjugated myself to what my mind perceived as the historical necessity to advocate revolution and blackness. We will do anything to keep from listening to the lonely sounds of our hearts beating. We will hearken to any other music, pop our fingers, dance, and look upon the naked King, and be blinded by the rich finery of his robes. We are the executioners of ourselves.)

In the same year, I lost my marriage and the revolution. With no place to hide, and nothing to obscure the loneliness, I died, for nothing and no one affirmed my existence. I had wanted one woman to be there always, carrying me inside her. How Freudian it sounds. The desire to return to the womb, but no! One is always expelled from the womb. I merely wanted someone to know me as I knew myself, for I had no race, no country and no family to give me a perfect reflection. Was it irrational to expect that there be one person in all of creation who would affirm my being?

Arlene had been that, no matter how imperfectly. Or at least I had been able to use her for that. Now there was nothing, and I didn't know why we had failed. We had started out to write a poem with our lives and ended with an old grocery list lying crumpled on the floor of the car, next to the candy wrappers, ends of ice cream cones, and beach sand. Had our failure begun when she collapsed before the prospect of her life and become pregnant? Had it started when I went south the summer of 1964? Or was it with my first affair? And which was that? Laurie, the sixteen-year-old with whom I'd shared silence the same summer I met Arlene? Or was it Yvonne, our bodies rippling like ribbons through still Atlanta nights? I searched every scrap of our lives and found that

Arlene and I never knew each other. She could not accept what she could not understand, and I was constantly changing, like patterns on a bank of snow blown by the wind. Arlene had watched the patterns, and never saw that the snow always remained. But one cannot vow to love unto death while kneeling at the altar of loneliness.

3

Thanksgiving morning, 1970. Carol and I flew back to Cambridge from the weekly trip to New York, and as I walked into the apartment, the voice spoke: "I am leaving." For the first time in my life, I wanted to live alone, and two weeks later, I returned to New York, moving into the Hotel Chelsea, the overrated hotel of literary fame, where Mark Twain, Thomas Wolfe, Brendan Behan and Dylan Thomas, among others, had lived. Living there was another dream which I quickly purged. A hotel, however, was a limbo, and that was what I needed. I was incapable of creating a home and had no desire to do so. I preferred the impersonal hotel furniture and being surrounded by transients, even if they were a very special kind of transient like the Jefferson Airplane and, the following year, Clifford and Edith Irving.

Carol and I continued seeing each other until the morning early in February when I awoke, and the first sound I heard was the voice: "It is over with Carol." As suddenly and mysteriously as we began, we ended. It was as if someone had flashed a Kodachrome slide onto a screen and then taken it away, leaving the screen shimmering with the white light of the projector. I did not understand, except that Carol had been the bridge between leaving Arlene and a tentative acceptance of my loneliness. It was as if she had been sent for that purpose, and having fulfilled it, was no longer necessary.

Living alone was not difficult. I was more bored than lonely, and, sometimes, boredom is a healer. The monotony of my life was joyous.

I was afraid to write, however, uncertain if I could. I'd never written away from Arlene, and until our last year together, she had read every word of mine. But when *The New York Times Book Review* asked me to review Bob Hayden's *Words in the Mourning*

Time, I could not refuse. I approached the typewriter like an athlete recovering from an injury, afraid that the former suppleness of his muscles will not return. In the past, I would have finished the draft in one sitting, rewritten it in another, and added polishing touches while typing the final copy. At the most, that would have taken three days. This time, a week was required. When I finished, however, I was relieved to know that Arlene had not been my muse.

(ARTICLE: "Words in the Mourning Time," *The New York Times Book Review,* January 24, 1971)

The recent publication of Robert Hayden's new book of poems, "Words in the Mourning Time," once again brings us the work of one of the most underrated and unrecognized poets in America. Until the publication of "Selected Poems" in 1966, Hayden was unrepresented by a book of his own poems, except for two small, privately printed books and a volume published in England. Now 57 years old, he has had to wait too long for the recognition that his work has merited for 20 years. But that is primarily because he is black.

If there was scarcely a market for black writers before the sixties, black poets must have been regarded as something odd indeed, particularly a poet who refused to be pressed into anyone's preconceived mold of what a black poet should be. Yet, Hayden persevered—teaching, writing, publishing where he could and giving occasional readings.

When I entered Fisk University in the fall of 1956, he had already been there 10 years in that miasma of black bourgeois gentility. On the campus, he was regarded as just another instructor in the English department, teaching 15 hours of classes a week, from two sections of freshman English to American literature to creative writing. No one at Fisk had the vaguest notion of what a poet's function was, not that they gave it any thought. Yet, somehow, Hayden continued to believe—in himself and poetry—though no one except his wife and a few students and friends in New York ever cared.

Within these circumstances, being a poet could bring him no joy. Despite his pain and loneliness, he always made it clear to those of us who were foolish enough to think that we wanted to write that perhaps our experiences would be different. In creative writing classes, he tried to teach us that words were our principal tool and no matter how important we considered our "message" to be, it was the words that expressed it. Assuming that we had something to say, the importance of saying it as well as our ability allowed us could never be underestimated.

When I read his poetry I know that I am in the presence of a man who honors language. His images give the reader a new experience of the world. In his "Selected Poems" are found such lines as: "Grave-black vultures encircle afternoon"; "palmleaf knives of sunlight"; "autumn hills/in blazonry of farewell scarlet." And in "Words in the Mourning Time" these lines appear: "His injured childhood bullied him"; "God brooms had swept/the mist away." He chooses words with the care of a sculptor chipping into marble and, in his poem "El-Hajj Malik El-Shabazz," from "Words in the Mourning Time," a vivid historical portrait of Malcolm X is presented in six short lines:

> He X'd his name, became his people's anger,
> exhorted them to vengeance for their past;
> rebuked, admonished them,
>
> their scourger, who
> would shame them, drive them from
> the lush ice gardens of their servitude.

Such a simple phrase—"He X'd his name"—but it sets up reverberations that extend back to August of 1619.

I left Nashville in 1961, and though I saw Mr. Hayden a few times afterwards, our relationship slowly diminished. I, his "son," had to find my own way, and he found new "sons" in succeeding classes. The last time I saw him was in May, 1966. I was working for the Student Non-Violent Coordinating Committee and had just come from the meeting in which Stokely Carmichael had been elected chairman. Black power was just a few weeks away, but Mr. Hayden had already felt the heat of its approaching flames. At a writers' conference held at Fisk a few weeks before, he had been severely attacked as an "Uncle Tom" by the students and other writers. When I walked into his house, his first words to me were a tirade against "the nationalists."

He had also just been awarded the Grand Prize for Poetry at the First World Festival of Negro Arts at Dakar, Senegal. That honor was not enough, however, to offset being rejected and attacked by black students and black writers. He had always insisted on being known as a poet, not a black poet, and he could be belligerent about it. I listened to him again as he angrily maintained that there was "no such thing as black literature. There's good literature and there's bad. And that's all!" I couldn't wholly agree then (and I'm still not sure), nor could I understand why he was so vociferous in denying that he was a black poet. After all, he was the man who had written "Middle Passage," "Frederick Douglass" and "Runagate Runagate," three of the finest poems about the black experience in the English language. Why couldn't he admit that he was a black poet?

271

To be a black artist has always been difficult. The mere fact that he is black means that he is associated with a "cause." It is his birthright, whether he wants it to be or not. Yet, while no one expects Philip Roth, for example, to be a spokesman for Jews, it is the black writer's fate to have his work judged more on the basis of racial content than artistic merit. This is because whites only grant the right of individuality to whites. A black is not an individual; he is the representative of a "cause." Unfortunately, blacks concur in this evaluation. They see each other as "causes" and have little, if any, use for a black writer who does not concern himself with "the cause." Both races think the black writer is a priest, offering absolution to whites or leading blacks to the holy wars.

The prevailing black esthetic was summarized succinctly by Ron Karenga when he said, "All art must reflect and support the Black Revolution and any art that does not discuss and contribute to the revolution is invalid. Black art must expose the enemy, praise the people and support the revolution." In other words, art should be the voice of political ideology and the black artist must comply or find himself with an indifferent white audience and no black one.

To a black artist, like Mr. Hayden, who was not conceived or reborn in the womb of black power, such thinking is not only repugnant, it is a direct assault upon art itself. By its very nature, art is revolutionary, because it seeks to change the consciousness, perceptions and very beings of those who open themselves to it. Its revolutionary nature, however, can only be mortally wounded if it must meet political pre-scriptions. That, however, is now being demanded of the black artist.

Robert Hayden refuses to be defined by anything other than the demands of his craft. He does not want to be restricted solely to the black experience or have his work judged on the basis of its relevance to the black political struggle. First and foremost, he is not a pawn in some kind of neo-medieval morality play. His task is, in his words, merely that which has always been the poet's task: "to reflect and illuminate the truth of human experience."

Now, I know that his desire to be regarded as nothing more or less than a poet was not a denial of his blackness, but the only way he knew of saying that blackness was not big enough to contain him. He wanted to live in the universe.

In the ninth part of the title poem of "Words in the Mourning Time," he writes:

> We must not be frightened nor cajoled
> into accepting evil as deliverance from evil.
> We must go on struggling to be human,

though monsters of abstractions
police and threaten us.

Reclaim now, now renew the vision of
a human world where godliness
is possible and man
is neither gook, nigger, honkey, wop, nor kike
but man
     permitted to be man.

If we ever reach that time when man is permitted to be man, one of the reasons will be men and women like this poet, Robert Hayden, who, when pressed into the most terrifying corners of loneliness, refused to capitulate to those, who in the screaming agony of their own pain and loneliness, could do nothing but return evil for evil.

At the time, I did not recognize the symbolism in writing about my mentor, but it was the literal return to the beginning after months of knowing that that was what I must do. I was embracing my past and the man who had been my symbolic father, who had midwifed the writer in me. And I was doing it in the way it had to be done—in public.

The symbolism of the literal return continued, for the next writing I did was a review for *The New York Times Book Review* of Thomas Merton's first posthumous book, *Contemplation in a World of Action.*

(ARTICLE: "Contemplation in a World of Action," *The New York Times Book Review*, March 14, 1971)

The sixties were a time when American youth engaged this society in a moral confrontation and challenged it to make the rhetoric of peace and democracy a reality in each of its citizens. America responded to the challenge with flags on its police cars. While some youth reacted to this by trying to make a moral virtue out of violent revolution, others withdrew from the picket lines and mass demonstrations to establish communes, where they could concentrate on creating the new society within the context of their own lives.

This important cultural development not only reflected a basic and fundamental dissatisfaction with the quality of American life (and a refusal to compromise with it), it also represented the beginning of new ways of thinking and living. The politics of confrontation is being replaced by a politic strangely akin to the essence of monasticism. The first person to recognize this was Thomas Merton, the Trappist monk who died in 1968; he saw in the youth culture "an attitude toward the world which is analogous to that of the monk."

In this book, Merton presents his finest and clearest statements on the monastic life. Although the world could more easily relate to him as Thomas Merton, religious writer, poet, translator and scholar, he knew himself only as Father Louis (his religious name)—Trappist monk, and, at the end of his life, Trappist hermit. His concern was for the fullest and most complete contemplative life and, though his other writings discussed the results of that life, it is in the 21 essays of this book that we are asked to consider directly the contemplative life itself.

While most conceive of the cenobitic life as a retreat from the world and its problems, Merton viewed and lived it as "a certain protest against the organized and dehumanizing routines of a worldly life built around gain for its own sake." The monastic life could only be positive, because its concern was being, not doing. "The monk is not defined by his task, his usefulness . . . he is supposed to be 'useless' because his mission is not to *do* this or that job but to *be* a man of God . . . his business is life itself." The monastery was not a place where the weak came because they could not succeed in the world. Those who entered with such an attitude would not survive the internal demands of a cenobitic life, for "monasticism aims at the cultivation of a certain *quality* of life, a level of awareness, a depth of consciousness, an area of transcendence and of adoration which are not usually possible in an active secular existence." This not only states the aim of the monastic life, it is also the aim of the most serious elements of the youth culture. Both challenge America to stop "making a living" and simply live.

Merton was never wholly satisfied with being merely a monk. In *The Sign of Jonas,* one of his earlier books, he writes of his frustration with being unable to spend all of his time in solitude and prayer. He always felt called to the eremetic life and, though he was denied permission to transfer to the more eremetical Carthusian Order in 1967, he was finally allowed to live as a hermit on the grounds of his monastery.

Six of the most interesting essays in this collection present a militant case for eremetism, essays Merton probably wrote when he was trying to convince church authorities of the legitimacy of his request. The popular conception of a hermit is that he is one who withdraws from people because he hates them. Merton spoke the truth of the matter when he wrote, with characteristic simplicity, that "some of us *have to be* alone to be ourselves." But, being alone is not a way of being which this society condones. And, the fear of the "loner" seems to have extended inside the walls of the monastery. Merton does not concern himself with the fears of others, but with the demands of the eremetical life itself. It is a life to which few are called, but, for those few, it is the only way they can feel their oneness with humanity.

The other essays in this volume are a call for revolution within the monastic life. For Merton, the cenobitic community had become an institution more concerned with its own preservation and rituals than with the quality of the inner lives of the monks. As Novice-Master of the Abbey of Gethsemani for many years, he had seen many young men come and leave; all they were offered was a habit and rules to which they were required to conform. They came as pilgrims into "being"; the monastery offered them little more than membership in a religious order. These essays offer many suggestions for reform, including the possibility of married men affiliating with a monastic order on intimate terms. Most interesting is the fact that in earlier works, Merton presented many arguments for celibacy. In the present one, the concept of celibacy is conspicuous by its absence. Merton's call for *aggiornamento* is militant, reflecting what must have been a deep personal discontent and, in all probability, will create quite a controversy in some religious circles.

At a time in American society when new forms of living are being attempted by a significant number of youth, this collection of essays is especially important, even for those who find formal religion repugnant. Merton writes: "To love our brother we must first respect him in his own authentic reality, and we cannot do this if we have not attained to a basic self-respect and identity ourselves." This insight from a Trappist monk parallels insights coming to us from the youth culture, the women's-liberation movement, as well as the writings of R. D. Laing and C. G. Jung, among others. Merton's consummate virtue was a humility that would never allow him to act or be used as a recruiter for the Roman Catholic Church. He did not believe that the cenobitic life was the only way. It was merely his, and it afforded him certain answers to the personal and social problems that each of us must address. The answers in this book come from a tradition as ancient as Western civilization itself, and a significant part of any prognosis for this civilization must incorporate the attitude toward the world found in monastic life.

I continued shedding the last remnants of my false public self, and once again, it was in the pages of *The New York Times Book Review,* an odd setting for making peace with one's self.

All praises are now given to the name and memory of Malcolm X. In his person he represented the apotheosis of blackness; but, except for the last 11 months of his political career, he articulated the aims and ideals of the Nation of Islam as the number one spokesman for the Honorable Elijah Muhammud. This is important to remember because as the most important black political figure of the sixties, Malcolm X brought the thought of Elijah Muhammud to a larger audience and thereby increased its influence. That fact is not recognized or acknowledged today, but it is very evident in "The End of White World Supremacy," a collection of four previously unpublished speeches given during 1962 and 1963, Malcolm's last year in the Nation. Here we find the concepts that, three years after his death, would be gathered under the rubric black power and forwarded as a secular philosophy: pride in blackness; the necessity to know black history; black separation; the need for black unity; black control of the political, economic and social institutions of the black community.

Malcolm X was more feared than loved by blacks while he lived, and these speeches are the best examples in print of why, even dead, he is a man to measure one's self against. One reads these four speeches from almost a decade ago and trembles. He speaks not as a political leader or social analyst (though he was both), but like one of the Old Testament prophets. He is the voice of doom from the maelstrom of American history. He does not exhort his followers or threaten his enemies. He lives in a place where such rhetorical weaknesses do not exist, for he represents Truth. He is one of the redeemed, and it is irrelevant to him if he is heeded or ignored. Being ostracized or vilified will not affect him in the least. Like Noah, he is building his ark, and if he is the only one who will be saved, then, all praises be!

It was this undoubting belief in the teachings of Elijah Muhammud, this vision of the wheat being separated from the chaff, that gave Malcolm his diamond-like integrity. He knew Armageddon was coming, and he was as sure that he was on the side of good as he was that the sun would rise each morning. I envy him his faith. For him, it was all so simple. Blacks were the chosen people, and their time had come. The white world would fall, and the black one would rise; he was one of the saved.

Unfortunately, it is not that simple, as Malcolm himself may have begun to learn in the brief months left to him after quitting the Nation. Shorn of its religious framework and the cosmological dimension Malcolm was able to give it, the thought of Elijah Muhammud is black nationalism, with all the necessary and painful contradictions that have to exist when there is no physical nation in which the nationalism can root itself, when so much of the history of the people is forever lost in the lower depths of white-sailed slave ships.

But Malcolm made an existential leap, over the abyss and into the faith of blackness. Many have made the leap with him, but there are those of us who have hesitated, knowing that there is no such thing as Truth, except the abyss itself. Faith is comforting, but it is blind. And though having sight can sometimes make one long to be blind, ultimately, it is only by seeing that we fully live. Black history reached a necessary apex through Malcolm X. It must proceed beyond that point, however, if blacks are not to become, like everyone else, hapless puppets of history, the blindest force of all.

The logical successor to Malcolm X was Stokely Carmichael, a young civil-rights organizer for the then Student Non-Violent Coordinating Committee. A year-and-a-half after the assassination of Malcolm, the thought of Elijah Muhammud was distilled into two words, which history spoke through Carmichael's lips—*black power!* And the seeds planted by Malcolm X exploded in the black psyche. "Stokely Speaks" is a collection of 14 speeches and essays covering Carmichael's political career from the civil-rights movement to black power to his present politics of Pan-Africanism. As such, it is a curious collection. If it is supposed to be a documentary record of Carmichael's political evolution, it is incomplete. Missing is the important interview Carmichael gave to Robert Penn Warren in 1965 (printed in Warren's "Who Speaks for the Negro?"), as well as his letter of resignation from the Black Panther party and, one of his best statements on Pan-Africanism, which appeared in the first issue of The Black Scholar.

What we have are the thoughts of a civil-rights organizer, a black radical and a Pan-Africanist, but the relationship of the three voices is vague. There is no introduction to indicate how the evolution occurred, and the speeches themselves lack the substance that might show how Carmichael's thought developed. He was one thing; then, he's another. Sometimes he's a little of all three. Thus, the book lacks a clear and definite focus.

Having been present when Carmichael delivered two of the speeches in this volume and, having helped in the writing of one of them (given at the meeting of the Organization of Latin American Solidarity in Havana, 1967), it was with some anticipation that I picked up the volume, expecting to relive some of the memories of those years. Oddly enough, I found the speeches boring, tedious and repetitious.

Carmichael is an electrifying speaker, but that electricity does not carry over to the printed page, as it does with Malcolm. Though dead,

Malcolm is terrifyingly alive in his speeches; Carmichael is alive, but his speeches are depressingly dead; I found myself wondering why the country had been so upset by Stokely. Then, I remembered. He spoke against a backdrop of burning cities and the sound of bullets in the night. Without such scenery, his words are a confusing mixture of black nationalism, quasi-Marxism-Leninism and New Left rhetoric, from which no coherent whole emerges. The speeches are replete with insights of brilliance, but insights alone do not make a political ideology.

At present Carmichael is a Pan-Africanist and is seeking to create an international black consciousness around the concept of a land base for black Americans in Africa. It is a revival of Marcus Garvey's concept of Pan-Africanism in which a strong Africa would be created that would offer protection to the black minorities of the Western Hemisphere. It is a unique solution for the dilemma of a landless people. However, Carmichael ignores Africa's complexity and the fact that African nations may not think that Pan-Africanism is in their own self-interest. Carmichael also bases his thesis on the assumption that the West will allow such a land base and, given the extent of Western economic interests on the continent, this assumption could be fatal for those who make it.

More distressing, Carmichael gives no indication that he is aware of living in the 20th century. He speaks of capitalism and imperialism, as if these were the primary sources of the problems confronting people. It is increasingly apparent, however, that the effects of technology and the electronic media on the psyche of contemporary man are as devastating as capitalism and imperialism—perhaps more so.

Today's world cannot be adequately defined by concepts that came out of the 19th century and, unless the problems are accurately defined, any solutions offered are going to be inadequate. Like Malcolm, Carmichael puts his faith in blackness, but the mystique of blackness does not exempt blacks from the subtle erosions of the soul caused by technology and media. Carmichael grew up identifying with Tarzan, he says in several speeches; today, young Africans in some urban areas are growing up identifying with American cowboys. That land base Carmichael is trying to create may turn into Disneyland before he realizes it.

Carmichael is historically important, but this collection makes it clear that his importance comes from the fact that he happened to be saying certain things at the precise moment when poor blacks were lecturing America with Molotov cocktails. Malcolm X was one of the makers of history. Carmichael was a reflector of it. Malcolm X was John the Baptist, preaching in the wilderness. We still wait for Jesus and, this time, I don't think he's coming.

Finally, the return was completed with a eulogy written on the suicide of an acquaintance. It was not only Robert Starobin's death I commemorated, however, but the internment of what I no longer was.

(ARTICLE: "On the Suicide of a Revolutionary," *Liberation*, Spring, 1971)

Sometimes someone falls so deeply into the pit of self that there is no rope long enough for a friend to throw to him. There is no ladder with enough rungs that he can grab on to and climb out. And, there is no love vibrant enough to warm the chilly air of the night.

For most of my life I've lived at the brink of the pit, and, sometimes, have lost my balance and fallen in. Each time (thus far) I have managed to emerge, mainly because of an uncommon fortitude which persists in maintaining my life even when all conscious desire and will is to the contrary. Bob Starobin wasn't lucky enough to have such a fortitude. Or, maybe he fell into a recess of the pit deeper than any I have ever explored. Maybe there is a corner of the pit from which no one returns, but once there, it is impossible to resist the seductiveness of death.

A .22 is such a tiny weapon. It is only effective at close range. Sirhan Sirhan used one on another Bob. It's such an ignominious weapon and is hardly worthy of either Bob. A samurai sword has more nobility; a .45 has more manliness. It's really difficult to take a .22 seriously. But, one is forced to, because it works. It exists to injure or kill and it is indiscriminate. Pull the trigger and it spits out a bullet, which spins through time, space and history until it explodes on contact with anything—a wall, a lamp, an arm or a human skull. It doesn't care. A .22 simply obeys whoever commands it.

Bob and I weren't close friends. If we were friends at all, it was only because he had a high regard for my writings, and, in that way, knew me better than I had the chance to know him. We met only once, at a meeting of historians at Wayne State University in Detroit in the spring of 1970. He read a paper on the attitude of accommodation in slave letters and I was on a panel with Sterling Stuckey and Eugene Genovese to respond to his paper with critiques. It was one of those situations that are unavoidable when blacks and whites come together in post-Black Power America, a situation in which people are not individuals, but historical entities, playing out a drama whose beginnings are now so submerged that we will never find them. And, in these days, any white man who devotes himself to teaching and writing about black history must have the fortitude and strength of a bull elephant, because blacks will let him know that his presence is unwanted and undesirable. Whether this attitude is just or unjust is scarcely a question. In absolute terms, it is obviously unjust. Historically, it is the present reality, and, that day at Wayne State University my heart ached for Bob, though I didn't know him, but I knew what I had to do to him. He had to be attacked and I did so, employing every forensic skill which two generations of ministers in my family had bequeathed to me. I bowed to the demands of history that day and will loathe myself forever for having done so. History makes its demands, but one does not have to accede to them. History is not just, but is as unfeeling and uncaring as a .22, and, unless it is questioned and challenged, it will function with the same vulgar efficiency. All too often we let ourselves be History's willing victims, and, that day History demanded that I treat another human being as a category and I, not without hurting inside, acceded.

It was fortunate for me that Bob and I had a close friend in common and through him, word reached me that Bob wanted to write to me. I was relieved to have the opportunity to try and undo what I had done, for Bob would have been more justified in hating me until the end of recorded time. We began writing each other and I apologized to him and told him that the incident had given me an idea for a short story in which I would explore how one can be black, in the fullest political sense, and yet, inhuman. He was kind enough to respond by saying of the story, "I hope I won't look as bad as I must have on that awful day." No. I was concerned about the danger I was in, recognizing the necessity for nationalism and yet not sacrificing my humanity to it as I had done that day. But, that was something I really couldn't explore with him, just as he couldn't explore with me problems he may have had as a white teacher and scholar in black history.

The last letter I received from him was in August of last year. He was very excited about the release of Huey Newton from jail. He was euphoric, in fact, and spoke of his increasing political commitment and of his fear: "I have been struggling all year, especially this summer, with the contradiction between my scholarly interests and profession and my desire to do more revolutionary deeds. The biggest hangup is, of course, the question of terrorism, for though I am armed to the teeth, I still can't figure out under what circumstances to use them, and I still am afraid of violence and death, though I guess this is related to my white privileges, my class background, and my loved ones."

I never answered the letter. I had been shoved into the pit once again and had found that it was deeper and more narrow than I had ever imagined. When his letter came I was struggling to reglue a marriage and, realizing that this time it couldn't be done, struggling to reglue myself and discovering that before I could do that I had to find myself and there is no Keeper of Souls to whom one can go to see if any lost selves have been turned in. Eventually, I died and passively waited for the resurrection to come or for my death to be complete. So, I couldn't write Bob, but if I had been able to, I wonder if I would have. I wasn't sure that he could have heard what I would have told him: Bob, don't be ashamed of being a scholar. There is no contradiction. To be a good scholar, as you are, is to be constantly involved in committing revolutionary deeds. Don't let others tell you how you should express your revolutionary commitment. You must insist upon the right to define that for yourself. And, don't be frightened into a corner because you are white. Being white is a category; you are a person.

But, I didn't write it, and, of course, now, I must live with the thought that maybe it would have made a difference. I don't think so, however. If his politics couldn't save him, how little, then, could they do who cared about him. It was his politics which served as the motor of his life and it is in that motor one must look for the defects which stopped the life. To say that he was killed by the forces of death which permeate this country is all too convenient. It is true, but only partially. Those same forces of death also permeate the politics to which Bob was committed, and, the ultimate responsibility for his death must be charged to those politics.

It is a politics which has no place in it for a quiet scholar like Bob Starobin. It is a politics which regards violent rhetoric and military action as the *sine qua non* of revolution. It is a politics which made Bob feel that he had to have guns in his house, though, in his uncommonly honest words: "I still can't figure out under what circumstances to use them." The revolutionary politics of our time made him feel that without a gun, he couldn't be a revolutionary. His weapon was his mind, and, there is a certain poetry in the fact that when he found the circumstances in which to use his gun, he killed himself by shattering his brain.

The revolutionary movement had no place for a Bob Starobin, but, because he cared, because he was committed to revolutionary change, because he couldn't exist without doing something to bring about that change, he had to twist himself out of shape to fit the accepted definition of what a revolutionary is. He had to abuse his soul, because the revolutionary movement could not provide a welcome and a home for that soul. And, it is only a short step from violating one's soul to destroying one's physical being.

Bob wanted to "do more revolutionary deeds," and the revolutionary movement did not tell him that a typewriter and a keen mind are revolutionary weapons. The princes of the revolution told him that if he wasn't part of the solution, he was part of the problem, and, not wanting to be part of the latter, he tried to be part of the former as it was defined by others. He didn't make it and has told us so in the most direct way he could.

Suicide is the ultimate act of anger. The one thing each of us truly possesses is our life, and if we find that there is no space anywhere in society where that life can breathe, we take a .22 and kill ourselves, because we have been given no other option than to deprive others of our self. Suicide is a totally selfish act, too, which is why there is such a strong taboo against it in our society. No individual is to feel so strongly about himself that he would totally remove that self from the world. He is to go on because he has a responsibility to others. But, the person who commits suicide knows how ridiculous that is. The suicide victim exercises that responsibility in the most hurting way possible. Generally, the overwhelming emotion he feels is complete despair and hopelessness, but, beneath that despair is rage and anger that he has not been given the psychic space he needed to live. Without that space, he has no choice; he must die.

The first stage of that death is spiritual, the descent into the pit, there, to struggle, as Jacob struggled with God. It is the Armageddon of the Soul, and, if one is able to identify and slay his attacker, he ascends from the pit, like the phoenix from the ashes. Death and resurrection. It is the life process itself. Most, however, die to themselves and passively wait for their bodies to cease functioning forty or fifty years later. Some, however, cannot accept a compromise. Their bodies are mere repositories for their souls, and if they can see no way to rise from the death of self, they will not tolerate the blind functioning of their bodies. Suicide has its own integrity.

Revolutionary politics should have within it the nourishment and comfort necessary to sustain us when we enter the inevitable dark nights of the soul. And, the fact that these politics could not sustain Bob Starobin is the most serious indictment possible of those politics. To be deprived of life is to be deprived of what is vital in ourselves. And, that vitalness, as he exemplified it, cannot be replaced. Each individual is unique, and the revolutionary movement must have within it the space to allow each individual to express his uniqueness. If it does not, it is not revolutionary. Bob has hurt us in the best way he could; he has absented himself permanently from our midst.

If the finest in our ranks take their lives, have not, then, our politics become the politics of death? Our rhetoric may blind us to that reality, but it was that reality, like a *tsunami*, which engulfed Bob. If his death is to be something more than a cause for momentary sadness and despair, it is the reality of that politics of death which the revolutionary movement now represents that we must confront. We must descend into the pit and be re-born. If we don't, then we will be writing eulogies for people like Bob Starobin for a long time to come.

As suddenly as the requests for my writing from various publications had begun almost two years before, they stopped. *Evergreen Review* published only irregularly; *Nickel Review* was forced to stop publication by its printers; and with the eulogy for Robert Starobin, I knew that I would not continue my column in *Liberation*. I would not receive a request for an essay or review for more than a year. I did not mind. It was time to be silent.

4

For two years, my inner and outer worlds were as still as summer forests. (Joanne and I began the winter of 1971. She was a woman of sensuous grace, one of the quiet ones. We did not try to create the illusion of a couple, and though we started living together that summer, she retained her own apartment. Because of her, I began creating a home, something I'd never had, besides the desk which occupied a corner of the living room in the various apartments and houses in which Arlene and I had lived. Joanne and I created a temple, where the sun held statues of ballerinas and nudes, African masks and statues, lithographs and block prints, Ethiopian rugs and baskets, Guatemalan fabrics, a table of inlaid tiles where we sipped *café au lait* and ate croissants on Sunday mornings, and a six-foot-long wooden Spanish desk where I worked. We shared what was important: food, frisbee, laughing, watching television and silence. We didn't burden each other with declarations of love. Our life together was that.)

In January of 1972, I discarded the last remnant of my previous existence and quit my radio show. I could not fly jessed by blackness and my efforts to transform the show from a forum for the black point of view to something which would reflect all of me had failed. (I returned to the air nine months later to do a morning show two days a week. I called it "Uncle Tom's Cabin" and for the next three years it would be a place where listeners awoke to the sounds of whales singing, Bach cantatas, Gregorian chants, and me talking about whatever came to mind.) In the autumn of 1972, I began teaching in the W. E. B. Du Bois Department of Afro-American Studies at the University of Massachusetts in Amherst. I had to test my self in the world once more, prove to myself that, at long last, my identity was held in my hands. There was no better way to do that than to place myself once again among blacks and see how comfortably I lived with myself with so many of "my people" disapproving of that self. I surprised myself, for I was so wholly who I am that I did not notice if others approved or disapproved. Nothing mattered anymore except that I be.

Then, during the spring of 1973, I had an affair, the most intense and voluptuous I'd ever had. Instead of preening myself in its bath, however, I cried as if I were kneeling before my own bier. When Joanne and I had begun, I had promised myself that there would be no other women. Marital fidelity was a way of honoring one's self, and I was more married to Joanne than I had ever been to Arlene.

With this new woman, whose voice had the gentle lilt of the white South and so much of my past, I feared that I was on the verge of repeating my life with Arlene, and if that were so, nothing justified the continuation of my own life. Joanne was as different from Arlene as anyone could be. If I could not be monogamous with her, there was no salvation for my rutting soul.

Once again, I craved Death with the anguish of an addict for his narcotic. I walked into the bathroom many times each day to look at the bottle of Excedrin tablets, and this time, it was only the thought of my children which stopped me. Did I have the right to shroud their lives in the winding sheet of their father's suicide? Reluctantly, I accepted that I did not. But being deprived of the right to die was the ultimate injustice.

I decided to go south. It was a healing country for me, and it had been six years since I'd been on the backroads of Mississippi and Alabama. I would submerge myself in the racial unconsciousness and there be cleansed.

5

Even after twelve years in New York, I considered myself a southerner. The South shaped and formed me and its speech remained on my tongue; its slow, easy rhythms were the rise and fall of my breathing. I was as bewildered by northern blacks as I had been in 1961 when I lived in Harlem. I looked at the black students in my classes who had not known segregation, or what it was to grow up without hope, and they were more angry at whites than I'd ever been, carrying faces grim as death masks. I did not understand.

I spoke to the black students at a small liberal arts college in Maine late that spring of 1973, and was not surprised when the evening began with, "Brother Lester. We understand that you have a white wife. How do you justify that?" I'd heard the question so often by then, it was boring. I wanted to tell them that I was divorced from the white wife they were referring to and was now living with a gentle lady with long, red hair. I decided I'd better leave well enough alone.

"Love is its own justification," I said, knowing how little that meant to an eighteen-year-old who mistook genital palpitations for love. I continued, using the question as a means of talking about how people turn each other into abstractions, which is the beginning of hate. To call myself black was to do nothing more than modify a definition imposed on me by centuries of Western history. If one knew himself as nothing more than black, he'd simply inverted nigger, Negro, and colored, not transforming himself but continuing to live by someone else's description of his reality. It was active participation in one's own objectification. We must live ahistorically, I told them, ceasing to be products of our times and leap, blindly and joyously into Time and live as if we were stars shining from where the ticking of no clocks could sound. I wondered aloud if this had not been the peculiar historical mission of blacks. We were Outsiders, living beyond the edge of the society and therefore, able to see its sicknesses and defects. Inherent in being a victim is a living hindsight, because the victim is the embodiment of the society's crimes. The victim is, therefore, the only one who can cut the way to salvation, but only if he accepts the existential pain of refusing to become an executioner. When the victim becomes an Insider, he ceases to be a victim and becomes what he previously condemned. "Who wants to be integrated into a burning house?" Malcolm X had asked. But we didn't listen, and the minute we called whites "honkies," we ceased to be Outsiders. The instant we yelled "Power to the People," we entered the society's psycho-historical frame and embraced the concepts by which our executioners lived. Instead of leaping into the void, we entered the maelstrom, and in redefining ourselves as blacks, we automatically redefined and imposed racial definitions on the rest of humanity. Murder is the act of defining another as separate from myself.

I talked, knowing that I was ordering my own being. "Are you saying that we must love all white people?" someone demanded to know. I wanted to tell her, yes, but I wasn't sure that I could accept that yet. "No, but I am saying, don't *hate* white people, because you hurt yourself. And I think white people are the best proof of what I'm saying. You hate injustice, not people. And, to be frank, you don't have the right to hate another human being." I might as well have told her to love white people, because the response could not have been more overwhelming had I walked in with two blondes in miniskirts and see-through blouses.

Finally, a young woman asked, "Well, what do you believe in?" It was an odd question and a horrifying one, because she was really saying, "If you don't hate white people and don't believe in black liberation, then, I don't understand you." My answer was inadequate: "Love and integrity." I really was a child of the fifties, wasn't I, because those concepts still retained a shadow of meaning during my college years. I had read the Platonic dialogues with intense excitement, because to define virtue, honor, love, and courage was to know values which supported life. But to talk of "love and integrity" dated me as surely as if I was wearing wing-tipped shoes. Virtue. That was the word I should've used. *Virtus* in Latin, meaning manliness, strength, capacity, from *vir*, man, and it had evolved into meaning, "the quality of moral excellence, righteousness and responsibility." Now that was a word to paint on a shingle and hang from one's soul.

The evening with the black students ended in forced politeness, and I drove away in a chilly rain, feeling very old and very tired. Virtue! Was I some fair-haired white maiden locked in the castle tower, braiding my hair as the barbarians approached, their penises tied around their waists in bows? No, I was the maid (fair-haired and white?) lying on the castle stairs, her dress bunched at her waist, her bodice torn in ribbons and her thighs smeared with semen-thickened blood.

I had to go back home, for it was in the South that I learned something of virtue from the old ones who never knew a day of ease, who accepted the indignities and atrocities inflicted upon them, but were never resigned to them. That was crucial, for they knew that "to wait upon the Lord" was not to sit on the porch and rock passively. "To wait" also means to serve, and serving God means refusing to hate the perpetrators of evil, because to hate the evildoers is to wait upon them. The old ones accepted their living hell, but did not serve it and were redeemed by their suffering. Young blacks today sit on the porch with their hands in their laps, the blood-stained machetes in their hands.

6

Nashville. My parents were out of town when I arrived, but I didn't have any trouble convincing the neighbors to let me have the spare key I knew Mother left with them (if she hadn't changed). ("Boy, you look just like your daddy. Sho' do! I woulda knowed you was Reb'n Lester's boy anywhere.") They didn't know when Mother and Daddy would be back and I hoped it would be a while, for I wanted the time alone in that house where I'd lived from age fourteen to twenty-two. Much of me remained, particularly in the basement studio where I painted. My paintings and drawings from high school were still tacked to the walls—a pencil portrait of Uncle Fate, Aunt Rena's husband, dated 1954; a watercolor copy of Edward Hopper's famous painting of a Maine lighthouse; and a charcoal sketch of a skull and candlestick holder, dated 1956. I'd forgotten that one, and it was only significant because I now owned a skull, a much-desired Christmas present from Arlene in 1968. There are recurring symbols in our lives, motifs which sound their notes like hunting horns. The skull is one of mine. (I used to stand outside the church when I was a child and watch the caskets being carried in before funerals. Inside would be Mrs. Johnson, who, I'd heard the grown-ups say, died because she ate strawberries and she was allergic to them; or Mr. Grant, a large man whose funeral was held quickly, because, Daddy said, the undertaker had done a poor job and the body had begun to smell, or Mr. Williams, who died suddenly on a hot day because he drank too much cold water. I did not like Death, because one could not predict or see its coming. It came in ordinary street-clothes, overalls, or even barefooted, and while you were sneaking into the refrigerator to eat a few red-luscious straw-berries, it seized your soul and ran through the back door before you had the chance to know you were dying. It was always there, watching, watching, waiting, and when you came home from work, hot and tired on a July day, and drank a cold glass of water to wash the dust of the day from your innards, it did not give you the chance to put the empty glass in the sink before it froze your heart. Less than a minute before, you'd said hello to your wife and children, walked out of the room and into Death. It was the unseen authority figure in our house, present, acknowledged and honored every Sunday morning at breakfast. "Oh, Lord," Daddy would pray, "one of us might not be in your presence when the next Sunday morning rolls around," and during the week I would beg God, or Death (they were confused in my young mind) to please not take any of us before the next Sunday, and when it came, I was relieved until Daddy bowed his head and I would see Death assume a thousand shapes in the vapor rising from the hot bowl of grits. I was afraid Death would take me before I became a writer or a concert pianist, and I wanted to be the first Negro to play in Carnegie Hall. Please, God! Don't let Death come yet.

Death came, not to our house, but to houses of those we knew, and I followed it on the days there were funerals at the church, waiting while the undertaker placed the coffin before the altar of the empty church, opened it and went outside for a last cigarette. I sneaked into the church then and stood before the casket, staring at the person I'd known. I looked and looked and could not under-stand. The person wasn't there. Somebody lay with their hands folded across their chest, but it wasn't the person. Where had he gone? What was it Death took which left you dead? I thought that if I stared intensely enough at the dead person, I could make him breathe again. Not that I cared about most of the dead I saw. I simply could not accept the threat to my own breathing they represented.

During the funeral I played outside, but, as the end approached, I rushed inside and stood in the back to watch Daddy walk out of the pulpit while the undertaker closed the coffin and the pallbearers lifted it. Then, the final procession began, with Daddy walking in front of the casket, intoning, "I am the resurrection and the life: he that believeth in me, though he were dead, yet shall he live; and whosoever liveth and believeth in me shall not perish." I loved that part of the funeral, though I did not understand how someone who was dead could live, but I hoped it was true, for my sake, and for all the corpses dancing around my childhood like children playing Ring Around the Rosie: Francita, a classmate whose bathrobe caught fire as she walked past the open, lighted oven, which was heating the house, and as I passed her house on the way to school that morning, I knew that her charred body still lay within; another classmate fell out the door of his father's moving car and was killed; a friend of my parents was shot by gangsters and sat down on the curb to patiently await the ambulance and Death; there was a girl at Highlander that summer after I graduated from college, who went from playfully flirting with me at lunch to swim in the lake, and I was there when Guy surfaced with her body in his arms, her exposed breasts breaking the surface first. And there was Thomas, seventeen, who went to the hospital on Thanksgiving and while I sat playing the piano on Christmas Day, the phone rang. A moment later Daddy announced that Thomas was dead, and the odor of the cooking turkey pinched our nostrils. I have never been able to celebrate Christmas since. Thomas was in my Boy Scout troop, and at the funeral the scoutmaster volunteered me to stand beside his coffin, a fifty-six-inch, twelve-year-old honor guard who, for weeks afterwards, saw Thomas every time I closed my eyes and that was when I began learning to live in the night, lying in my bed and staring at the moon. Death has rested astride me as if I were its mount, but so it is placed on us all. Some of us know it, however, and learn to gallop, though the rider is heavy.)

So, a skull sits on my desk between the antique miniature butter churn filled with pencils, and the Japanese-style earthenware cup made by Nancy Holloway, Jim's wife. I call that skull Friend, for it reminds me that we are all skulls and one day we might sit on someone's desk. The charcoal drawing of the skull on the wall of my adolescent studio was covered by an eleven-year layer of dust and soot, but I did not brush it off. Nothing can obscure it.

The boy I had been still lived in that house, but I could not find him outside. Nashville had been urban-renewed into Anywhere, U.S.A. That boy grew up in a southern town, where slums bordered middle-class neighborhoods, corn grew in vacant lots and everybody sat on porches in the evenings. The slums were gone, replaced by housing projects and brick dwellings that look as if they came from the toy ads of a Sears-Roebuck catalog. No one sat on the porches, not even of the houses that had them, except the few old ones who remained.

My past was trucked to landfills and dumps. The vacant lot where we used to play football with the white boys (and, to our chagrin, get beat) was now occupied by the Country Music Hall of Fame, and I could not find the library I had integrated single-handedly. I went past my high school, but did not go in to walk its corridors. I know that I am not there, for Pearl High is integrated now. I felt like an old Klansman, because I wanted to grab a shotgun and run the white kids out. How proud we'd been of that school, for it was one of the best black high schools in the South. My past had been integrated into oblivion.

Atlanta. Many people with whom I'd worked in SNCC were here, and most of them seemed to be living the same lives that would have been theirs if they'd never sung "We Shall Overcome." It is almost as if "the movement" had not existed for them, until they start the "Do you remember that time in–?" I don't, even if I do. What is more sad than an old radical. At least be a crazy one, like the IWW organizers sitting in dingy offices in Seattle, plotting the revolution and singing "I Dreamed I Saw Joe Hill Last Night," which they probably did. Could any of us sing "We Shall Overcome" now without being ashamed of ourselves for once having believed it? It had given meaning to our lives, but many who had sung it had entered the middle class anyway. The new values which "the movement" tried to birth never became a part of them. Through it all, they remained securely bourgeois, which is another reason why "the movement" did not succeed.

Alabama. Worth Long and I traveled together that spring of 1966, and he has continued his peripatetic ways, driving throughout the South twelve months of the year looking for old musicians. It was good to be traveling with him again.

It was raining when we left Atlanta. He drove, and I looked

out the window, my cameras in my lap, waiting for the inevitable photographs to come toward me.

Worth began remembering as we went through Selma. He had been SNCC's organizer there before King's Traveling Civil Rights Circus arrived in 1965. We drove past the building that had housed the SNCC office on the second floor. It was across the street from the city jail, where the infamous Jim Clark had reigned.

Worth laughed. "Jim Clark must have thought I was crazy to not only come in his town and organize, but to rent an office across from his jail." We both laughed, recalling the boldness of SNCC organizers. Then he was serious. "But, that's what you had to do to show people that you weren't afraid." He paused, chuckled, and added, "Even when you were more scared than they were."

I was driving now, having taken the wheel when we crossed from Georgia into Alabama. Maybe it was remembering, but Worth didn't like to drive in Alabama. I'd known other ex-SNCC people who wouldn't drive in Mississippi. Time had not diluted the emotional memories of being chased by Klansmen, stopped by state troopers, of the constant fear of a bullet crashing through the windshield, unheard until the fraction of an instant before it imploded you into nothingness.

I slowed as we passed the Chicken Shack, in whose dark booths I'd sat many nights drinking beer and moonshine and watching an incredibly thin, black-skinned girl named Rosie dance as if she didn't know that she wasn't in Africa. She took the basic steps of whatever dance was then current and improvised, working her way into the rhythms of the three-minute jukebox record. Her blackness blended into the shadows of the dimly lit cafe and suddenly, the darkness was a visual rhythm. When the music stopped, she was only an ordinary woman, but when she danced, I could have married her.

We turned another corner and passed the cafe from which the Reverend James Reeb had emerged one evening during the spring of 1965 to be struck by a baseball bat and killed. We continued and crossed the Pettus Bridge.

"The Lawd was with me that day." Worth laughed. "I'd been in jail somewhere and had been released that morning. I was just coming back into Selma when I saw people running off the bridge.

People were lying in the middle of the street, screaming. Man, if they'd let me out of jail an hour sooner, don't you know I would've been on that bridge, too. Thank you, Jesus!" he exclaimed. "That's one march I'll never be sorry I missed."

It was late afternoon when we passed through Lowndes County. We remembered Mrs. Viola Liuzzo, the white woman from Detroit who was murdered as she drove a young black kid back to Selma after the Selma-Montgomery March. The roads of Lowndes County were as long and straight as I remembered, bordered by deep forests which opened out occasionally into cotton fields before closing in again. It was still a fearsome country, particularly at dusk when it was almost possible to believe that the trees carried shotguns.

We drove slowly through Hayneville, our eyes turning toward the courthouse in front of which Jonathan Daniels, a young white Episcopal seminarian, was murdered. "Damn!" I muttered. "What're we doing, Worth? Taking the atrocity tour?"

"It *is* getting kinna depressing, ain't it?"

We stopped to see the Jackson Brothers, whose father had been the backbone of the Lowndes County Freedom Organization, whose symbol was a black panther, later dishonored by the group in California. He was dead now, but his sons carried on in his stead. It was good to sit and talk with them.

Across the road from their house was the old Freedom House, as the SNCC office and home of the local organizers was called. The word does not adequately describe the leaflets and flyers stacked in corners, the books and radical newspapers scattered over desks and chairs, the poster-covered walls proclaiming freedom for everyone from Mississippi to Vietnam and points between, and the mattresses flung over the floor where, invariably, someone lay sleeping, day and night, for a Freedom House was, also, a way station for traveling organizers, friends, sympathizers, or someone with no place to sleep who knew freedom only as a word.

I'd slept on that floor several nights, but what I remembered most was the outhouse in the back. It was a three-sided tin shed with no roof, which fronted onto a field. There was no toilet, only a board stretched over a deep hole. One sun-dancing spring morning in 1966, I sat there, the wind brushing lightly against the exposed parts of my body, and watched a man plowing the field. It was a moment outside history, a moment which had no relevance to the social struggle taking place in Lowndes County and the country. I was performing a simple, elemental act, and in just such an act, performed in that way, was the meaning of life. There was no aspect of reality with which I was not at peace as I sat there, and though I shrugged this feeling off as ridiculous, the memory of the experience remained with me, linking itself to my experience on the train in 1959.

I wanted to cross the road and see if the outhouse was still there, but, afraid that it wouldn't be, I didn't.

Mississippi. It was good to be back. I loved Mississippi, because of the blues, though many young blacks now consider the blues passé, an expression of self-pity which blacks can't afford. Maybe that is what they feel in themselves, because the blues is a willingness to dance with life, no matter how painful it becomes. The blues is the knowledge of hell and a way of saying, with Dilsey, that we "endured." To endure is to learn how to extract the true, the good and the beautiful from existence when it is not offered.

The present generation of blacks is unworthy of its forebears. That is a harsh judgment, but in finally letting ourselves be unashamedly angry after centuries of repressing anger, we have lost what was absolutely essential—a way of being in the world and living with adversity, without being controlled or dominated by it. (When I led singing at mass meetings throughout the state nine years ago, I could only stare at the emotions loosed by the prospect of longed-for, cried-for, died-for freedom. Poor freedom. It got entangled with revolutionaries a few centuries ago and has never been the same. Is relief from an abusive political system the same as freedom, or is such relief only a change in the political environment and totally alien to freedom? I could sense the madness of the late sixties being born then and wanted to flee from the churches when the audiences reached near-hysteria and someone would yell, "FREEDOM!" And the response crashed into our lives: "NOW!" "FREEDOM!" "NOW!" "FREEDOM!" "NOW!" Sometimes, I would manage to slip unnoticed outside and leaning on the hood of a car, smoking a cigarette, I wondered if we were leading people on the road to freedom, or taking them so far away that they might never find their way. I was not even sure that some of them might not know more about freedom than us, who were young and angry, for they had lived their lives in the palm of Death's hand and had survived. Yet, they were not as angry as we who came later. They knew that freedom cannot be wrenched from someone else's grasp, like a pocketbook snatched from a woman's hands by a fleet-footed thief. We tried to create the illusion of hope by relieving ourselves of the burden of mortality. The individual disappears in the revolutionary promise of a better tomorrow, and thus, we forget today. The old ones had no tomorrow, so they used today as a chalice.)

The younger generation looks upon its ancestors as weak because they accepted their oppression, or so it seems. But the old ones had the greater strength, for they learned to live without hope, without succumbing to despair. My God, what a feat that was! The young ones rage at their hopelessness and impotence, and, thereby, are consumed.

I wanted to learn more from the old ones, to become worthy of them, but from what I saw of Mississippi that June, I would have to rely on what I already knew. That architect left Nashville and brought his Erector sets to Mississippi.

I was ashamed of myself for hating this change. The living conditions of poor blacks were being improved. Why, then, was I depressed? Because a house is more than a structure. It is a value system, and I was afraid of what formica and plastic-wood paneling do to the soul. There was a difference between a lawn and a yard, and now there were more of the former. A lawn existed to be mowed and looked at, but one sat in a yard with a six-pack or two of beer by his chair, offering a can to anyone walking down the road.

Maybe I was romanticizing the poor and their picturesque shacks. But Grandmother lived in a shack, and when I was there, I never missed the "conveniences" of home. Grandmama didn't have electricity, or running water, and the outhouse was on the other side of the chicken yard (and ain't nothing more scary than walking through a chicken yard in your pajamas at midnight). Despite her children's attempts to get her to change, she never thought her living conditions needed improving. Her water was delivered once a week in two big barrels by a man with a mule wagon, and there was another one by the corner of the house to collect rain water. I realize now that, because I dipped water from those barrels, I know water in a way that is not possible by turning on a faucet. I know water! Getting it from a faucet is more convenient, but I can't say that dipping it from a barrel or a bucket was inconvenient. Only slower.

But we're given two choices only: A shack, or a house that looks like it came in a cereal box. If I reject the latter, it seems that I am saying, "Let them live in shacks." But, no. I am simply refusing the proffered alternative. I do not want to retain the shack, but there is something about its spirit which it may be fatal to lose. "I was made by a person," it says, standing shakily at the edge of a cotton field. One looks at the wood and in its fibers, one touches the rains and the winds which have aged it, the cold which cracked it, and the sun which turned it gray. Through the cracks in the floor at Grandmama's, I could see fifty years of junk which had been shoved underneath the house and forgotten. Having cracks between the floor boards is not a prerequisite for a house, but, at least, it is human. Vinyl is not.

In Grandmama's world, a person made his/her life with their hands. Our lives are prefabricated on assembly lines. My great-grandfather decided how he was to live and put up a four-room shack. I was astounded as I drove through the South by the number of trailer parks bordering the highways. People live in metal coffins and call them home. At one time, only hoboes lived in boxcars. Now we call them trailers, raise our children in them and say it is normal. We think our lives are better than my grandmother's, because for ninety-two years, she chopped kindling wood, washed her hair in rain water, trimmed the wicks of the coal-oil lamps and refused to ride in a car. When human decline is called progress, when the insane takes on the appearance of the normal, one has a moral obligation to go mad.

I'd always thought the South would be there, but it won't be. I was the old Indian watching the tribe give up its time-honored ways, helpless to stop it. The young do not know what I know and thus, cannot even understand me when I talk. My father's past overlapped my present, and I was his son. The degree to which my past overlaps my children's present is nil. They even have northern accents. I can see in the eyes of the young that I am a corpse to them and future generations. People now live in warm houses and I want them back in tepees. Ah, old warrior. Go mutter to the wind.

7

I returned to New York, grieving for myself, unable to tell Joanne about the desert of my life, about what it was to be thirty-four years old and know that nothing I'd ever done mattered. On a shelf above my desk rested the nine books I'd published, most of them bound in leather. I stared at them, for they had been my *raison d'être*. I'd always thought that if I could not live well, the books I authored would balance the scales and justify the pain I suffered and inflicted on those who tried to love me. I looked at those books, and they were only books, words lining pages and bound between covers. The most that I could say was that they were competent, and that was all any book I would write would be. At best, my talent was a modest one, and I marveled that I had done so much with so little. I was Vivaldi, not Bach, writing the *Gloria* and knowing that I could not even conceive of the first measure of the *St. Matthew Passion*. Yet the ultimate irony was that the agonies and suffering of the minor artist were as great as those of the major ones. But what was the merely competent artist's compensation? Pride in his competence? Satisfaction at knowing that he'd done the most with what he had? If so, the suffering was not justified.

I looked at those nine books, held them in my hands, turned the pages, read my name on the title pages. But they did not tell me who I was. Only what I had done.

I sobbed, day after day, and Joanne held me, trying to convince me that I was a good writer and teacher, that many had been affected for the good by my radio show, but I knew that if that were true, it had been accidental. Seeing that she could not convince me, she cried, for in my own nothingness, I made her know hers. I told her to move to her apartment.

She did, but one evening when she came over to walk Misha, our Russian wolfhound, she turned as she went out the door, and said, "Well, I guess since I stayed during the good times, I might as well stay during the bad ones." Perhaps when we are no longer acceptable to ourselves, it is essential to know that we are acceptable to another. Just that and no more. If she had said, "I love you," which she seldom did, it would have been a rebuke, for one cannot love nothing. There was nothing she could do for me, but she made a decision about her life, saying, I will remain vulnerable to you, even at the risk of my sanity and life.

I said nothing, but as the door closed behind her, I emerged from the desert. Nothing had been resolved except that I no longer wanted to die. Instinctively, I picked up my cameras, which I had used only once on the southern journey, and, for several days, photographed Joanne's body. It was as if the way back to life was through its primary medium—the physical—and my primary medium—Art. With the camera at my eye, her exquisite sensuality massaged the aches of the emptiness, and one evening in my closet darkroom, I took a print from the fixer, and smiled as I looked at the image of her perfect breasts.

8

On the first of July, we left New York, with no destination or itinerary. We had a month before she had to return to work and I had to speak at a conference at the School of Religion at the University of Kansas.

I'd always wanted to drive across country, but Joanne was apprehensive, certain that America was nothing more than gas stations, Burger Boys and superhighways. I told her it wasn't, but I was not convinced that we would find the mute remnants of the old, and sit in the shadows of near-forgotten ancestors. I needed to disappear from my life, to be unknown, anonymous, and nonexistent. Above all, I did not want to think about myself or my life.

> July 1–2
> Harper's Ferry, W. Va.
> (Journal)
> I came here to pay my respects to ol' John Brown, not expecting to find two beautiful towns with the same name, the modern one built on the side of a mountain overlooking the confluence of the Potomac and Shenandoah rivers, and the reconstructed old one on the banks of the rivers. Joanne and I have photographed every cornice, dormer, rooftop, stairwell, and doorway here, I do believe. I wonder what it must've been like to live in a time when people cared what a window looked like, when people took the time to carve a lattice, a decorative motif. Yet, their lives weren't better than ours. They killed Indians and held slaves. The beauty and grace of early American architecture was not reflected in their lives, but who said that it should be? I did! It should've made a difference, shouldn't it?

The Shenandoah River is beautiful, though I can't help remembering the people whose name it bore, whose name is all that remains. Does anyone else sit on its banks and see the Indians plying the white water instead of two white boys with orange life jackets in a canoe?

July 3–4
Bird-in-Hand, Penna.

Amish country. We are surprised by the number of tourists and wonder why they come. Are the Amish just a tourist attraction, or do the tourists sense the shadows here?

The Amish seem indifferent to us spectators. Their one-horse covered buggies trot along the two-lane highways as if the cars lined up behind do not exist. The black-suited, bearded men, the women in long, blue dresses and the children seem ignorant of their oddness, but then, I guess we're the odd ones. I experienced the presence of the Amish as a rebuke. Yet, there was nothing I wanted to do less than spend the summer harvesting corn which is as plentiful as weeds.

We visited the Ephrata Cloister, organized in 1732 by Conrad Beissel, a German Seventh Day Baptist, which is about the oddest religious combination I can imagine. Restored by the state and operated as a tourist attraction, the Cloister was a celibate community during its existence. We toured the community's buildings and a more depressing place I have seldom seen.

Beissel seems to have been one of those religious men who never knew the joy of God, for everything at the Cloister was designed to make one feel his worthlessness. (You only need reminding if you've never had it suck your blood.) Hallways are narrow, to remind you of the straight and narrow path; doorways and ceilings are low, forcing you to bend on entering a room, a way of enforcing humility. The rooms are small and constricting. The beds, of course, were boards and the pillows, wooden blocks. What a fearful view of the world they must have had to live in that place and call their lives religious. Had they never experienced the love, compassion and grace of God? We were happy to leave and return to the hilly, narrow backroads where corn tassels twinkled beneath the sun.

July 5
Waynesboro, Va.

How much of it I carry with me. That little black kid who grew up fearing whites and how much of that fear remains, particularly with Joanne beside me. Whenever we stop for gas or to eat, it is all I can do to get out of the car and act normal. But nobody seems to notice us, and believe me, I'm looking all the time for the least sign of trouble.

July 6
Charleston, W. Va.

I love the mountains of this state, but Joanne's emotions were as twisting and tight as the mountain curves by the end of the day. This is her first trip by car and I can't understand how she can be bored. She is accustomed to flying somewhere on vacation and staying in one place. I like to move. Each of us enjoys being alone so much that we're having trouble learning how to travel together. I have a horrible feeling that somewhere in the Midwest, I'm going to put her on a plane back to New York and that'll be that. I don't want to make this trip alone. No. That's not it. It's important to me to make this trip with her, because I've never been able to share my real joys before meeting her. And sharing is two people doing together what they would do if they were alone. So, we sat beside the Shenandoah and drank coffee from the thermos, and it was better because we were alone and together. God, I hope she learns to sink into the motion of the car and go with it, learns to see the trees, rock formations and rivers as we pass them. We've got a lot of days before us, and if I think about it, it is rather ridiculous to think that two people can be together twenty-four hours a day for thirty days and like it. Well, I'm a ridiculous person.

July 7–10
Berea, Ky.

We've been visiting Jim and Nancy Holloway and their three children. Though I've known Jim for five years, this was only the third time we've seen each other. I was anxious about coming, for a friendship which flourishes in letters may wilt under the exposure of personal contact. Thus, it was more than a little surprising that I felt as if I belonged to his family, that it was my family. And I don't know why, except that I am allowed to be. Plus, Jim and I share a love for the important things in life, such as *Hawaii Five-O, Mannix* and bourbon-and-water.

I don't know what's happening to me, but I have particularly enjoyed being with his children, and miss mine. But the older my children get, the more I *want* to be their father and cannot imagine my life without them. If I think about it too much, I

299

can almost cry that Joanne doesn't want children. Maybe we'll adopt a thirteen-year-old girl, and I've seen several on this trip I would propose as candidates.

Jim and I drove to the Abbey of Gethsemani today. I was a little apprehensive about going, confronting the place which has overshadowed my life. I was afraid that I would regret not having come twelve years ago, afraid to find out that my entire life had been a mistake since that night Arlene decided to save me from becoming a monk, and I let her.

We spent the day with Brother Patrick Hart, who was Merton's secretary. He had secured permission from the Abbot to show us parts of the monastery not usually seen by outsiders. After talking with Brother Patrick for a while, he took us through the monastery. My immediate response on entering the quadrangle behind the gatehouse was one of homecoming. The statue of the Virgin Mary which stands in the center, her arms extended from her body, palms outward, seemed to embrace me. I wanted to stay there with her, but didn't want to appear pious. We walked on, toward the Guesthouse over whose doors are the words: GOD ALONE. So deeply did those words pierce me that I seemed to stumble inside myself.

We entered the chapel, and it is the first church in which I've ever felt that God was present. It is a masterpiece of simplicity, with high, whitewashed walls. At the rear is the monk's choir, long and narrow, opening at the front into the main sanctuary where Mass is celebrated. There, a large marble slab serves as the altar and behind it a small simple cross is affixed to the wall. The windows are high and long, of pale, pastel yellows and blues, abstract in pattern, and the light coming through them dabs the colors on the whitewashed walls. The chapel epitomizes Cistercian silence, for the monks know that noise is also visual. Thus, the chapel did not clamor with stained glass windows depicting the life of Jesus, or with ornate columns. Everything had been reduced to essence. Nothing interposed itself between me and God.

I stood there, unable to believe that this place existed, yet knowing its existence more forcefully than anything I'd ever known. A few monks drifted in quietly, bowed toward the cross at the front and seated themselves in the choir to pray. Nothing was more natural than that chapel, those monks, and me there with them. I didn't feel that this was a world within the world, as with the Amish. Somehow, that cloistered Cistercian world *is* the world.

It was late afternoon when we left. I went without regret or longing, even glad that I had not come before now, for I would not have been ready to receive what was given to me today. We drove back through small, mean Kentucky towns, where the sight of my black personage caused people to stop and stare. I wasn't bothered, for their hatred has nothing to do with reality, and to respond with anything more than a chuckle would be to mire myself in illusion and perpetuate its existence. GOD ALONE. That is the world, the only reality. All else is unreality, a delusion, a nightmare. Saying that does nothing to pay the bills, or put money in the bank for the kids' college education, or buy gas for the car. Yet, GOD ALONE is the beginning, middle, and end.

July 11–12
Shakertown
Pleasant Hill, Ky.

Coming to this former Shaker Community, which I happened to read about in *Country Inns and Backroads,* underlined my experience at the Abbey. The Shakers knew something we do not, for they were able to free the creativity that is within each person, and in the furniture, agricultural innovations and cooking, we experience the grandeur that is each human being. The Shakers withdrew from the world because they thought the end was near. Yet, they lived as if tomorrow would always come. That isn't a paradox, but an acceptance of Truth, because none of us have anything except this day. To live without the promise of tomorrow is to confront death—one's own and/or the world's. To confront death is to embrace life. It is to imitate Christ, who knew of his end and when it would be.

The Shakers only expressed their belief in the coming end of the world by refusing to birth children. Yet, that was not the expression of despair I sense in so many young people who don't want to "bring children into this world." (I've read nothing about the Shakers, so what I'm saying is based solely on my perceptions of them from living here for two days in what was their community.) But I think their decision not to have children was more an expression of "Why?" than despair at the kind of world in which those children would live. That is the question so few parents ask. I never did.

It is a lovely place, though I wonder what the Shakers would think of men and women being allowed to sleep in the same bed in what was once their strictly segregated houses. In the evening, Joanne and I play frisbee, and I think the Shakers would approve of that. The joy of their lives is evident in everything they did.

301

July 13
Southern Ill.

This is a rather seedy motel off some Interstate, which our two-lane highway crossed. When we left Shakertown, Joanne started looking at the Mobil Travel Guide and the maps, because thus far on this trip, I have made all the decisions about where to go. No more. Thank God for women's liberation, because the worst part of being a male is having to be responsible for making decisions.

We ended up in New Harmony, Indiana, which the Travel Guide said was the site of two religious communities in the nineteenth century. For two people who haven't been to church in years, we certainly seem to be looking for something. Whatever it was, it was not in New Harmony.

Unlike Pleasant Hill, the religious community that was here had its buildings scattered throughout the town and I didn't have the energy to look for it. Quite by accident, we came upon the Roofless Church, which is just that—a "church" with walls but no roof, the reason being that the roof will be put on when there's peace in the world, or some such nonsense. There was something depressingly Protestant about it. The "church" features a sculpture by Jacques Lipchitz, which is thoroughly modern and secular. It stands beneath a dome, whose shadow, says a tourist brochure, creates the shape of a rose. The barn swallows, however, didn't read that, and what seems to be Indiana's entire barn swallow population has built nests on the inner ledges of the dome. They have also rendered critical appraisals and aesthetic judgments of Lipchitz's sculpture all over it, and have come close to making the thing an acceptable piece of art. Another few years and it'll be a masterpiece. The Roofless Church and its "art" is the perfect example of religion which has its beginnings in the mind instead of the Spirit. The whole place was very depressing.

The travel guide book informed us that Paul Tillich was buried in New Harmony and I was eager to visit his grave. I should not have been. He is buried a few yards behind a rather good restaurant, the Red Geranium, and he would've been better off being buried in the restaurant. His gravesite is in what is euphemistically called, Paul Tillich Park. This is a tiny labyrinth of paths bordered by pine trees. Each path leads to a stone table on which is carved a quote from one of Tillich's works. At the end of one path is a bust of Tillich, beneath which lies the urn holding his ashes, or at least, so I assumed. The whole place is infuriating, because it is a maze, and one wanders and wanders,

302

coming upon these quotes, all of which are Tillich at his most pedestrian. I alternated between anger and profound sadness. But when you die, your friends usually get their revenge. (Maybe our enemies should handle our last rites, because they perhaps know better what our life was about.) The "park" looked like the tailend of a Labor Day picnic, except that it was too ugly to even litter. A few flip-top tabs and cigarette wrappers would have improved things a little. A used condom or two wouldn't have hurt either. Well, if you're ever in New Harmony and need a place to make out, (there were no motels there, which is why we're here), even God won't catch you at Tillich's grave.

July 14
Nauvoo, Ill.

I have entered the country of my childhood and am surprised that I had forgotten it. All day we've been following back country roads to be as close as possible to the Mississippi River and I had forgotten just how open to life the Midwest is with its farm land gleaming green. Every summer during my childhood we traveled with Daddy to church meetings and revivals and I was always most excited when we crossed rivers, any river, but particularly the Mississippi. Today we crisscrossed back and forth across it, taking a small, free ferry across at Batchtown, a seldom used country bridge back across somewhere else, and the imposing bridge which traverses it at Louisiana, Missouri, a town I remember from my childhood. We drove on unmarked country roads, the ones designated on the map as tiny blue lines with no numbers. Sometimes they were paved, sometimes not, and occasionally we followed the road to its end in someone's back yard.

We stopped at a roadside table on the Illinois side of the river at mid-morning, drank coffee from the thermos and ate some of the coffeecake Joanne bought at the Red Geranium. Few cars passed in either direction on the road, and those were local people. (I know I've found a good road when I see no out-of-state cars.) After breakfast, we scrambled down the bank of the river, stood for a while, took some photographs, and left.

We photographed a lot, laughing as we realize that neither of us has taken one picture of a human being. Cornfields, barns, horses, churches and the remarkable white frame farmhouses, but no people. Joanne wondered idly if there was something wrong with her because she did not want people in her pictures. There isn't.

I had planned to stop for the night in Hannibal, Missouri, for

303

I remembered so vividly the time we visited it in my childhood, and going through Mark Twain's home, seeing the fence Tom Sawyer tricked the others into whitewashing for him. I wanted to share that with Joanne, but decided to move on when I didn't believe the Holiday Inn desk clerk when she told me they had no vacancies.

We've ended up in another religious community, or at least a former one, thanks to Joanne's meticulous reading of the Travel Guide. Nauvoo, Illinois, was established by the Mormons. Joseph Smith and Brigham Young had almost created an autonomous state here, when their frontier neighbors, feeling threatened, murdered Smith and a number of other Mormons. Brigham Young moved the survivors to Utah. Today Nauvoo is trying to capitalize on its Mormon past, as well as its wine and blue cheese industry, but without mentioning why the Mormons left.

It is a depressing little town, but maybe that's because I am so sensitive to the blood lust in the air, the Mormon ghosts moaning through eternity. But any trip across America is, in part, depressing, if one remembers the massacres that enabled whites to take this country from the Indians. It is surprising, however, how many Indian place names remain. We brought with us a Dictionary of American Place Names, and so many towns, rivers, and counties are named by Indian words—Illinois, Iowa, Mississippi, Peoria, Keokuk, Sioux City—and on and on and on. The settlers took their land and their lives, but retained their words. Why? It is like making a contract with the dead. America is a vast cemetery.

There is a small gallery on the main street here, with finer pottery, jewelry, paintings and drawings than anything I've seen in New York. All of it was created by crafts people from Iowa and Illinois, and being a New York snob, I was astounded that such fine work could come from places like Davenport, Iowa, and Moline, Illinois. But how good it is that there are people who did not feel, as I did, that they had to come to New York and be famous. I know that I had no choice, for I would have died if I'd remained in Nashville, but that indicates an inner weakness. One should live in obscurity, do their work, and not care if it is recognized. How I would have liked to have been a New England maker of tombstones, known only to those who had need of my services. That is the best way to be in the world.

I bought a framed piece of calligraphy at the gallery, done by a young woman from Rock Island, Illinois, named Chris Wooten. It reads: "Come, come, ye saints . . . All is well." I don't know why, but I had to have it. Maybe one day I will understand what it means.

July 15
Sioux City, Iowa

We left Nauvoo early this Sunday morning, crossed the Mississippi River for the last time and went in search of Boonesport, Iowa, a ghost town. Crossing the Des Moines River at Bonaparte, I noticed two attractive teenage girls standing on the bridge, smoking cigarettes. They were the small-town girls who know in their ripe, pubescent bodies that there is more to life than Bonaparte, Iowa, but don't know what or where it is. So they hang out in the corner luncheonette, watch the boys shoot pool and drop dimes in the jukebox. Life aches within them, but there is no release. A few will escape, but most won't, and in a generation, their daughters will take their places on the luncheonette stools. Life is a circle. So is a noose.

I would like to rent a bus and drive through all the small towns, looking for the young girls whose eyes are wounded, the ones who are always "in trouble," the ones who carry their bodies like offerings to the gods and know that there are none anymore, no sacrificial altars, no priests and priestesses to bring them eternal honor. All the gods have eight cylinders now and eventually come to rest on the outskirts of town, piled on top of each other, turning to rust. So the girls languish beside the jukeboxes, waiting for someone to recognize them and when no one does, they give up those young, pointed breasts to rough, hurting hands and those supple thighs part for callous conquerors on the altar of a car's backseat, and on Sunday morning, the girls stand on the bridge and stare into the river, no longer known by themselves.

When we found the gravel road to Boonesport, we passed a barn filled with junk and had to stop. It was run by two old women, a mother and daughter and never have I seen a more incredible collection of old farm tools, bottles, jars, and you name it.

In the back there was a pump organ and I remembered the time I had to go with the church choir to McMinnville, Tennessee, because the regular church organist couldn't. When we got there, I was dismayed to find that the only instrument in the church was a pump organ, but after the minister explained that all I had to do was pump the two pedals to keep air flowing through the organ, I had a good, but tiring time.

"Do you play?" one of the old women asked, seeing me at the organ.

"Oh, I haven't touched a keyboard in almost fifteen years," I demurred.

"Well," she began, coming over and opening the hymnbook resting on the organ, "there's nothing like a good hymn on Sunday morning, especially when you can't get to church."

So, I sat down and surprisingly, my fingers remembered more about the keyboard than I did, and we had church, as the rich tones of that old organ filled the barn and my legs pumped the pedals as if I were still a young man.

I bought a miniature butter churn, and one of the old women, seeing me staring in wonder at the barrel of gourds, told me to take a handful. That's good pay for an itinerant church organist.

Fifteen miles of gravel road and we were in Bonaparte, which sits on the banks of the Des Moines River, and because of its location, is a ghost town. The annual spring floods eventually made the town uninhabitable, though thirty people live here now and are trying to revive the town. While Joanne went to explore some of the old houses, I sat beside the river, drinking coffee, eating the now stale coffeecake and reading the paper. What is there about sitting beside a river and drinking coffee that makes me feel so at peace? Probably all I'll remember from this trip are those moments. But it is like sitting in a three-sided outhouse, feeling the wind and watching a man plow a field. Maybe that's what I'll do with my life—drive around the country and sit beside rivers and drink coffee.

July 15
Rapid City, S.D.

The world changed to wheat today. Everywhere the wheat shone yellow beneath the wide sky, and it was a little embarrassing to hear myself saying, over and over, "They really are amber waves of grain!" But they are! And the skies are spacious, and though I haven't as yet seen a fruited plain, I won't be surprised if, and when I do.

South Dakota is magnificent. I am not assaulted by the human ego here, for it is impossible for Man to dominate this world of land and sky. Houses, cars, trains, and grain elevators look as if they are being seen from a plane. People are reduced to the minuscule and insignificant place they occupy in the world. When compared to the sky, or the great prairie, people are overrated. Shakespeare should have lived in South Dakota and then he would have known that Man is not akin to the angels. Man is not even in the same category as a grain of wheat. If that sounds misanthropic, it isn't. I am just exultant to feel myself in proper relationship to the universe. I am a grain of sand on an infinite beach and the knowledge makes me deliriously happy.

It was mid-afternoon when we stopped in Martin to eat, and afterwards, decided to go to Wounded Knee. It was scarcely marked on the map, but looked to be at the junction of two gravel roads. When we returned to the highway, I noticed thunderheads piled on the horizon, lightning flashing in them, and I knew that the storm was over Wounded Knee. How I knew, I can't say, but the knowledge filled me, and I was reluctant to continue and risk the possibility of being caught in a storm on an unknown country road, miles from any help. Just as I was about to ask Joanne if we shouldn't change our plans and go to Wounded Knee another time, a strange, but certain confidence spread through my being, and slowly formed into words: "Do not be afraid. The Lord is with you." I wasn't sure that the words had not come from my mind, an expression of a hope rather than a definite knowledge. But it kept repeating itself: "The Lord is with you." I decided to see if He was.

Almost two hours later we turned onto a gravel road. The storm cloud hovered beside us now to the right, as we followed the road up and down the hills for ten miles, through pasture lands where the cattle were as likely to be standing in the middle of the road as in the fields. There were few houses to be seen. Only us, the cattle staring with vacant eyes, and the storm cloud.

As we started down a steep hill, the sky darkened and the clouds rumbled with low thunder. Suddenly, there was no sun as we came to the bottom of the hill, where, ahead of us, was a junction with a large sign board announcing that this was the site of the Wounded Knee Massacre.

As I stopped the car at the junction, the lightning flashed, the thunder reverberated and the rain came down in hard torrents. And I understood why the Bible described the shepherds as being "sore afraid" when the angels announced the birth of Jesus to them, because I trembled inside, and my fear had nothing to do with the storm.

We got out of the car to stand in the rain and read the description of the massacre, to look into the soft mountains and visualize the cavalry coming out of them to sow blood into the land at the spot where I stood.

Joanne pointed out the cemetery on the rise across from the junction, and we drove to it. It was so dark now that I had to turn on the car lights. We got out and stood at the graves of the murdered Sioux. Flowers lay on each grave and I nodded to myself, thinking that, yes, someone should place fresh flowers on those graves every day. And then, it was only slowly that my mind allowed itself to accept what my eyes had been trying to tell it. The flowers were plastic.

We left, the rain now so heavy that it obscured the mountains and turned the sky to night. We drove less than a mile when, suddenly, the rain ceased. The highway was dry and the sun was shining with languid evening light. I turned off the car lights.

We drove in silence for several hours through the deserted lands of the Oglala Sioux Reservation. No cars came toward us; there were none behind us. Occasionally we passed a house or trailer, or saw a wrecked car at the bottom of a gulley. We were alone, and the fear was palpable inside the car. I was afraid to know that the mysterious storm, which had begun with our arrival and ended with our departure from the junction, had been more than a coincidence. Finally, I broke the silence, asking Joanne if she thought it had been coincidence. She shook her head, and the silence returned, trembling with a knowledge we could scarcely comprehend and did not want to accept. But it was a knowledge so profound, it could not be denied.

I wished that I were an Indian shaman, a priest of the Great Spirit, who was accustomed to going off into the hills and being spoken to by God. I sensed in myself vestiges of just such a priesthood, but I live in a society which does not admit the possibility of God speaking as directly to us as He did to Samuel and Saul. We are systematically educated to believe that knowledge is perceived only through and with the mind. If God spoke to any of us, we would consider it a psychological delusion, a manifestation of the id, or some such. We have civilized ourselves into deafness before God.

But why am I, too, not deaf? Why me, Lord?

July 17
Rapid City, S.D.

We were stuck here today while I had the car tuned and the oil changed, and now I know what Hell will be like. Block after block of motels and take-out places, the neon signs glowing like coals. Rapid City is a literal desecration of the holy, as it is built at the entrance to the Black Hills, which are hallowed ground to the Sioux. But I know that the Great Spirit will have its revenge. Indeed, Rapid City itself is that revenge. Americans seem to have a genius for ugliness.

July 18–21

Little Big Horn, Mont.

I came here to celebrate Custer's defeat, but the first evening when we went to the battlefield and stood at the top of the rise where Custer himself fell, that was suddenly unimportant. I looked down toward the trees behind which was the Little Big Horn River. Beyond were the mountains at the horizon and I knew that I belong to this land. It is me and I am it. I looked out upon the rolling prairie and the blue-curved sky, and it is the same world I experienced at Gethsemani. I am alive as part of the land and the sky. I am a clump of sagebrush! What a beautiful thing to be, for didn't God choose to speak to Moses through a bush?

We had not planned to stay here long, but there was no reason to leave. Indeed, I know now that this is where we were being led to.

We spent the days playing frisbee in a field while evening languished on the horizon. We spent the days listening to evening wind in the tall grasses and I felt the spirits of Crazy Horse, Sitting Bull and the Great Spirit itself. To be here at evening, alone as the wind whistles gently out of the north is to know holiness, all pervading yet solitary, awesome yet ridiculously ordinary, mysterious but devoid of mystery. This land, this sky are Truth, which is the simple recognition of what is and the acceptance of it. Having accepted, I give myself willingly.

The monastery is the world.

July 22

Lovell, Wyoming

We spent the morning looking for the Pryor Mountain Wild Horse Reserve, but the rain and fog hid it. We drove on a gravel road from St. Xavier to Grass Lodge through sensual hills, and finally into Wyoming. I was sad to leave Montana, for I've never been anyplace where I felt myself so expressed by the physical environment, except Gethsemani.

"I could spend my life photographing here," I told Joanne.

"The mountains would be your cathedral."

309

9

August 3
Lawrence, Kansas

We spent our last week together driving through Wyoming, and saw herds of deer, laughed at magpies skimming over currents in the awesome Wind River Canyon, fell in love with horses standing with their heads at each other's flanks, swishing flies from the other's face, visited my beloved friend, Nancy, who lives in the mountains of Colorado with her horses, chickens, prize-winning rooster, dogs, and John. Joanne flew back to New York from Denver, and I stayed at the airport until I could not distinguish the lights of her plane from the stars. Then, I sat in the car for a while, crying quietly.

Without her, I was not interested in back roads and took the interstate across Colorado and Kansas, wishing she was with me to tell me why the sky of Kansas is flat and Montana's is like a dome. She would know.

I've just completed five days of listening to theological discussions and it was almost enough to turn me into an infidel. I felt out of place among religious professionals—ministers, teachers and seminarians—who couldn't talk without quoting Bonhoeffer, Tillich, Barth, and others with whom I wasn't familiar. I wondered if they lacked the words of their own because they had never experienced God, except through theologians. Tell me about *you*, I wanted to yell at them.

Eventually they did, but not with words. I listened to their emotions and perceived that they were people without hope, and thus, in despair. They felt abandoned by God, which was not surprising, because their religion was a politicized Christianity. They feel that the Church is called upon to save the world, and I kept wondering, what gave them the right to think they should save the world? And what did they want to save the world *from*? Or for? Contemporary Christianity seems to find its *raison d'être* in good works—feeding the poor, marching in Selma, giving money to Indians—all of which is fine, but it isn't anything which an atheist couldn't do and doesn't do. The irony, of course, is that when these "good works" do not change the world in even its tiniest part, they fall into despair and wonder what's wrong with the world. Nothing. The world hasn't changed since Adam.

I spoke on the third day of the conference and I told them that there is no hope, and as long as one thinks there is, he/she is saying that life only has validity to the degree that one's impact on the world is for the good. But the meaning of life is not to be found in the effect we have upon the world, or what we think to be the world. We are called upon to live our lives and be instruments of God. That should be enough. It isn't, because we cannot accept that we are not God. Only He can change the world. We are merely human, curls on the waves, clouds that billow at midday and disappear at sunset. As long as the Church thinks, however, that it should and can change the world, it will be a caucus within the Democratic Party. Christians want Jesus to be President. But Christianity is supposed to be the alternative to Caesar, and so intent in its virtue that Caesar will not be able to withstand the intensity of its light. Instead, Christianity has become a wing of Caesar's Bureau of Propaganda.

It was good to be with people with whom I could speak only about religion. In all the times I've appeared in public, this was the first occasion on which I felt wholly myself, hiding nothing. I did feel a little arrogant appearing with such prominent theologians as Gregory Baum and Rubem Alves, for what do I know? I've never read theology and for most of the conference, I didn't have the slightest idea what people were talking about. The morning I addressed the group, I prayed before leaving my room, telling God that it was His show, because what could I tell people who knew more than I did? But once I got up to speak, words came from me that I cannot even recall ever uttering even to myself. They came from somewhere within me that had never before known words, but it was the place which I want to be my only voice. I'm not ashamed anymore of being one who hungers and thirsts for righteousness. I want to be a saint, for there is no other reason to be alive. GOD ALONE. The human vocabulary should be reduced to those two words.

I was ashamed of my life when I compared it to those of some of the people I've met here—the minister of a suburban Chicago church, who was struggling with the racism of his members, the young seminarian recently separated from his wife and trying to upend his life, the campus ministers who didn't know how to communicate with black students, and Mitch, a minister from Vinita, Oklahoma, with whom I played frisbee when too much theology threatened to give me a migraine. We founded the Church of the Holy Frisbee, and most of the conference participants had joined by the end. These people gave me more than I them, because my life is so solitary, lived within the confines of my book-filled apartment, shared wholly only with Joanne and the typewriter. The people I met at the conference confront American despair daily and struggle with the pain of it in themselves and those they must counsel. I was humbled by their unknown and unseen courage.

I was most affected, though, by the Catholic nuns, particularly Sister Adrienne, whose smile was surely the one God had at the creation. The nuns did not seem to be concerned with hope, despair, alienation, or theology. They were simply themselves, as ordinary as dirt and as holy.

August 4–6

Kansas City, Kansas

It has been twenty years and I want to come here and walk the streets of my childhood. Instead, my parents told some friends that I was coming and they arranged a public gathering, which I should not have consented to. I am now a thing to them, someone they think is famous, and they want to shine in my "glory." Well, I had to insult the most persistent and I did not care. I am almost fatally ill with people trying to impose their idea of me on me. I am not an idea, dammit! And anything anyone ventures to say about me will not be true. I will not be pinned by anyone's words, particularly my own.

I did manage to get away by myself and drive by the houses we lived in. How tiny they looked now. How narrow the streets are. In my mind everything was so large, which it was to that boy-child. I will retain his perception of this town, though it has not changed since I left.

Being here, I realized that part of this summer has been a journey through my life, looking for myself, and in some places, finding nothing, and in others, making visible what had always been within me, but until now, only dimly perceived.

August 8–10

Peru, Indiana

My brother has become a middle-aged man. Those were my first thoughts when I saw him. It has been ten years and I had remembered him as tall and very handsome. Maybe he was, but his hairline is receding like Daddy's now, revealing the skull beneath.

We sat up late, talking, and there was much that I wanted to tell him, but how do you become brothers after you've both lived a lifetime? I wanted him to know what my journey through time had been, but he seemed to take my presence as a chastise-

312

ment, saying things like, "Well, I'm glad one of us did something with his life, because I sure didn't bring any glory to the family name," and "You keep on writing so Daddy can be proud of one of us." I didn't know how to tell him that I had not come to judge his life, but for him to know mine. But can we ever know another's life? Not really. We can only have varying degrees of knowledge about that life, but I think I accept now that I am alone. And having accepted that, I will never again be in danger of killing myself. I am alone. Thus am I born.

10

August 13
1 P.M.
Abbey of Gethsemani
Trappist, Ky.

Spent a few days at Jim and Nancy's, looking at the mountain which keeps guard over them, riding the horse with their children, and generally, settling into the stillness of my being before coming here for this brief visit.

Am in Rm. 215 in the Guesthouse. Outside my window, the water tower, a tree and the sound of locusts.

The silence is heavy but not oppressive. It overlays everything like fog and I nestle snugly within.

Am here until Thursday morning. Don't really know why, except it has been a long time coming. Not here to think about becoming a monk. Oddly, that is very far from my mind, which must mean that I am becoming free of at least one romantic notion.

I'm here to better learn how I can live the essence of the monastic life in the world. In other words, to more clearly define who I am and how I must live to be a more fluent tongue of God's. This, of course, will not be easy. Particularly since it is at the level of "dailiness" that I must find and use that tongue. How much should I withdraw? How much be involved? How do I shape my days so that they sing?

Rule #1—Move slowly. If there is the urge to rush, exaggerate slowness.

. . . Do not
Think of what you are
Still less of

313

What you may one day be.
Rather
Be what you are (but who?) be
The unthinkable one
You do not know.

—Merton—

5:00 P.M.

It's funny, feeling that I'm supposed to *feel* a particular something by being here. As if what it's all about is feeling. I do,
however, feel something special looking at the cemetery behind
the chapel, the statue of the Virgin outside the gatehouse. But
feeling has little or nothing to do with Being, so I laugh at myself when I feel nothing (or almost nothing) except fatigue,
sleepiness, annoyance at the inevitable noises and presences of
others.

7:50 P.M.

Compline was beautiful!!

August 14
1 A.M.

Went to bed at eight and awoke at eleven, after dreaming of
Compline, and in eager anticipation of Vigils.

Am rereading *Sign of Jonas*, perhaps my favorite book of
Merton's.

"The inviolability of one's spiritual sanctuary, the center of the
soul, depends on secrecy. Secrecy is the intellectual comple-
ment of a pure intention. Do not let your right hand see what
your left hand is doing. Keep all good things secret even from
yourself. If we would find God in the depths of our souls we
have to leave everybody else outside, including ourselves.

"If we find God in our souls and want to stay there with Him,
it is disastrous to think of trying to communicate Him to others
as we find Him there. We can preach Him later on with the
grace He gives us in silence. We need not upset the silence
with language."

1:35 A.M.

I think it is better being here than anyplace I've ever been.
Maybe that is a typical first day reaction. We'll see what I feel
on leaving Thurs. morning.

". . . poverty, conceived as a function of solitude or 'nakedness'—detachment, isolation from everything superfluous in the

interior life. Renunciation of useless activity in your natural faculties."

4 A.M.

Vigils was not worth the anticipation. I'd expected a service permeated with mystery. It was a lot of words.

"Going into Louisville the other day I wasn't struck by anything in particular. Although I felt completely alienated from everything in the world and all its activity I did not necessarily feel out of sympathy with the people who were walking around. On the whole they seemed to me more real than they ever had before, and more worth sympathizing with."

I wonder if it isn't easier to "sympathize with" people when one doesn't have to be actually and continually with them, i.e., one can apprehend their essence because one doesn't have to confront, on so many irritating levels, their "unreality." Thus, the problem becomes to communicate and respond to essence in the midst of "unreality."

7 A.M.

Lauds was beautiful and I just don't mean aesthetically. Listening to Gregorian chants on records is an aesthetic experience. Hearing them in the chapel here is experiencing Art at the service of God. Indeed, the chants here make even Bach cantatas seem secular. Bach, whom I loved more than anyone, I realize now, calls attention to his music. One is aware that this is great music, that this is a beautiful phrase or line, of the interplay of instruments and voices. In the chants the music does not direct attention to itself, but to God. There is no other way I can put it. Listening to it is not an aesthetic experience; it is a religious experience which goes beyond emotion to parts of the self which have been lying famished. I wish I could pray, really pray, i.e., lower my body and kneel, bow my head, and fold my hands. I envy the Catholics who come in, bow to the cross, make the sign of the cross, kneel and pray. I can't bring myself to do it. And anyway, what would I say? "Hi, God. What's going on?" Doesn't seem quite right.

One of the problems of being a guest at a monastery is resisting the impulse to act pious. I think this is what I was hinting at yesterday when I was wondering about "what to feel." When you're here, you think you should feel "religious," and I sense that in the other guests who look so serious. So I laugh at myself a lot.

I don't think I could be a Trappist. Monks are people and people move and movement is visual noise.

1 P.M.

Finally got to sleep at eight and awoke around eleven. (What is this three hours' sleep at twelve-hour intervals?)

The food here is plain, but quite filling. Surprisingly so. Last night's supper was a bowl of clam chowder, bread and fruit salad and not having eaten since eight that morning, I despaired that it would fill me. It was more than sufficient. The brown bread is a meal in itself. Really delicious.

I stay mainly in my room, except for meals and the chanting of the Offices. I like being alone. Haven't spoken in twenty-four hours and don't miss the human contact one bit. The rules of the Guesthouse only allow conversation a half-hour after each meal and it is such a relief not to have anyone ask me where I'm from, what do I do, what do I think of the place, and all those dumb questions which wouldn't really tell them a damned thing about me. I don't dislike people, but they seldom reflect my inner reality or even point toward it.

> ". . . in the plans of Divine Providence, there is no such thing as a defeat and that every step is, or ought to be, a step forward into the wilderness and that even publicity can nourish humility. It must be neither loved nor hated for itself, but simply accepted with indifference from the hand of God, that His will may be done."

August 15
8:40 A.M.

Lauds was simply exquisite this morning. I think it will be with more than a little regret that I'll leave tomorrow. Not because I dread going back to the world so much as not wanting to leave reality.

Noon

Just can't get into Mass. Today is the Feast of the Assumption of the Blessed Virgin and I sat through as much as I could, but I could believe little of what I was hearing, could not feel God in the people around me and it all felt like church. And church is church. I cannot worship with others. One's life should be a continual act of worship anyway.

I do enjoy the other Offices—Lauds, Sext, Nones and Compline, but not Vigils and Vespers. But I touch something very real in the minor Offices.

I find myself looking forward to the Offices. Not only do I feel some small portion of God's presence, but they serve to break up the day, ease the burden of time.

"God makes us ask ourselves questions often when He intends to resolve them. He gives us needs that He alone can satisfy, and awakens capacities that He means to fulfill. Any perplexity is liable to be a spiritual gestation, leading to a new birth and mystical regeneration."

2:30 P.M.

Went to Nones. In came two young girls in shorts and there went Nones. Ah, Julius.

4:20 P.M.

". . . it will not hurt me at all to realize that everyone who loves Truth is, in this world, called upon in some measure to *defend* it."

Rule #2. Begin each day, not with the news or rock music, but with Bach cantatas, Gregorian chants for one half-hour. Better Gregorian chants because Bach can get emotional. The Spirit is beyond feeling. Then, read something that further communicates the Spirit—Merton. Find others.

Say the prayers which God has given you here: "O Lord, come to my assistance. Thank you for this life. May I live it well and according to Thy will."

"O Lord, it is good to be possessed by You. Make me worthy."

Afterwards, eat a simple breakfast. Bread and butter, tea or coffee, cereal and fruit. Do this whether you want to or not, even if you don't think you have the time.

"Emotion does a man great injury in this monastic life. You have to be serious and detached and calm all the time. Faith is the antidote: Cleansing yourself of impressions and feelings and the absurd movements of a half-blind understanding by a clear penetration into the heart of darkness where God is found."

Is this what Merton means by "interior silence"?

6:30 P.M.

Vespers was good. I always enjoy the Offices more when I can sit to myself. Also it is better to sit in the back, where I cannot see the monks in the chancery below, but only the ceiling, the light coming through the windows.

I am glad to observe in myself that I do not feel that my spiritual life has been less or will be less because I am not a monk. Being here convinces me even more that my way is in the world, a cigarette in one hand and a bourbon-and-water in the other.

I am glad, too, that Joanne is Catholic, though not a practicing one. But I remember early in our relationship how I just opened up to her when she told me that she'd been raised in the Church. The fact that she is Catholic gives me a kind of support, i.e., she understands and empathizes and I doubt that I could have come here without someone else being able to actively share this with me. I guess what I'm trying to say is that she respects the monk who is me.

August 16
6:30 A.M.

I will be leaving in a few hours. I could stay indefinitely, because I like who I am here.

Yesterday morning when I awoke, I considered leaving. Why, I'm not sure, except a noisy neighbor in the next room had disturbed my sleep with his snoring. I napped, read, worked on a poem during the day. Then, during Compline, it began to happen. Exactly what, I really can't describe. But a feeling of utter sweetness began to permeate me. It took me over, quietly and definitely.

I sat in the monks' cemetery, walked to the top of the hill across the highway, lay in the grass and the feeling remained. It was a happiness unlike any I'd ever known. I seemed to be rocking gently back and forth in the bottom of the sky.

I came back to the monastery to sit in the chapel, but the outside door was locked. So I walked around the quadrangle and stopped before the statue of the Virgin Mary which stands at the center. As I looked up into her face, I became transfixed, immobilized. I tried to move and could not. It was a more beautiful feeling than any I've ever known in the arms of a woman. And I, who during Mass yesterday could not understand how grown men could be singing about Mary ascending into heaven, suddenly knew that it was true! I looked at her and thought of the Immaculate Conception and, awe-struck, I whispered: "Why not? Why—*not*?" If God *is* God, then, of course, He could and can do anything He so desires. Anything! And that yes, it was true, all of it—the Virgin Birth, the Crucifixion, Resurrection and Assumption! It was true!!

I stood there, hugging myself in delirious joy. I sat on the ground before her, my eyes never leaving her face, resting in the

318

warmth of her embrace. Eventually, the feeling began to dissipate, but not the knowledge. That is within me now and I will never be without it again.

I do not regret leaving this morning, and, in fact, am looking forward to going out there, because I know now that there is no "out there," that there is no separation between this monastery and that pained world. They are one. The monastery is simply the world without its infinite facades. Here is pure Being and life dedicated to It. That is the world, but one can never know that as long as he is of what is presented as the world, as long as he takes seriously what the world decrees as real. And one can never know himself as long as one confuses self with what that world defines as real.

I am eager to leave, to go into the world and more and more, not be of it. I cannot save the world: I cannot change the world. All I can do is say Lord, Here I am. Use me. To submit one's life to that Divine Will is not to find peace, but to struggle and suffer. God does not provide answers because there are no questions. There is only that Divine Essence. There is no other reality, no other world.

It is time to go back to my students, my radio show, to blacks who hate me because I love, the bills and all the rest. It will be enough if I become so real that I am ordinary, like prairie sagebrush. And maybe, just maybe, God will set me ablaze.

If He does not, it is of no moment. All is well.